ANZIO
EPIC OF BRAVERY

ANZIO
EPIC OF BRAVERY

By Fred Sheehan

UNIVERSITY OF OKLAHOMA PRESS : NORMAN

Library of Congress Catalog Card Number: *64-20763*

Copyright 1964 by the University of Oklahoma Press, Publishing Division of the University. Composed and printed at Norman, Oklahoma, U.S.A., by the University of Oklahoma Press. First edition, November, 1964; second printing, December, 1964.

IN its way, this book is dedicated to every member of the VIth Corps who fought at Anzio and who put the lie to the manufactured term "Master Race":

To those who out-blitzed the Blitzkrieg

But if an individual were to be singled out as the prototype, I suppose it should be my old First Sergeant, whose advice and friendship I cherished through four years in the army and for many years afterward:

Patrick H. Mackey
born into the Choctaw Indian Nation,
but a full-blooded American.

Preface

AS the years slip by into decades, it still seems incredible to those of us who were there that so much of the world's attention could be focused on so tiny a piece of the world's topography for so long, then pass into limbo so quickly and almost so permanently.

For four months in 1944 a semicircular strip of Italian seashore fifteen miles long and seven miles deep kept much of the world on tenterhooks. For the Germans, it was "an abscess" to be lanced. To the Romans, it was a long-pending hope of deliverance from unwanted occupation. To the British, it was inconceivable that what was happening there should be happening. To the Americans, it was agony, more proof that we should never have allowed ourselves to become so thoroughly enmeshed in the Mediterranean toils.

Anzio was one beachhead in World War II where we came within a hair's breadth of being pushed back into the sea. Yet the complete story of Anzio is difficult to come by. Millions of words have been written about it; it is repeatedly alluded to in references to the war in the Mediterranean, in fact in the over-all picture of World War II—a passing mention here, a reference there, sometimes a whole chapter devoted to four momentous months. There are mountains of material in the basement of the Pentagon and at the War Office in London, official records, tactical, statistical, logistical; there are the file folders containing the testimonials acknowledging the awards of Congressional Medals of Honor and Victoria Crosses; there also are the records of courts-martial. Unit, regimental, and divisional histories are kept on file in the Army's archives at Frederick, Maryland. This abundance of written matter, cold facts, only begins to tell the story of what happened at Anzio.

Although as a member of a rifle company on special duty to division headquarters at the time, I had a broader scope of information available to me than to others assigned to lower echelons on the military scale, yet I was astonished when I discovered during research for this book what was really going on at certain periods on the beachhead. No one person has the ability or the capacity to keep up with the many elements involved in a single battle, even one going on in so restricted an area. Like a jeweler studying a diamond, he can view the over-all stone but not each separate facet simultaneously. So it was with everyone at Anzio. We knew what was going on immediately around us, but one had to be other places to know what was going on there. A rifleman in an infantry squad has a different version of what went on at Anzio than a signal company messenger, the artillery forward observer different than the T/5 who scheduled the loading and unloading of the LST's at the badly battered dockside.

When it came to day-to-day existence, the Allied soldier at Anzio made his bed as best he could where he could. In some cases men literally lived in caves carved into the side of wadis or the

Southern Italy, showing relationship of Anzio to Rome

reverse slope of the banks of the Mussolini Canal. In other places, the men dug deep pits in the sandy soil then roofed them over with any material that could be found, preferably old doors, and on top of this mounds of dirt were piled high as further protection against shell fragments and antipersonnel bombs. In still other places, men were forced to lie in soggy slit trenches only inches deep because it was impossible to dig deeper on account of underground water. Others were billeted in villas and in the buildings lining the waterfront at Anzio and Nettuno and enduring the nerve-shattering, incessant shellfire from the enemy long-range guns.

I remember the delight of discovering an uninhabited enemy pillbox along the shorefront at Nettuno. It was hemispherical in shape with concrete walls and roof several feet thick, built originally to defend the harbor at Anzio but never used. It was located a short distance from the foot of the steps of the Church of St. Anthony. After only one night in that pillbox it was evident why we had no difficulty in laying claim to it. The church steeple was being used as a point of registry by enemy artillerists, and, because of the purpose of its design, the pillbox had a large opening at its back end, which now, unfortunately, was its front. The following morning we, too, abandoned it and sought a safer nocturnal refuge farther inland.

Anzio brought to World War II that relic of World War I —the sandbag. Because of the static nature of the fighting and the proximity of the subsurface water, it was necessary to "dig in" above ground, using sandbags for the purpose. And when the demand far outstripped the supply, the cylindrical cardboard cartons that 105-mm. artillery shells were packed in proved acceptable substitutes. These, filled with sand and stacked in rows, provided good protection from flying shell splinters.

These are the things that are left out of the official histories, the minutiae that figure greatly in the story of a battle although they may have no connection with the outcome: such details as latrines, or the lack of them, while the soldier is on the front line—a minor detail, although one of paramount importance to the man involved.

And the ludicrous side of officialdom—the general charged with solving traffic congestion in so confined an area served by two main roads. The solution was simple. A priority system was put into effect with various windshield stickers signifying the varying degrees of essentiality for vehicles traversing the important arteries. But overlooked was the fact that the windshields on all vehicles were folded down over the hoods and covered with canvas to prevent the sun's reflection from alerting enemy observers. Result—the windshield stickers were very neatly covered up, and the general's priority system was for naught.

The purpose of this narrative is to tell as complete a story as possible of the Anzio Beachhead, not as military history or critique, but as the account of the individual soldier—why he was sent to Anzio, what he did when he got there, and what was going on around him at the time.

Where possible I have indicated the source of the historical facts and quotations, but a word of gratitude must be said to a great number of other persons who were also at Anzio in various capacities—from generals to war correspondents to BAR men—for permitting me not only to jog their memories but to peruse their own personal records.

Fred Sheehan

Norwood, New Jersey
September 18, 1964

Contents

---

xiii

Illustrations

---

xv

MAPS

ANZIO

EPIC OF BRAVERY

CHAPTER ONE

Operation Shingle

T
HE Allied soldier went to Anzio much as he went anywhere else. He went because he was ordered to go.

To him Anzio was only another Italian town, a little easier to pronounce perhaps, but just a spot on the map that few persons had ever heard of. If they had, they knew it as the birthplace of the Roman Emperor Nero, and if they looked on the map they would find it some thirty-seven miles almost due south of Rome. But to the Allied soldier heading for Anzio it was just another noplace, just another beachhead, and he had been on beachheads before. There had been North Africa, Sicily, Salerno, and the leap-frogging amphibious assaults along the Adriatic coast of southern Italy. All these had gone before. Boats were nothing new to these soldiers heading for Anzio, and they were sure that Anzio would be nothing new.

One thing was certain. This would be a short hop, no days or weeks of discomfort aboard ships where boredom is the worst enemy before anxiety sets in to wipe away that boredom. No washing and shaving in salt water, no continuous and endless chow lines. This one would be quick, and the soldier would be back in his own element—on land. A ship was no place for a soldier regardless of how many invasions he had been in before, regardless of all the amphibious training he had gone through getting ready for this. He had been on more ships than half the sailors in the Navy, but once he had seen the bow of his ship, there was nothing left but the stern, and he had seen bows and sterns many times before. They all look alike; worse, they smell alike. To a soldier, a ship is a prison. There is no place to go, nothing to do—just wait and think, reflect upon why he was there on that ship at that time and heading for Anzio.

It all started in an atmosphere of fine cognac and good cigars, this Anzio thing. V stood for Victory. It also stood for Vindication.[1] Vindication for something that had happened some twenty-eight years earlier but which continued to torment the man sipping cognac and smoking the big cigar. Twenty-eight years earlier, at another time and another war, and Winston Churchill had just turned forty years of age. He was a brash young politician with a fine future ahead of him. Already he was a member of the cabinet, First Lord of the Admiralty, and men of substance were listening to him. He was formulating policy, running the world's largest navy in what was then the world's greatest war. One of his ideas caught the imagination of the Allied high command. It was bold, audacious, but it had merit. He proposed landing troops on the Gallipoli Peninsula in Turkey, forcing open the Dardanelles, capturing Constantinople, knocking Turkey out of the war, and finally linking up the western Allies with the Russians in the Crimea. This was in 1915, the second year of World War I.

The Dardanelles, where Europe is separated from Asia. On

[1] Dwight D. Eisenhower, *Crusade in Europe*, 221, 222.

April 24 a vast armada of naval ships steamed up to the mouth of the Turkish straits, cannonaded the landing sites, and began unloading troops. Englishmen, Australians, and New Zealanders poured over the beaches and up into the hills on the European side of the straits; the French went in on the Asian side. Later the French would give up their foothold in Asia to go to the aid of the beleaguered British on the European side. The Turks, under the command of the German General Otto Liman von Sanders, were resisting stubbornly. Days became weeks, weeks became months, and more and more Allied troops were being thrown into the battle. The people at home were increasingly alarmed at the mounting casualty lists. Commanders were changed, but still they got nowhere. Then, the decision to give it up. The last troops to get out left January 9, 1916. They left behind mountains of equipment and 55,000 dead, wounded, and captured.

Gallipoli was a disaster, a disaster of such proportions it toppled the government, and the young politician with the bright future went into the trenches in France as a major carrying his own *Croix de guerre*—Gallipoli.

A government inquiry officially exonerated the former First Lord of the Admiralty of blame in the Turkish debacle, but as a politician he knew that in the public mind Winston Churchill and Gallipoli were synonymous. One day he must erase this blight that historians were bound to insert next to his name in the pages of time. This was the torment that haunted him for twenty-eight years.

And then in the fall of 1943, opportunity presented itself.

In the fall of 1943, the war in the Mediterranean was over so far as the military planners were concerned. It had been determined the previous May at the Washington conference of the combined chiefs of staff that with the capture of Sicily, the American fighting divisions in the Mediterranean would be removed from the area and sent to the United Kingdom to get ready for the direct assault across the English Channel. Churchill's "soft underbelly" theory of invading the Continent through the Balkans into Middle Europe had been ruled down. It was regarded as still another peripheral engagement, a strategic sideshow whittling around the edges of the enemy but never meeting him head-on. The soft-underbelly theory was visionary but impractical from a military standpoint. The British Prime Minister favored pushing through the traditional invasion route—the Ljubljana Gap in Yugoslavia—into the middle of Europe, defeating the Germans and at the same time saving that part of the Continent from what he rightly feared would be virtual annexation by the Russians. But the military forces needed for such an undertaking simply could not be supplied through the limited port facilities in that part of the Mediterranean.

Churchill was ruled down but not out. The British Prime Minister was a determined man. With the departure of some American divisions from the Mediterranean following the capture of Sicily, he redoubled his efforts to retain those divisions ticketed for future transfer from the area.

The Allied invasion of Salerno had been in the planning stage for months before Sicily fell, but it was to be on an if-needed basis. It had already been decided that the British Eighth Army would follow up the capture of Sicily, push across the Straits of Messina and on up the Italian peninsula. In the over-all strategy, all that was wanted from Italy were the big airfields around Foggia which could be used as bases for our heavy bombers from which we could reach the industrial heartland of Germany. The combined chiefs of staff, dominated by General George C. Marshall, had determined that the main ground effort against the Germans was to be made across northern France and straight toward Berlin. There were to be no diversionary sideshows. The Eighth Army was to take those airfields around Foggia and the big ports of Naples and Bari for supply purposes. If needed, Clark's Fifth Army could be called on to help.

General Marshall, with the complete backing of President

Roosevelt, the previous May had stated flatly: "The Mediterranean is a vacuum into which America's great military might could be drawn off until there is nothing left with which to deal the decisive blow against the Continent."

But between May and August the situation had changed. With the capture of Sicily, the Italian government collapsed, Mussolini was overthrown, and Italy surrendered. Part of the surrender terms included the promise of Allied troops to insure Italian sovereignty and to keep it from becoming a German vassal. This was playing right into Churchill's hands. Mark Clark's Fifth Army would be needed after all.

In the seven days from the overthrow of Mussolini to the actual invasion of Calabria by the Eighth Army, both sides were in a quandary. The first of the Axis partners was suing for peace, but there were terms attached. As for the Germans, Hitler conferred with his two field marshals in Italy—Erwin Rommel and Albert Kesselring. Rommel, so soon after the defeat of his Afrika Korps, was pessimistic, but Kesselring, already in command of the German troops in southern Italy, expressed confidence in his ability to hold off the Anglo-American forces and establish a line of defense south of Rome as well as to maintain order within German-occupied Italy.[2] He already had taken advantage of the political confusion in Rome and ordered the Italian army disbanded. The Nazi Führer deliberated and finally adopted the Kesselring plan as a political expedient.

As for the Allies, there was no alternative; the Fifth Army must be sent into Italy. Those American fighting divisions not immediately slated for transfer to Britain would be retained in the Mediterranean, would comprise most of Mark Clark's army. They included the U.S. 3rd, 34th, 36th, and 45th Infantry divisions, the 1st Armored Division, the 82nd Airborne Division, three Ranger battalions, and other smaller combat units as well as great numbers of supply and administrative troops. It was quite

[2] Albert Kesselring, *A Soldier's Record,* 221.

7

an array, and the British Prime Minister was determined to keep the Americans in the Mediterranean while he continued to promote his soft-underbelly theory.[3]

The British Eighth Army crossed over the Straits of Messina from Sicily into Reggio Calabria on September 3. On September 9 the first of the Fifth Army's assault boats touched shore in the Salerno Bay at Paestum at 3:30 A.M. By the first of October Naples fell, and the Allies had in their possession all that was wanted in Italy—the airfields around Foggia and the two big supply ports of Naples and Bari. Fall was settling in, and the Germans were taking full advantage of the weather and the rugged Italian terrain in their slow withdrawal toward Kesselring's defense line south of Rome, delaying the Allied advance long enough to permit the labor battalions of the Nazi Todt Organization to construct what was to become the Gustav Line, that impregnable series of fortifications literally dug and cemented into the sides of the lateral spurs of the Apennines. The methodical Todt workers had taken months to construct a bastion of steel and reinforced concrete, alternate layers of railroad ties, stone, and earthworks across the natural and traditional defense line south of Rome from the Tyrrhenian to the Adriatic. Traditional, in that for generations Italian military cadets had been taught the natural defense characteristics of that very line across Italy's midriff. Youthful Italian officer candidates at the Military College worked out paper problems and fought imaginary battles along that very line from Cassino to Ortona much as West Point cadets work out on paper the tactics over and over again of the Battle of Gettysburg, all of it designed to drive home to the aspiring generals the advantages of terrestrial relief in the art of defensive warfare. Unfortunately, our generals had not studied at the Italian Military College. Such was not the case among the German military; they were all too familiar with that memorable example of a natural defense barrier, so much so that now they improved upon it. And all the while, their rear guards exacted tremendous energy and large

[3] Albert C. Wedemeyer, *Wedemeyer Reports*, 231.

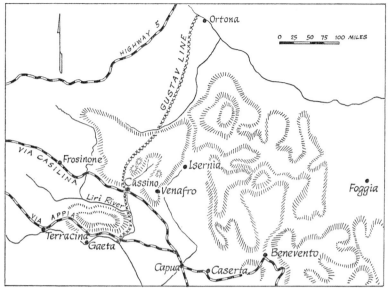

The Gustav Line

numbers of casualties from the slowly advancing and unwary Anglo-American armies. In merely passing through the outposts leading to the Gustav Line, the Fifth Army, consisting of eight front-line divisions, advanced only seven miles at a cost of some 16,000 casualties in the month and a half it took to get from the Volturno to the Rapido.[4] And winter was setting in.

Winter in southern Italy is misery at its utmost—rain and leaden skies day in and day out. The rain began to fall the day Naples fell, October 1, 1943. It started as a light rain, almost welcome after months of a droughtlike existence hardly a harbinger of what lay in store. Throughout October it continued intermittently and the skies became increasingly overcast until, by the first week in November, it turned into an interminable drizzle spotted by heavy, drenching downpours. There were only three days during November in which it didn't rain throughout the daylight hours, but those were spoiled by rain after dark. The fields in

[4] Mark W. Clark, *Calculated Risk*, 261.

9

the valleys were turned and churned into impenetrable quagmires. Wheeled vehicles off the hardtop roads literally sank to their crankcases in the mud. It was not uncommon to see the wheels of jeeps and trucks banded by heavy hawsers, improvised skid chains, in an effort to gain traction in the ooze. Virtually everything on wheels came to a standstill, and the Allied armies were forced to resort to mules for transport. November became December, and still the rains came down, now cold and mixed with sleet. In the higher reaches of the Apennines, the sleet was mixed with snow. Frozen feet and frozen hands were replacing the term "trench foot" on the medical reports. Infantry companies were suffering more from the weather than from enemy mortar and artillery fire, and the enemy mortar and artillery fire were not diminishing.

Huge boulders, ledges, caves, reverse slopes, towering peaks—all were utilized by the Germans for defenses, and the overcast and snow were additional advantages. Allied progress was necessarily slow. There were no routes other than those interdicted by enemy guns, and the German artillery increased as the Allies got closer to the Gustav Line. Through holes in the overcast, the *Luftwaffe* reappeared.

The Allied soldier was digging in deeper here than at any time previously in the war. Then forward progress stopped completely. The war in Italy developed into a prolonged artillery duel with constant patrol action. From behind their prepared positions, the German gunners concentrated on preregistered targets, and the B.B.C. was describing the town of Venafro—a tiny, but important road junction—as "the hottest spot on earth." And it was.

Venafro stands at the head of the valley of the Volturno River, and immediately behind the town the mountains rise to a height of more than three thousand feet. One road, paralleling the river, leads into the center of town then cuts at a right angle to hug the floor of the valley northeastward to Isernia. The road, a two-lane hardtop, was the only access for vehicles and artillery pieces. Worse, it is almost beeline-straight from Presenzano leading into

Venafro, ideal for the German gunners on the mountaintop looking straight down that road. Virtually nothing moved along that road during the daylight hours. There was no official order, none was needed. Only the foolhardy ventured along it in the daytime. Not even the rain, the sleet, or the snow could bring about a respite from the enemy artillery fire along that road.

The combination of austere weather and rugged terrain took its toll among the Fifth and Eighth Armies. Casualty lists were gradually wearing down the fighting divisions to the point where, in some cases, line companies numbered only twenty-five effectives. The battle of attrition was underway. The apprehension of the American high command was fast approaching realization. The Italian campaign was indeed the vacuum that General Marshall had predicted, a maw into which American troops were being poured. And at Whitehall, a perplexed British Prime Minister was seeking a way around the expected Washington reaction.

The Fifteenth Army Group, comprising the American Fifth and British Eighth Armies, was under British command and, as such, "thought British." General Sir Harold R. L. G. Alexander was in command of the Fifteenth Army Group and in constant touch with his prime minister. Churchill received daily personal briefings. As early as October 3, Alexander informed Churchill that the Germans showed all apparent intentions of staging a slow and costly-to-us withdrawal up the Italian boot to an ultimate stand along a lateral line from Pisa to Rimini. Further, Alexander saw an orderly Allied advance which would shortly place them along a line above Rome.[5] But three days later, Alexander noted for Churchill a definite change in German resistance. Eisenhower, too, was advised, and the Allied planners set up schemes to circumvent any determined German effort to halt the advance. Most of these involved amphibious end runs. Some, along the Adriatic, were actually carried out.

By late in October a crisis developed in Italy. Our intelligence reports indicated that the Germans were moving additional con-

[5] Winston S. Churchill, *The Second World War,* V, 213.

tingents below Rome and that they might soon be in a position to launch a crushing counterattack.[6] Churchill reacted with what the American high command then considered undue alarm. He and the British chiefs of staff expressed the belief that if the Allied position in southern Italy became worse, it might be necessary to pour additional troops into the Mediterranean and even postpone the proposed invasion of northern France beyond the May 1, 1944, deadline.[7]

At a meeting in Bari on November 8, General Eisenhower and his deputy Theater commander, General Sir Henry Maitland Wilson, listened as Anzio was mentioned for the first time. Alexander proposed the establishment of a bridgehead behind the German lines on the plains south of Rome.[8] An attack would be directed against the Colli Laziali (Alban Hills) with the intention of disrupting German supply lines and eventually capturing Rome. To carry out the expedition, the necessary landing craft would have to be borrowed from Overlord,[9] and a date, December 20, was selected as the latest on which such an amphibious operation could be staged. By then, it was reasoned, the main Allied armies would have breached the German winter line and would be in a position from which they could link up with the amphibious forces within a week following the invasion. Then the borrowed landing craft could be released and dispatched to English ports well within time to participate in the Overlord operation in northern France.

As proposed by Alexander, the amphibious effort at Anzio would involve only one division with seven days' supplies, enough to sustain it until the linkup with the forces driving up from the south. The U.S. 3rd Infantry Division was selected for the task.[10] It was withdrawn from the line, rested and refitted, and prepared for the end run which was to take place on or about December 20.

---

[6] Kesselring, *op. cit.*, 226.   [7] Churchill, *op. cit.*, 254.

[8] Eric Linklater, *The Campaign in Italy*, 152.

[9] "Overlord" was the code name for the planned invasion of Normandy.

[10] Lucian K. Truscott, Jr., *Command Missions*, 288.

As November wore on into December, the weather worsened. The Allied advance was completely stalled. That December 20 deadline came ever closer, and finally the thought of an amphibious assault at Anzio had to be abandoned. The Allied armies were fully engaged in the laborious battle for the frozen heights of the Apennines. Eisenhower breathed more easily. He was about to leave all this behind, depart the Mediterranean to head up the Overlord operation, and he did not want his assault craft tied up in an Italian end run.[11]

The 3rd Division, now rested and refitted, was ready for battle, but it would not be used in the amphibious engagement after all. Rather, it would spearhead a new assault against the Gustav Line in a desperate effort to bring to an end the winter stalemate.[12] At a meeting in Naples on December 18, Generals Eisenhower and Clark went over the new plans for breaching the German defenses. The 3rd Division was to cross the Rapido below the town of Cassino, storm through the German positions, and open a pathway into the Liri Valley for the tanks of the U.S. 1st Armored Division. The U.S. IInd Corps was brought over from Sicily to command the renewed frontal attack. The Corps had been under the direction of General Omar Bradley in Africa and Sicily; now it was headed by Major General Geoffrey Keyes, and it was moved into the center of the Fifth Army line. Eventually the Corps would bring into the line three new divisions—the U.S. 85th, 88th, and 91st Infantry divisions—as well as the 1st Special Service Force, a specialized group of some eighteen hundred picked Americans and Canadians. For the moment, however, the 3rd and 36th Infantry divisions and that part of the 1st Armored Division already in Italy would come under its command. These units had been part of VIth Corps.

The addition of IInd Corps would not mean much for the moment, other than to add to the tactical command in the important center of the Fifth Army line. To its right, the now depleted U.S. VIth Corps held the line to the juncture with the Eighth

[11] Eisenhower, *op. cit.*, 243.   [12] Truscott, *op. cit.*, 293.

Army. To IInd Corp's left was the British Xth Corps. It might be noted that while the U.S. Fifth Army was predominantly American in its makeup, it always had British elements attached to it. It was an obvious effort on Churchill's part to still any possible accusation that the British were not carrying their full share of the fighting.

The first elements of the French Expeditionary Corps also were arriving in Italy in December of 1943 from Africa and from Sicily,[13] and this unit, consisting in the main of Algerian and Moroccan colonials under the command of General Alphonse Juin, eventually would take over the right flank of the Fifth Army line.

The generals were hard at work poring over plans of attack, but they still had not been informed that all this planning would come to naught. Other forces had been at work weeks earlier that would tie the American generals' hands. On November 28 at Teheran, the Big Three—Roosevelt, Churchill, and Stalin—began a momentous meeting that would last three days and change the entire complexion of the war in the Mediterranean. A new element was entered into the lengthy debate between the American and British planners in the person of the Russian Premier. Here in the first face-to-face meeting of the Big Three political leaders, Stalin could personally push his demands for the opening of a second front, demands which under the circumstances now seemed unwarranted. The Russians no longer were in great peril. The Red Army had been built up to huge proportions, and Soviet industry was turning out all the needed sinews of war. For more than a year on the battlefront the Russians had held the tactical upper hand over the German armies in the east. Still, Stalin went on voicing demands for a second front. He could see the mounting military might of the Americans still mostly uncommitted in battle. Only a relatively few American divisions were actually fighting. American production capacity was outdistancing all previous predictions and still had not reached its peak.

This, plus Churchill's continuing clamor for pushing the war

[13] *Ibid.*, 288. See also Linklater, *op. cit.*, 137.

into the Balkans and moving on into Central Europe, posed a political problem that the Russian leader preferred to circumvent. But at that three-day meeting, opportunities presented themselves to both Churchill and Stalin for arriving at what for the moment was a mutual agreement. Churchill at first was shocked when Stalin agreed with the American plans for simultaneous invasions of France, one from the northwest, the other from the south. He saw in it still another effort to distract the Western Allies from the Balkans and Middle Europe, thereby keeping this area open for future Russian domination. But the wily geopolitician saw also a perfect opportunity. With Roosevelt, he could listen to Stalin continue his plea for the opening of a second front; agree with the American President that it was still too early to launch a direct assault against the Continent across the English Channel; sympathize with the Russian leader that the Red Army was carrying the brunt of the ground war against the Nazis; and then, in one move, he could quiet the Russian and keep the Americans in force in the Mediterranean. At Teheran, for the first time, the term "third front" was brought up.[14]

The proposal was simple enough. The threat of a second front would be enough to tie down German divisions in northern France, but enlarging the campaign in the Mediterranean into a full-scale and active third front would bring about the expenditure of additional German troops and material, thereby alleviating the pressure along the Russian front. It would also keep alive Churchill's hopes of ultimately succeeding in carrying out his soft-underbelly theory.

General Eisenhower reported in Crusade in Europe:

> The British still favored a vigorous and all out prosecution of the Mediterranean campaign even, if necessary, at the expense of additional delay in launching Overlord; while the Americans declined to approve anything that would detract from the strength of the attack to be delivered across the Channel early in the following summer. The Americans insisted upon examining all projects for

[14] Churchill, *op. cit.*, 352.

the Mediterranean exclusively in the light of their probable assistance to the 1944 cross-Channel attack; on the other hand, the British felt that maximum concentration on the Italian front might lead to an unexpected break that would make the Channel operation either unnecessary or nothing more than a mopping-up affair.

The prime minister and some of his chief military advisers still looked upon the Overlord plan with scarcely concealed misgivings; their attitude seemed to be that we could avoid the additional and grave risks implicit in a new amphibious operation by merely pouring into the Mediterranean all the air, ground and naval resources available.[15]

The minutes of the Big Power meetings of World War II still have not been made public, but this much is known:

Churchill dusted off Alexander's proposed Anzio operation, more than doubled the original number of troops to be involved, turned it into an Anglo-American enterprise to soften the blow to General Marshall, then added the clincher—the capture of Rome, the first of the Axis capitals to come within the sights of the Allies. The operation would be Gallipoli all over again, but this time he would succeed. The idea held out wonderful prospects to the British Prime Minister.

Leaving Teheran for London, Churchill stopped off in North Africa for a short rest. He was physically exhausted and wanted a moment of relaxation. He chose a villa at the ancient city of Carthage, just outside Tunis. There he developed pneumonia and was bedded down for several weeks, and while he recuperated his newest idea marked time. So it was that the still uninformed generals in Italy continued their plans for a renewed frontal attack against the Gustav Line.

Along that line, the two Allied armies divided the front roughly in half. The Fifth Army was strung across the western side of the narrow peninsula from Isernia westward through Venafro, San Pietro d'Infante, both sides of the Mignano Gap, along the

[15] Eisenhower, *op. cit.,* 225.

rain-swollen Rapido and Garigliano rivers to Minturno, and on to the Tyrrhenian Sea. The Eighth Army was dug in along the crest of the Apennines from Isernia eastward, along the Sangro River to Ortona on the Adriatic.

The Germans had an estimated six divisions opposing the Fifth Army, only two opposite the Eighth.[16] From their commanding positions, these were enough to hold the two Allied armies in check. But neither the British nor the Americans were willing to settle for a winter-long stalemate despite the fact that everything of military importance in Italy so far as the Allied chiefs of staff were concerned already was in their hands. The cluster of air-fields in the Foggia area were in operation, the giant Flying Fortresses and Liberators were taking off and landing on regular 'round-the-clock bombing missions against the factories of the Third Reich. The supply ports of Bari and Naples long had been secured and cleared and were alive with dockside activity.

On Christmas Day, 1943, Mark Clark called a conference at Keyes's IInd Corps headquarters. In addition to the army and corps commanders, Major General Lucian K. Truscott, Jr., was called in to discuss the role his 3rd Division would play in the forthcoming attack against the Gustav Line.

Christmas Day of 1943 to most was just another day. But to the frostbitten men in the line across the snow-capped southern Italian mountains, it was a day on which the Army kept its promise of hot turkey dinners to celebrate the festive day. But as the day wore on, it became evident that the traditional Christmas feast left something to be desired. It was a long way from the turkey farms in the United States to the front lines in Italy, somewhere along the way refrigeration had broken down, and what had been meant as a holiday treat suddenly developed into gastric distress. Fortunately, the wave of diarrhea was mild if uncomfortably inconvenient.

At the IInd Corps war tent in the muddy fields back of the

[16] Clark, *op. cit.*, 240.

line, Christmas Day was filled with discussion, anticipation, apprehension, but most of all with determination to carry out the plans for the breakthrough into the Liri Valley.

Across the Mediterranean at Carthage, still another Christmas Day conference was underway, this one called by the British Prime Minister. In attendance were Generals Alexander and Eisenhower, and at that conference the broad idea of landing in force some sixty miles behind the main German defense line in Italy was spelled out.[17] It was to be a tour de force not only to quiet the Russians but also to still the voices in Commons and in Congress rising against the seemingly senseless casualty lists coming in each day from the supposedly static Italian front. And Churchill was making Rome a military necessity.[18] On the previous October 4, Hitler had signed the orders to hold onto Rome and to defend the Gustav Line. Now he was boasting that Rome would never be taken.

From a practical military standpoint, the capture of Rome was of little significance. Italy already had capitulated, the Italian Army behind the German lines had been deactivated, the Allied occupation of the Italian capital meant only a million or more additional mouths to feed. It would be a further strain on our supply lines, a sapping of the necessary stores for the buildup in Britain. But to the British Prime Minister, the taking of Rome was of paramount political importance. Rome must be taken, if only for the prestige value.

All plans, not only those concerning operations on the southern Italian front, were about to be overhauled. A dictum from the topmost level was altering the war. The earlier denial of even enough craft to mount a one-division amphibious operation at Anzio suddenly was reversed by a cablegram from Carthage to Washington.[19] The ensuing reply granted the British Prime Minister the necessary shipping to turn a spot on the map into the focal point of world attention. And he dubbed the entire undertaking "Operation Shingle."

[17] Eisenhower, *op. cit.*, 242.   [18] Churchill, *op. cit.*, 436.
[19] *Ibid.*, 436.

CHAPTER TWO

"*Anzio Will Astonish the World*"

T HE headquarters staff of the 3rd Division spent Christmas Day, 1943, reconnoitering the sector through which they would launch their frontal assault against the Gustav Line—the approaches to Mount Porchia and Mount Trocchio, the gateway to Cassino from the south. From a command post atop a height south of the twin peaks, the 3rd Division's operations officers had an excellent view of their immediate objectives—Porchia and Trocchio and the tiny town of Sant'Angelo, which stood on a slight rise above the overflowing Rapido River. Beyond Sant'Angelo lay the Liri Valley.

Securing the heights of the twin mountains would pose no problem for the veteran 3rd Division, nor, they reasoned, would it be excessively difficult to push the infantry across the flooding river. Getting the armor and field guns across, however, would be the difficult feat.[1] Studying the terrain, it was obvious that the Germans would hold the dominant positions along both flanks of the point at which the river would have to be crossed, also that enemy light artillery would be in position to knock out any bridges that might be thrown across the river. The most foreboding obstacle was the town and the mountain immediately behind it that juts up almost perpendicularly some seventeen hundred feet, the town and the mountain of the same name—Cassino.

Nothing had been mentioned about taking either the town or the mountain; yet these were the commanding positions, and in enemy hands they posed a considerable deterrent. It was an altogether dismal assignment that faced the 3rd Division, yet the staff felt they were up to it.

However, on December 28, just three days after the fateful meeting at Carthage, General Clark notified Truscott that his division after all would invade Anzio; Truscott could forget about the river crossing and concentrate again on the amphibious end run. Also, he would not be alone this time. The British 1st Division would accompany the 3rd, and there was a promise of an almost immediate buildup of the initial force.

As Clark put it, "Prime minister Churchill is back in the Mediterranean picture as a sort of super commander-in-chief, a role he likes to play."[2]

Operation Shingle was to be conducted by the U.S. VIth Corps which had been relieved of further operations on the Fifth Army's right flank by Juin's French Expeditionary Corps.

Army, Corps, and Division G–3's had a job to do and not much time in which to do it.[3] An amphibious landing is an extremely complicated maneuver requiring infinitely minute attention to detail, split-second time tables, and intricate traffic patterns worked out in advance for transport both at sea and ashore,

---

[1] Truscott, *op. cit.*, 294.   [2] Clark, *op. cit.*, 254.

[3] G–3, designation of plans and operations section of headquarters on division, corps, and army level. Plans and Operations Section on the battalion and regimental levels are designated S–3.

tons of paper work to insure that each man is landed at the right place at the right time with his equipment and supplies readily available when needed.

The planning for Anzio was hurried. The Fifth Army planning board actually had less than a month to prepare for the operation. Its first and biggest task was to overcome serious restrictions placed on such an undertaking by the diversion of shipping and materiel already allocated for the buildup in Britain. Shipping in particular posed a knotty problem. There were not enough large landing craft available in the Mediterranean to mount an invasion force and to sustain it in the approved fashion. Even with the additional craft reluctantly lent to Operation Shingle by the Overlord planners, the Fifth Army planners had to rely on improvisation. And improvisation is the pathway to disaster.

The United States and Royal navies managed to accumulate a meager eighty-four LST's,[4] relinquishing them only for an additional month away from their assigned duties at English ports. The deadline for their return—February 29. These eighty-four craft were barely enough to land the initial force of two beefed-up divisions and to bring up the remaining units and supplies from Naples on the turn-around runs. From Anzio to Naples was a full day's voyage for an LST, a distance of roughly 120 miles. Loading and unloading in the accepted manner took an interminable amount of time, and time was of the essence for the soon-to-disappear landing craft. A plan had to be worked out for their maximum use, a plan to get around the delays involved in loading and unloading. Such a plan was evolved by the G–3's closeted in the ancient palace at Caserta.[5]

[4] LST, Landing Ship Tank, an ocean-going flat-bottomed craft 328 feet long that can be beached to permit egress of personnel and vehicles through its huge bow doors and ramp.

[5] The palace, almost two centuries old, housed Fifth Army headquarters. Construction of the palace was begun in 1752 by Charles III of Naples and Sicily. Built for his wife, it was designed to rival the grandeur of Versailles. Late in 1943, the Fifth Army took over the palace for its rear echelon headquarters. Although still ornate after two centuries, the palace was dreary, dank, and pitted by the ravages of time. It was definitely not designed for habitation during those bitter

Inside the palace, numbed by the cold, the tacticians and logisticians plotted their course and wielded their slide rules against the double deadline of a hurried invasion and the loss of the all-important shipping. It was determined that the LST's would be needed for at least a month after the initial landings, and with their departure scheduled for the last day of February, D Day for Anzio would have to be on or before January 30.

Weather, the phase of the moon, and other factors governing an amphibious assault ruled the twenty-four-hour period of January 21–22 as the only practical time to stage the invasion. That gave the planners barely three weeks in which to fit the myriad pieces together.

There was another obstacle—the experience of the troops themselves in amphibious operations. General Truscott rightly believed that his 3rd Division should be permitted a dry run, a mock rehearsal in preparation for the real thing.[6] His division long had undergone amphibious training in the States, had already taken part in two D Days—in French Morocco in November, 1942, and again in Sicily the following July—and it had landed at Salerno, although not in the assault force. However, the division had absorbed large numbers of replacements in the intervening time, and these men had been exposed to little or no amphibious training before joining the 3rd. The figures showed the division had 115 per cent turnover in platoon leaders since the invasion of North Africa,[7] and these young officers were the ones on whom the success of an invasion would rest. Truscott also argued that the Navy might find a refresher course stimulating, even beneficial. After considerable and lengthy argument to get his point across, Truscott finally received the necessary Army and Navy approval. Clark admits that "it was only with the greatest difficul-

---

winter months of 1943-44. It was in this palace, by the way, that General von Vietinghoff, commander-in-chief of the German Southwestern Army Group, formally signed their unconditional surrender on May 2, 1945.

[6] Truscott, *op. cit.*, 302.

[7] Kent Roberts Greenfield (ed.), *Command Decisions*, 255.

ty that we managed time for a rehearsal of the Anzio landing by the Third Division."

It was fortunate the mock invasion was staged, for it was a complete shambles and virtually everyone concerned was in a furor. Truscott was scathing in his report on the dry run. To VIth Corps commander, Major General John P. Lucas, Truscott stated:

> No single battalion landed on time or in formation. Transports were so far offshore that assault craft required up to four and a half hours to reach the beach. No single element was landed in hand and on its correct beach. Some beaches were missed by as much as a thousand yards. No anti-tank weapons, artillery or tank-destroyer guns were ashore by daylight. No tanks were landed. Ship-to-shore communications were defective if not totally lacking.
>
> To land this division at Anzio as it was landed during the rehearsal would be to invite disaster if the enemy should counterattack at daylight with 40 or 50 tanks. In my opinion, there is grave need for additional training.[8]

Brief and bitter, Truscott's memo only began to tell the story of the rehearsal debacle on the beaches below Salerno. The infantry companies were strewn about the practice beaches in a crazy-quilt pattern. The division's artillery, placed aboard those large, floating two-and-one-half-ton trucks which the Army labeled DUKW's and the GI's more appropriately nicknamed "Ducks," ran into especially choppy water. In relatively calm water the Ducks could perform admirably. In this instance they flooded and capsized, and spilled their precious cargoes fathoms deep into the Mediterranean.

Copies of Truscott's bristling critique of the landing rehearsal were dispatched by officer courier to General Clark and the naval commander concerned, Rear Admiral Frank W. Lowry. Clark, however solicitous, pointed out there was not enough time for another rehearsal. He was well aware of the proportions the dry run had reached in proving that everything can go wrong at once,

---

[8] Truscott, *op. cit.,* 303–304. See also Clark, *op. cit.,* 268.

more than aware of the serious loss of materiel. In all, some forty-three Ducks had capsized, more than twenty howitzers and a number of anti-tank guns were lying at the bottom of the sea. Admiral Lowry, commander of Naval Task Force 81 charged with the actual Anzio landings, shared Clark's chagrin and Truscott's desire for another try. But there was no time.

The ill-fated mock invasion was staged from January 17 through January 19, leaving barely enough time for everyone concerned to get back aboard the ships and head for Anzio. The loss of the Ducks would not be too serious; the sunken howitzers would be made up temporarily by the attachment of a battalion of 105's from the 45th Division.[9] The whole force would go with the solemn promise from Admiral Lowry that his men would perform perfectly in the actual invasion.

The invasion fleet of some 250 ships and craft would set sail from Naples in the early hours of January 21, destination Anzio.[10]

Actually, the amphibious assault was only one part of a three-phase operation designed to open the Road to Rome.[11] The Anzio invasion was to be the third in a series of simultaneous maneuvers, the crowning blow. The orders were spelled out:

1. The British Xth Corps was to force a crossing of the Garigliano River, turn northward to threaten the approaches to the Liri Valley, while the U.S. IInd Corps was to push across the Rapido, on past Cassino, and into the mouth of the Liri Valley.

2. The French Corps would wheel to its left across the mountains behind Cassino to secure the commanding heights, while—

3. The U.S. VIth Corps would land some sixty miles behind the German lines, cut off the main German supply routes, capture the *Colli Laziali,* and throw the enemy into a complete rout.

All three corps were to link up within a week and prepare for the final and glorious push on Rome. This was the way General Alexander's order read. This was the dictum of the British Prime

[9] John Bowditch III (ed.), *The Anzio Beachhead,* 12.   [10] *Ibid.,* 13.
[11] Linklater, *op. cit.,* 154. See also Clark, *op. cit.,* 267.

Minister at that Christmas meeting at Carthage. But this was not the way it was to happen.

Historically we have been taught that all roads lead to Rome. Actually, very few do. For the Allies in the winter of 1943–44, only three roads led to Rome, and each was quite effectively blocked by the German armies. Highways 6 and 7 led north and northwest to Rome through the Fifth Army sector; but the German redoubt at Cassino lay astride Highway 6, and Highway 7 wends its way through the razorback Aurunci Mountains before opening onto the easily flooded Pontine Marshes. Highway 5 leads to Rome, but it runs in an east-west direction and was behind and paralleling the Gustav Line.

So, in effect, no road led to Rome so far as the Fifth and Eighth armies were concerned.

However, from the other direction, it was a different matter. It was from Rome that all the needed supplies and reinforcements poured in to the Nazi defenders of the Gustav Line—from Rome, along Highway 5 and fanning out to the south along the road spurs servicing the German defense line. And from Rome, almost due south along Highway 6 to the main strong point at Cassino flowed the German sinews of war.

Highway 6, twenty-five centuries old and known when it was first laid by the ancients as the *Via Casilina*, the inland road connecting Rome with Naples had seen military traffic virtually since its inception. Roman legions as far back as the fourth century B.C. stormed down the *Via Casilina* to do battle with the invading Samnites in the very mountains into which the Nazis had constructed their *Winterstellungen*.[12] Hannibal traversed the road some one hundred years later in an unsuccessful attempt to sack Rome. The Byzantine general Belisarius in the sixth century A.D. was the first to lead a successful attack on Rome from the south, and he did it along the *Via Casilina*. Other armies in other times fought up and down Highway 6. The Allied soldier

---

[12] *Winterstellungen*, literally "winter positions."

25

in 1944 was just another in the seemingly endless parade of militant humanity treading its way over a well-worn path.

Oddly, this more militarily important of the two highways connecting Naples with Rome is the less famous. The *Via Casilina* is little known to the average person, yet the *Via Appia* (Highway 7) is familiar to everybody. Possibly it might be that death and destruction rode the *Via Casilina*, whereas pomp, pageantry, and romance were the wayfarers along the *Via Appia*. The Appian Way was the route of the returning Roman heroes wheeling their chariots up the cobbled avenue for the traditional welcome of a grateful nation for yet another piece of overseas territory added to the ever expanding empire. Actually, the *Via Appia* is the newer of the two roads to Rome from the south; construction did not begin on it until 312 B.C.

But as the new year 1944 A.D. began, it was the *Via Casilina* that was again the workhorse of Mars, this time denuded even of its rather melodious name. It was merely Highway 6 in all the communiqués. Its more popular sister artery would retain its name and its romantic nostalgia. Only in terse military reports would the *Via Appia* be referred to as Highway 7, otherwise it was always the Appian Way. Even the least imaginative of the war correspondents could write of the glorious and ceremonious past of the *Via Appia*. So Highway 6 remained with only a number to separate it from any other road in Italy.

The Appian Way was insignificant from a military standpoint. Its use by the Germans was impractical for anything other than a purely supplemental supply route; it hugged the coast too closely and was too easily interdicted by offshore naval fire to be of any appreciable value. As for the Allies, the Appian Way's traversal through the narrow gorges of the rugged Auruncis was within too close range of the enemy guns that could be set up along the many vantage points studding those mountains. Also, the fact that it led out into the Pontine Marshes, which could be so easily inundated by the enemy, ruled out any possible thought of pushing northward along that avenue.

Then there was the weather. We had our all-weather Navy to seal off the enemy use of Highway 7, but we had only our Air Corps to cut the flow of German supplies southward from Rome along Highway 6, and in the winter of 1943–44 the weather was such that our Air Corps was limited to only two flying days in any week. With the rains and heavy overcast on their side, the Germans supplied the Gustav Line with relatively little interference.

The main rail line leading south from Rome paralleled Highway 6, and the same circumstances governed the German use of the rail line. A second rail line paralleled Highway 7, but, like the road route, it too carried only a small amount of military traffic.

If Rome were to be reached, it would have to be by storm up the *Via Casilina*. The only other avenue of approach was from the sea. And Churchill wanted Rome.[13]

Kesselring was aware of the Allied alternative of an amphibious landing near Rome, but he was not sure just where or when the amphibious assault would strike.[14]

The topography of the Italian peninsula limited the number of possible invasion sites. The mountainous spine of the peninsula tapers off eastward toward the Adriatic in a series of ridges almost the entire thousand-mile length of the country, leaving a coastal plain rarely wider than five miles. On the western side, the mountains meet the Tyrrhenian more abruptly but at varying intervals, leaving in some places plains as wide as twenty-five miles. These militarily maneuverable plains, however, are very few.

In addition to flatland on which to move about, there are other military requisites that must be met when planning an amphibious assault: a suitable beach on which the smaller craft can land their personnel and cargoes; with port facilities, and within range of aerial protection. Of all this Kesselring was aware, and he narrowed the Allies' choice to two possible sites—the area south of Rome around Anzio and, north of Rome, the better-suited possible beachhead at Civitavecchia. He was not aware, however, of the role the British Prime Minister played in selecting the site, nor

[13] Clark, *op. cit.*, 255.   [14] Kesselring, *op. cit.*, 231.

did he realize the tightness of Allied shipping and the deadline imposed on its use.

What Kesselring could reason, so could we, and we were in an ideal position to resort to subterfuge. For months, since the city fell to the Allies on the first of October, Naples had been a hotbed of espionage and counterespionage. Not all the Fascists fled Naples with the retreating Germans, nor were those who remained all behind bars. Although the volatile Neapolitan would swear on the good name of his mother and all the other things a Neapolitan would swear on that he had never been a Fascist and that the only good thing Mussolini ever did was to bring a modern sewerage system to at least some parts of Naples, no one really could be sure of his beliefs or his reactions. The modern Neapolitan is an enigma, a sparkling clown one moment, ruthless and animal-like the next. And regardless of the lip service paid to Mussolini for his attempt to install sewers in the largest city in southern Italy, most of Naples refused to be converted from the ancient practice of dumping its sewage into the streets, often from four or five floors up, and allowing the rainy season eventually to carry it out to sea. That such a widespread practice was far from sanitary and could breed all manner of disease bothered the Neapolitans not one whit; they had been living with it for so many centuries they had developed an immunity to virtually every known disease and many that are not known. Besides, the Neapolitans with their phenomenal birth rate are the greatest unsuspecting adherents to the Malthusian tenet that famine and pestilence will keep the population within bounds until a war comes along to get mankind back on an even keel. The average Neapolitan never heard of the nineteenth-century English economist-philosopher, but he thoroughly believes and practices the Englishman's theory that Nature itself will keep the population aright.

However, when not immediately concerned with living and dying and procreating, the Neapolitan is extending the range and diversity of his wily ventures. And in this atmosphere, the Army's intelligence and counterintelligence discovered Elysian fields for

gleaning and spreading both reliable and spurious military information—among the latter, the constantly recurring report that
the Fifth Army was planning an amphibious landing near the small
seaport some forty miles northwest of Rome, Civitavecchia.

The area around Civitavecchia was the more suitable for such
an undertaking. It figured that this was where the Americans
would strike. Anzio? Possibly—but it was only second best and
was not mentioned by the underground operatives. It had to be
Civitavecchia. And just as certain as the Germans were, we were
equally as certain that the Germans believed our planted story.
They had spent too many years indoctrinating the world on the
precision of the Prussian mind.

While German intelligence had its shortcomings, so too did
ours. G–2 reports on German formations in the Anzio area just
before the landing were extensive, actually more accurate than
many other pre-operation appraisals of enemy strength.[15] But
even at their best, intelligence reports lag behind existing situations
by at least two days. Many times the information is a week old.

It would have been impossible for our G–2 to have known, for
example, that the Germans had withdrawn a full division from its
beach-watching chores south of Rome just one day before the
Anzio landings,[16] or that on that same day the garrison at Anzio
and neighboring Nettuno had been whittled down to three engineer companies of the 29th Panzer Grenadier Division. The remainder of the division had been dispatched to the Cassino front.
Such information is acquired only after days of questioning captured enemy soldiers.

The information on enemy troop concentration we actually
did have was accurate, comprehensive, and virtually complete.
The location of practically every enemy division in Italy was pin-
pointed immediately prior to embarkation for Anzio, and a timetable was worked out denoting which German units could be ex-

[15] Truscott, *op. cit.*, 305.
[16] The 90th Panzer Grenadier Division. See Kesselring, *op. cit.*, 231, and
Bowditch, *op. cit.*, 16.

pected to arrive to battle the invading forces and when to expect their arrivals.[17] By the end of D Day, it was reasoned, one full division and miscellaneous units from the nearby area totaling some 14,000 men would be facing the invading Allies, and that by the third day, the Germans would have three complete divisions plus random units amounting to a fourth division to hem in the two Allied divisions and their attached units. But man for man, both sides would be about evenly matched, and we would have the greater firepower plus the guns of the naval ships offshore to tilt the scales.

Where our intelligence did fall short, and Fifth Army G–2 cannot be held completely responsible, was in not knowing of the intricate plan worked out for just such contingencies by the Nazi Field Marshal Albert Kesselring.[18] Had he not worked out such a plan in view of the evidence at hand, he would have been derelict in his duty and guilty of a heinous crime, inasmuch as he was just as much responsible for the lives and safety of the men under his command as was any theater commander on the Allied side similarly responsible. It should be noted that up until the time of his death, more than fifteen years later, Kesselring retained the respect not only of those men who served under him but also of those who opposed him on the field of battle.

Although a personal friend of Hermann Göring dating back to the early days of the *Luftwaffe*, Kesselring was a professional soldier, not a party puppet. As such he was tolerated but rarely favored by the hierarchy of the National Socialists.[19] Only his cold, hard reasoning enabled him to retain his command when it already had been determined that Rommel would head up the German armies in Italy. His logic and ability won out in that early September meeting with Hitler. Since then, he had lived up to his claims.

The details of Kesselring's containment plan were simple

[17] Truscott, *op. cit.*, 305.
[18] Greenfield, *op. cit.*, 258–59. See also Truscott, *op. cit.*, 307.
[19] Kesselring, *op. cit.*, 19.

enough. Not having the manpower to spread out along the lengthy Italian shoreline to insure against surprise invasions, he set up a system to utilize his rear echelon troops, antiaircraft personnel, those in rest areas. In effect, everyone not on the firing line was in an emergency manpower pool to act as a fire brigade in the event of an Allied invasion. On a code signal—in this instance, "Case Richard"—[20] these troops plus the mobile units and reconnaissance elements of every front-line division were to be rushed to the threatened area to form a defense line against the invaders until larger units arrived to take over.[21] A simple plan, one that worked despite the efforts of our Air Corps to isolate the battlefield for our advantage.

For weeks, while the ground and naval forces had been preparing for Operation Shingle, the Air Corps was also preparing for the Anzio landing. "Operation Strangle," they called it, and it was designed to cut rail and communication lines leading into the forthcoming field of battle to prevent the movement of enemy troops and supplies from the north.[22] That the fliers added a tremendous burden to the German supply system was indisputable. Allied air attacks inflicted great damage and necessitated a gargantuan effort in repairing it; but the fact remains that Kesselring was able to rush troops from as far away as Yugoslavia, from southern France, and from Germany itself to mount against the new attack behind his regular line,[23] and that these troops were never tactically short of ammunition or other supplies. Troops and supplies arrived in time and in sufficient quantity over the very road and rail lines that supposedly had been completely ruptured.[24] Our G-2, knowing that our ground and naval forces were restricted to only two good days of weather out of any seven during this

[20] The German code was literally "Fall Richard"; the term *Fall* is translatable into English as "Case." We used much the same in our designations of military maneuvers as "Operation Shingle" or "Operation Webfoot."

[21] Siegfried Westphal, *The German Army in the West*, 242. See also Greenfield, *op. cit.*, 259–61.

[22] Bowditch, *op. cit.*, 12–13. See also Truscott, *op. cit.*, 306.

[23] Bowditch, *op. cit.*, 20.   [24] Truscott, *op. cit.*, 306.

miserable winter of 1943–44, should have realized that our Air Corps, even more dependent upon good weather, would have been severely restricted in its Operation Strangle, and G–2 should have taken this factor into consideration when appraising the pilot reports on assignments carried out. The end result of Operation Strangle was that it failed to isolate the Anzio battlefield.

In the days immediately after Germany's final collapse, Kesselring was interviewed by American correspondents following his surrender at Saalfelden, Austria. He was quoted as saying our biggest mistake at Anzio was in landing a force too small to accomplish its mission. The German Field Marshal was overly modest. It would appear that our biggest mistake at Anzio was in underestimating the ability of a highly competent opponent—namely Kesselring—to perform well the tasks assigned him.

It is interesting to note here that no one below Army level really believed that a two-division effort at Anzio would panic the Germans into withdrawing from their prepared positions along the southern front,[25] nor were they at all convinced of Churchill's sagacity in promoting such a tenuous operation. The two American generals—VIth Corps's Lucas and the 3rd Division's Truscott—who would head up the new amphibious assault each attempted to impress upon the higher authorities the necessity of planning for a period of time longer than the seven days it was believed that Anzio would remain isolated. This anxiety was expressed at a high-level meeting on January 7.

By this date, Winston Churchill had recovered from his bout with pneumonia and had moved on from Carthage to Marrakech in Morocco. He had called a conclave of the topmost British and American military and naval leaders in the Mediterranean.[26] The object: to discuss in further detail what was now his special project. On Christmas Day he had talked over the Anzio invasion with Eisenhower and Montgomery, but only in the broadest terms since neither commander would be involved in the Italian campaign any longer. Both men were giving up their Mediter-

[25] *Ibid.*, 298, 306.   [26] Churchill, *op. cit.*, 447.

ranean commands to assume their new roles in the preparation of the Normandy invasion.

By January 7, British General Sir Henry Maitland "Jumbo" Wilson had taken over as commander-in-chief of the Mediterranean Theater. American General Jacob L. Devers assumed the Eisenhower role as theater commander of U.S. troops and was Wilson's deputy. Both men, as well as Churchill and Lord Beaverbrook, listened to Lucas and Truscott spell out their trepidations that Anzio in all probability would remain a beachhead for longer than the expected week that it was estimated it would take the armies in the south to link up with the invaders, and that this possibility should be taken into consideration in the final planning.[27]

Devers indicated that he shared the field commanders' misgivings and gave his personal assurance that the new beachhead would be fully supported, that the necessary shipping and landing craft would be kept on as long as was needed beyond the supposedly strict deadline for their transfer to English ports.

For his part, Churchill ruled out the apprehensions of the field commanders. Churchill voiced no misgivings. He was exuding confidence, unearthing every possible resource to strengthen the operation, expending every ounce of his abundant energy, boasting the optimistic belief that the landing at Anzio would almost immediately result in the Allies' overrunning all of Italy.

The Anzio invasion, he said, will "astonish the world and certainly frighten Kesselring."[28]

He was convinced the plan would work. After all, it was literally his plan!

[27] Truscott, *op. cit.*, 298–301.   [28] Greenfield, *op. cit.*, 255.

CHAPTER THREE

Preparation for Invasion

BACK in Italy, Lucas and Truscott began preparing for their roles in Operation Shingle. Truscott was very much concerned with the dry run at Salerno for his 3rd Division, now that he had garnered Mark Clark's reluctant approval. Interestingly, that rehearsal was brought up at the Marrakech meeting, and Churchill had written it off as unnecessary and time-consuming, contending that one experienced officer or noncommissioned officer in each platoon was sufficient to get the division ashore.[1] But Truscott continued to plead for the rehearsal, pointing out the small number of his troops who actually had that experience, and Churchill was overruled on the matter.

[1] VIth Corps report on January 7 meeting at Marrakech, minutes filed by Colonels E. J. O'Neill and William H. Hill.

34

Not so, however, another suggestion brought up at the same time. It had been proposed from the point of view of supply that rather than having one American and one British division stage the invasion, two American divisions should be assigned to the operation. The British used different-caliber rifles and field guns, drove different vehicles, and even ate a different type of food than the Americans. In essence, two separate systems of supply would have to be set up. But these arguments were rejected by the Prime Minister, who wanted his new Mediterranean venture to be strictly an Anglo-American show. Churchill was adamant on this point, which was to give rise later to the suspicion on Mark Clark's part that, having been first to enter Naples, the British also wanted to be first into Rome.[2]

Churchill was immovable, and Anzio was to be a joint British-American undertaking regardless of the additional problems it posed.

By January 18, most of the naval vessels were concentrating back at Naples and its satellite ports from the shambles of the dry run south of Salerno. The Neapolitan waterfront was bursting with activity as Allied port battalions and Italian longshoremen worked side by side loading supplies, ammunition, and finally troops aboard the many and varied ships nosed in along the entire harbor front. The larger ships were berthed at those docks that had been restored to operation following the earlier destruction caused by our bombers and the demolition by the fleeing Germans. The smaller, shallow-draft vessels nosed in to shore where they could.

The tiny port of Pozzuoli just north of Naples was ideal for these latter. The ancient fishermen of Pozzuoli had paved the beach with huge, flat stone blocks as a matter of convenience for themselves in landing their hauls of fish and spreading their nets to dry. The paved beach was equally convenient centuries later for our snub-nosed LST's to pull right up on the big stone blocks,

[2] The King's Dragoon Guards were the first to enter Naples on the morning of October 1, 1943.

open their bow doors, lower their ramps, and admit a line of over-loaded two-and-one-half-ton trucks to fill up their vast insides and topsides while the infantry poured aboard to occupy the space in and around and under the vehicles.

The makeup of Admiral Lowry's Task Force 81 included virtually every imaginable naval craft below the category of battleship and aircraft carrier. Among them were two command ships, four Liberties, ninety-six LCI's, those all important eighty-four LST's, fifty LCT's, eight LSI's, and a varying number of cruisers, destroyers, minesweepers, repair ships, submarine chasers, destroyer escorts, and the like.[3]

Task Force 81 was divided in two—Task Force Peter (British, under the command of Rear Admiral T. H. Troubridge, R.N.) and Task Force X-ray (American, under Lowry). Each would deposit its troops and materiel at its respective beach, the British to the north and west of Anzio, the Americans to the south and east. It was Admiral Lowry's responsibility to embark, convoy, land, and support the troops until the beachhead was firmly established.

It was also Admiral Lowry's responsibility to scout the landing sites in advance, and the Navy's findings were hardly reassuring. The waters off Anzio were much shallower than those off Salerno,[4] and the Germans had forestalled the possible use of the port by scuttling at least one ship at the mouth of the channel leading into the port. Further, two offshore sandbars would impede all but the shallowest-draft landing craft from getting within hundreds of yards of the British beaches. In short, naval charts and intelligence showed that Anzio was not an ideal site to stage an amphibious operation, but that troops could be put ashore. Once on land, the narrow Roman Plain buttressed by the *Colli Laziali* and the Lepini Mountains was far from being an ideal site for a battlefield. However, the operation was underway and would be pursued.

At the Neapolitan ports vast amounts of supplies and ammu-

[3] Bowditch, *op. cit.*, 9.   [4] *Ibid.*, 7.

nition were being stored aboard the Liberty ships. Trucks and tanks and armored vehicles trundled onto the LST's and LCT's, and the infantry clambered aboard to fill up whatever space was left. An additional two thousand two-and-one-half-ton trucks were supplied for the operation by General Brian Robertson, chief administration officer of the Fifteenth Army Group.[5] Each would be overloaded to twice its regulation capacity and backed aboard the LST's, backed aboard to speed their unloading at the beachhead and to permit the LST's to get back to Naples that much sooner for another load to bring up to Anzio.

This was the plan worked out by VIth Corps G–4, Colonel E. J. O'Neill, a plan which, by the way, also was vetoed at that meeting at Marrakech but which was put into effect regardless of that veto. The reasoning behind the rejection of O'Neill's loading plan was that it was considered extremely dangerous to have trucks loaded with live ammunition out in the open atop the LST's. But the necessity for making full use of the small number of available LST's obviated adherence to the rules set up by those not immediately involved with the solution of the problem. The main thing was to get on with the job, conflicting orders to the contrary. Throughout the entire time that Anzio was to be supplied by ship, Colonel O'Neill's unorthodox trucking system was employed.

For those four months that Anzio was to remain an isolated beachhead, LST's arrived on regular schedule, disgorging their cargoes of overloaded two-and-one-half ton trucks roaring head-first out of the gaping mouths of the cavernous vessels only to be replaced by empty two-and-one-half-ton trucks which drove head-first into the ships to be brought back to the supply dumps at Naples to load up and start the cycle over again.

Back in at Naples, head in at Anzio; it saved precious minutes where minutes counted, when they were under the eyes of enemy 280-mm. railroad guns. Minutes saved on just one vehicle added

[5] General Brian Robertson, son of Sir William Robertson, chief of the Imperial General Staff of the British Army in World War I.

up considerably when more than fifty vehicles were involved. It meant hours saved in the unloading and reloading of just one LST at Anzio, hours that could give German artillery observers time enough to register their big railway guns on the bulky ships at the quay some twenty miles away. With no LST's to spare, regulations had to be ignored.

By the night of January 20, all was in readiness. The ships were loaded, the troops aboard, the plans gone over for the last time, and in the early morning hours of the twenty-first the invasion fleet set sail. It headed almost due west toward a rendezvous point off Sardinia and Corsica. The sea was calm, the weather perfect. The third phase of the operation to end the winter stalemate and capture Rome was underway.

Timed to coincide with the Anzio landings were the other two phases of the over-all operation. Actually, they had already begun when Admiral Lowry's armada set sail from Naples. As explained in the general order issued by Alexander, Fifth Army's new undertaking was: "To draw enemy reserves which might be employed against the assault landing; and then create a breach in his front through which every opportunity will be taken to link up rapidly with the seaborne operation."[6]

Fifth Army ordered the British Xth Corps, now reinforced by the addition of the British 5th Division which had come over from the Eighth Army front, to cross the Garigliano near the coast, then turn inland in the direction of Cassino. The French Expeditionary Corps, on the right, was to continue its push through the mountains, wheeling to its left to gain the heights above Cassino, while the American IInd Corps, in the center, was to force a crossing of the Rapido and break into the Liri Valley. All this was planned to take place on the eve of the Anzio invasion and was intended to throw the Germans off balance.

The night before the start of the entire three-phase operation, the daily summary issued by Fifth Army G–2 indicated that the Germans also were suffering from the daily attrition of static war and the weather.

[6] Clark, *op. cit.*, 271.

Within the last few days there have been increasing indications that enemy strength on the Fifth Army front is ebbing due to casualties, exhaustion and possibly lowering of morale. One of the causes of this condition, no doubt, has been the recent continuous Allied attacks. From this it can be deduced that he has no fresh reserves and very few tired ones. His entire strength will probably be needed to defend his organized defensive positions.

In view of the weakening of the enemy strength on the front as indicated above, it would appear doubtful if the enemy can hold the organized defensive line through Cassino against a co-ordinated Army attack. Since this attack is to be launched before Shingle, it is considered likely that this additional threat will cause him to withdraw from his defensive position once he has appreciated the magnitude of that operation.[7]

The daily intelligence summary seemed to be echoing the hopes and desires of Winston Churchill.

In any event, the British achieved their crossing of the lower Garigliano, established their bridgehead, and continued to push northward against mounting enemy opposition. Likewise, the French on the right continued their efforts to gain the heights overlooking Cassino. But both efforts were slower and more difficult than had been expected.

In the center, disaster struck.

In the center, the American 36th Infantry Division, newly back in the line after its reorganization following the devastating losses it suffered during the invasion of Salerno four months earlier, was charged with what any infantry soldier will readily admit is the most difficult of all infantry maneuvers—crossing a narrow, swift, unfordable river against a well-dug-in enemy. Under the best of circumstances from a military standpoint, only an experienced outfit well trained in the particular maneuver can have even a slight hope of succeeding. This was pointed out earlier by the staff of the 3rd Division when the river crossing was originally assigned to that outfit. The 3rd was experienced and well trained,

---

[7] Truscott, *op. cit.*, 306.

yet its officers had voiced serious doubts about the success of this maneuver.

The 36th at this time was a poor selection to replace the 3rd in such a difficult engagement. Where the 3rd was aggressive, high in spirits, and aware of its potential, the 36th was none of these. It was still suffering from the shock of having been severely mauled in its first encounter with the enemy. But the 36th was the only division available to Clark, and it had to be used.

The Rapido River is barely sixty feet wide and in the dry season is only a trickle of a stream. But in January, 1944, the Rapido truly lived up to its name. After three months of continuous rain, the Rapido was a torrent. Added to this, the Germans had methodically dynamited the upstream dams, further contributing to the cascade of water pouring down the length of the narrow river.

The Rapido, although nine feet deep and flowing at the rate of eight miles an hour, had not spilled its banks. If it had, it would have eliminated one obstacle facing the foot soldiers of the 36th— that of getting the assault boats into the water and the men into the boats. As it was, the Rapido was still some two or three feet below its vertical banks, and this presented an awkward situation when trying to lower the boats into the river and board them, all the while under fire of enemy guns only sixty feet away.[8]

These were not the only problems facing the men of the 36th. First, the division's defense perimeter was a mile back from the river. This circumstance afforded the enemy the opportunity to undo each night all the preparations that had been made under the greatest of difficulties the preceding day. Paths cleared through mine fields to the river's edge were easily resown with mines by German night patrols. This meant that for the men of the 36th, when the attack got underway, a mile's length from the line of departure to the river had to be crossed at night through a mine

---

[8] Since this book concerns primarily the Anzio operation, references to related actions must be brief. However, for the full story of the Rapido River crossing the author recommends Fred Majdalany's excellent *The Battle of Cassino*, in particular, Part II.

field and against murderous enemy fire, all this while weighted down with the normal battle paraphernalia as well as with assault boats to get them across the river. But it had to be done, and the 36th Division was charged with carrying it out.

At eight o'clock on the night of January 20, well after sunset, the assault companies of the 141st and 143rd Infantry Regiments set out on their mission. The 141st was to cross the river north of the town of Sant'Angelo, the 143rd to the south of it.

Sant'Angelo was a group of houses set on a knoll some forty feet high above the banks on the far side of the Rapido in an S-turn of the river a few miles south of Cassino. The Germans had been preparing their positions for weeks and turned the small group of stone buildings into a ring of fortresses from which it was impossible to dislodge them even with the most concentrated artillery fire. Further, they had ringed their bank of the river with foxholes and machine-gun emplacements, battlements which could be manned as soon as the American attack began.

Then there was the fog.

A thick ground haze settled in over the entire area shortly before the jump-off. An experienced formation would have considered it a boon. To the men of the 36th it only added to their misery. Groping their way across the mine field with their own artillery laying down a creeping concentration before them, the fog-bound men of the 36th became lost and intermingled with other units. Exploding mines and enemy counter-battery fire were taking their toll of officers and noncoms, requiring constant halts for reorganization, adding to the over-all confusion. As the supporting units overtook the assault troops, disorder became complete.

Nevertheless, the river was reached, and, with the enemy only sixty feet away, the American artillery was ordered to cease firing. In the lull and in the fog, German riflemen and machine gunners relied on their ears instead of the eyes to spot the advancing Americans, and at this range they couldn't miss.

Without further artillery support and with most of their

41

assault boats punctured or shredded by enemy fire, the men of the 141st and 143rd Infantry regiments began their crossing of the Rapido River. Of the boats that reached the bank intact, many were riddled before getting into the water, others were swamped and sank, still others went spinning off downstream as casualties of the swift current. Relatively few reached the far side of the Rapido.

An hour after setting out, portions of two companies of the 141st had gained a foothold on the German side of the river north of Sant'Angelo. To the south, the 143rd had almost a battalion across primarily on account of the fact that the division's engineers had succeeded in constructing two footbridges across the river. It was not until after dawn that the Germans discovered and knocked out the 143rd's bridges.

As dawn broke on January 21, the Anzio invasion fleet was well out in the Tyrrhenian heading for its rendezvous point off Corsica and Sardinia. The commanders knew of the action supposed to be taking place in the Cassino sector to draw troops away from the area where they would be staging their invasion, but they had no word on how the battle in the south was going. First reports would not be radioed to them for hours.

And as dawn broke over the tiny town of Sant'Angelo, the remnants of a battalion of Americans were digging in across the river south of that town, a relative handful across and digging in to the north of the town. The two groups were cut off from each other and had their backs to the river, each with distorted ideas of what progress the other was making. There was no communication. The lines connecting the field phones were cut, and those radios that had been carried across the river were waterlogged and inoperable. As the sun came up and burned through the fog, the commanders of the two groups of Americans could see for themselves the hopeless predicament that faced them. Cut off. Out of communication. No idea of when or whether reinforcements would arrive. And now they were under enemy observation from the heights above. They could see German tanks and self-propelled guns being wheeled into position to wipe out their bridgeheads. With this, Major David M. Frazior, commander of the 1st Battalion, 143rd, sent back a messenger asking permission to withdraw to safety across the river. But before the messenger returned with the order to hold where they were, Major Frazior had taken it upon himself to order an evacuation.[9]

Then there remained only the remnants of the two companies of the 141st still holding onto a fingertip of shell-pocked land on the far side of the Rapido. Curled up in their holes, conserving their ammunition, they awaited darkness so that they too might get back across the river. It would be a full twelve hours of agony. The enemy was turning loose every gun in the vicinity against that handful of Americans, everything from small arms up to the dreaded 88's.

At 36th Division Headquarters, meanwhile, General Keyes was conferring with the division commander, Major General Fred Walker.[10] Ordering would be a better word, ordering the 143rd back across the river into the positions it had too readily given up, ordering reinforcements for the two companies of the 141st still holding on to their tiny bridgehead north of Sant'Angelo. Keyes was doing his utmost to restore order to the chaotic situation. But his orders were slow in getting from division to the regimental command posts, and it was not until four o'clock in the afternoon that the 143rd pushed off in its second attempt to establish a foothold on the far side of the river. By this time the Germans had brought up reinforcements. The 211th Grenadier Regiment, the 115th Reconnaissance Battalion and part of the 104th Panzer Grenadier Regiment moved into position to augment the force already holding the far side of the Rapido.

The now seriously depleted 1st Battalion, 143rd, managed to get a small number of men back across the river only to run into stiffer opposition than that which had forced their earlier retirement. The regiment's 3rd Battalion had better luck, ferrying across three rifle companies and constructing a footbridge across

[9] Clark, *op. cit.*, 274.   [10] *Ibid.*, 275.

the river by nightfall over which the 2nd Battalion crossed during the night. Both battalions managed to push on for about five hundred yards. At daybreak the Germans unleashed the full fury of their reinforced counterattack, and by noon it was all over for the 143rd. Those who could got back to their former assembly areas, but the 143rd Infantry Regiment was considerably fewer in number.

To the north of Sant'Angelo, meanwhile, the 141st Infantry was expanding its bridgehead, pushing almost a thousand yards beyond the river bank. With his three battalions across the Rapido, Lieutenant Colonel Aaron W. Wyatt, Jr., commander of the 141st, appeared to be succeeding. Another fog was settling in on the battlefield, and attempts were being made to throw a Bailey bridge across the river to bring up armor and self-propelled guns.[11] Also, the division's reserve regiment—the 142nd—was being readied to be thrown in to continue the attack.

Actually, by this time and counting the hapless 143rd, a total of six battalions were across the river. On the strength of this, IInd Corps commander General Keyes later stated: "It was proper and sound to continue the attack."[12]

Fog or no fog, the German gunners had the bridging point too well registered. The Bailey bridge was never constructed, nor did the 142nd ever come out of reserve to reinforce the bridgehead.

The fog lifted again sometime in the afternoon of January 22, and the Germans renewed their efforts of systematically eliminating the American toehold on their side of the river. American gunfire, easily distinguishable by sound from that of the enemy, gradually diminished until it died out completely. As dusk settled in on the Rapido River Valley on the second full day of battle, the Germans again were in complete possession of their side of the river and the American 36th Division had suffered its second thorough mauling in less than half a year. It had lost more than

[11] Bailey bridge, a lightweight steel truss bridge of sectional design capable of being erected in the field with relative ease and speed.
[12] Clark, *op. cit.*, 276.

two thousand men in an unsuccessful attempt to score what had been hoped would be an important breakthrough on the road to Rome.

The 36th had tried and failed.

After the war, an effort was made in Texas by former members of the 36th Division, who banded together in an association, to force Congress to lay the full blame for the Rapido River disaster on General Mark Clark. They cited casualty figures of 155 killed, 1,052 wounded, and 921 missing in action. Total casualties in the unsuccessful engagement totaled 2,128. The group charged Clark with unjustifiably expending the lives of the men of the 36th in a foolhardy and impossible operation.

However, a Congressional board of inquiry headed by Representative Andrew J. May, the chairman of the House Committee on Military Affairs, ferreted out the facts of the Rapido River crossing. Clark's role was that of a middleman; the operation had been ordered by Fifteenth Army Group commander General Alexander both to score a breach in the Gustav Line and to serve as a diversionary movement to cover the amphibious landings at Anzio. The board also learned that the river crossing was far from impossible, that the British just a few days before had staged a successful crossing of the Garigliano, which is fed by the Rapido, only a few miles downstream from the point where the 36th attempted its crossing. Too, the 34th Division successfully crossed the Rapido under equal if not more difficult conditions farther upstream several days later.

In a letter to chairman May, Secretary of War Robert P. Patterson stated:

> ... I have carefully examined the reports in this case and it is my conclusion that the action to which the 36th Division was committed was a necessary one and that General Clark exercised sound judgement in planning it. While the casualties are to be greatly regretted, the heroic action and sacrifice of the 36th Division undoubtedly drew the Germans away from our landing at Anzio during the critical hours of the first foothold, thus contributing in

45

major degree to minimizing the casualties in that undertaking and to the firm establishment of the Anzio beachhead.[13]

General Clark was completely exonerated by the Congressional board of inquiry, but never within the borders of the state of Texas. Many years later, Texas legislators in Washington succeeded in blocking the appointment of General Clark as Army chief of staff purely because of the disaster suffered in Italy in January, 1944, by the Texas National Guard division.

Clark had his faults, as most men have, but the 36th Division's difficulties in January, 1944, were their own and could not rightfully be charged against him. They were handed a difficult but not impossible assignment, and failed. Clark's mistake may have lain in choosing the 36th for the role. He is quoted as saying later: "I selected (the 36th) for the tough, unglamorous job at the Rapido because I knew its men had the stuff to get across the river if anybody could."[14] Actually he had no other choice. His more experienced divisions already were on the line or en route to Anzio, and only the advance parties of the two new divisions—the 85th and 88th Infantry divisions—had arrived in Italy by this time. It had to be the 36th; there was no other.

The 36th Division was one of three National Guard divisions fighting in Italy. The other two—the 34th and 45th—were made of the same stuff basically: the hard core of National Guard cadre filled out with inductees who had been brought up to the divisions as replacements. All three had undergone similar training under similar conditions and in the same amount, the only difference being that the 34th had received the greater part of its pre-combat training outside the United States. The 34th was selected to be the first American division to be sent to the United Kingdom as a show of strength and intention following our declaration of war against the Axis powers. While the 34th completed its training in Britain, the 36th and 45th trained side by side in Texas, in the Louisiana maneuvers of 1941, in amphibious training on Cape

[13] Clark, *op. cit.*, 279.   [14] *Ibid.*, 280.

Cod in 1942, and in mountain training in Virginia before both divisions were shipped to North Africa in 1943.

The 34th received its battle baptism in the African campaign and suffered a severe setback at Kasserine Pass. The 45th saw its first combat in the invasion of Sicily. The 36th, however, was not committed to battle until it landed in the first wave at Salerno. "Operation Avalanche" they called that, and the 36th was swallowed up in it. Sloshing ashore on the heels of the 36th at Salerno was one regimental combat team—the 179th—of the 45th Division, still fresh and eager after a series of hard-fought triumphs in Sicily, and in the Texans' own words then, "We were never so glad to see that Thunderbird in all our lives."[15] The remainder of the 45th Division followed the 179th ashore and literally saved the hide of the 36th as well as the beachhead itself. Under one of the ablest commanders of World War II, Major General Troy H. Middleton, the 45th was thrown into the line at the darkest moment of the Salerno beachhead, and its 189th Field Artillery Battalion was actually barrel-sighting its 155-mm. howitzers against the onrushing Germans. At that point there was serious consideration given to evacuating the beachhead. At his command tent under a fig tree near Paestum, Middleton was overheard telling General Clark, "Mark, leave enough ammunition and supplies. The 45th is staying."

And stay it did. So did Fifth Army.

Middleton, a non-West Pointer, a graudate of Mississippi State College, a veteran of the Mexican border dispute, the youngest regimental commander in the A.E.F. in World War I, was to be given a third star as result of Salerno. Shortly, he was to give up command of the 45th, ultimately to lead the VIIIth Corps in its participation in the cross-Channel operation the following summer. Suffering with arthritis that had been aggravated by the

---

[15] The shoulder insigne of the 45th Infantry Division was the Indian thunderbird, designed as a yellow bird on a red background. Originally the division's insigne was the Indian good luck sign of a swastika. That, of necessity, was changed following our declaration of war against the Nazis.

miserable late fall weather in southern Italy, Middleton left the division in November of 1943 for a brief stay at Walter Reed Army Hospital. It was with a feeling of great loss that the men of the 45th watched him go. His soldiers appreciated him, he was a fine gentleman and a great commanding officer. His bent was not along the spit-and-polish line; he was a natural for a National Guard division. Inspections and saluting were for the Regular Army; fighting was for the National Guard. While still undergoing training in the States, he would address the men of his division: "All I want is just what you want—to get this war over with so I can get back to Louisiana and do some fishing."

At other times he would say without the slightest bit of reproach, "I know I have a fighting outfit. I can tell that from the Provost Marshal's report." The 45th did manage to get into its share of mischief while it was undergoing Stateside training.

A commanding general like that was bound to be missed, and he was bound to be appreciated. Appreciation of Middleton's generalship extended up to Eisenhower, who wanted him to lead a corps in Normandy. He was advised that Middleton was hospitalized and crippled with arthritis, but Eisenhower cabled Marshall in the Pentagon: "You send the man and I'll send him into battle on a litter, because he can do better that way than most commanders I know. I'd rather have a man with arthritis in the knee than one with arthritis in the head."

He got the man.

Eisenhower was to take still another general from the 45th and give him command of a corps in northern France, Raymond S. McLain, an Oklahoma City banker who, as a brigadier general, was artillery commander of the 45th in the Mediterranean.

Both men went on to greater accomplishments in the cross-Channel operation, McLain to take over the 90th Infantry Division and later to be given a corps command. It was Middleton's VIIIth Corps that secured the Cherbourg peninsula and later was to figure as the prime mover in setting up the eradication of Von Rundstedt's salient in the Ardennes.

Fifth Army troops wading ashore from LCI's
at the beachhead near Anzio, January 22, 1944.

Signal Corps

The 3rd Division comes ashore at Anzio on D Day.

Signal Corps

Tanks and infantry of the British 1st Division assembling
on the beach on D Day for their drive inland to the Albano road.

Imperial War Museum

British self-propelled "Priest" gun unloading from LST at Anzio.

Imperial War Museum

Major General John P. Lucas, VIth Corps commander at Anzio.

Signal Corps

Major General W. R. C. Penney,
commander of the British 1st Division at Anzio.

Imperial War Museum

The anti-aircraft units were always on the alert.

Signal Corps

The infantry patrol invades No Man's Land
to blast Germans out of a farmhouse.

Signal Corps

The George Patton legend to the contrary, it was Middleton who saved the Battle of the Bulge. It was his order to stand and fight in place, to build up islands of resistance, knowing that they would be surrounded, but all the while to slow down the German advance and gain time in which to bring up reinforcements. He was criticized at first by Patton for ordering the 101st Airborne Division to hold the important road hub of Bastogne. Later, old "Blood and Guts" admitted it was a stroke of genius.

Rather, it was a page from Middleton's handbook. He long had instilled his theory in the soldiers under his command: "If you want to hold a position you can do it; the other fellow will quit first." It had worked at Salerno and it worked again at Bastogne.

Middleton turned over command of the 45th on a rainy November afternoon at the division's forward command post in a muddy olive grove near the town of Presenzano. His successor was Major General William W. Eagles, who had been the assistant division commander of the 3rd Division. The two men shook hands under the dripping trees, and Middleton climbed into his staff car and was driven off. No formalities. Middleton was like that. He just drove off.

The 45th would continue to be fortunate in the selection of its commanding generals. Eagles, at first suspect because he was a West Pointer and had come from the Regular Army 3rd Division, was tall, lean, gray-haired, and wore glasses. He was mild mannered, soft spoken, and still retained his Hoosier accent. He smoked a pipe and appeared studious. But, like Middleton, he was constantly on the go, invariably up front with his infantry regiments determining for himself the situation that confronted his division. He took over a well-operating military machine and made no changes, and in a comparatively short while gained the confidence and respect of his new command. He was an excellent choice to succeed Middleton, a solid person, a good soldier.

Eagles' new command may have been National Guard, but it was the equal of the other units assigned to the Anzio operation. As a National Guard division it was treated like a country cousin by the Regular Army men who were running the war, but it was always thus. Nevertheless, the 45th asked no favors. It had the self-assuredness, the *esprit de corps* that comes from the knowledge that it had performed well all the tasks alloted to it. It was a proud division with a willingness to tackle anything it was asked to do. These attributes it shared with its sister National Guard division in Italy at the time—the 34th. The 34th originally was from Iowa; the 45th from Oklahoma, Colorado, New Mexico, and Arizona.

The 36th was from Texas. It should have been proud, cocky to the point of belligerence, but it was not. After its initial introduction to combat at Salerno, the division's attitude was almost apologetic. Its character was hangdog, dejected. The 36th at a later date would find itself, would redeem its promised potential as a fighting unit. One day it would drink from the invigorating cup of victory that would restore its self-esteem, but that would come long after its assignment to cross the Rapido.

The 34th and 45th, on the other hand, presented a different countenance. Possibly after its defeat at Kasserine Pass, the 34th might have felt much the same as the 36th did after Salerno, but that was several battles ago. In the meantime, the 34th swallowed the bitter herb of Kasserine Pass, rose again, and went on. As for the 45th, it had not known defeat.

On January 9, the 45th was relieved on the line by the newly arrived French. It was enjoying virtually its first respite since landing in Sicily the preceding July. Back in the area around Piedimonte d'Alife and Telese, that tiny mountain resort famed through the centuries for its mineral waters and sulphur baths, the Thunderbirds were more interested in the wines of the region than in its mineral waters, and the rain-swollen rivers were less odoriferous for bathing purposes than were the famed sulphur baths. And there was a taste of home. Movie comedian Joe E. Brown was touring that part of the world with a USO troupe consisting of himself and a piano player. It should be noted that relatively few of the members of the fighting divisions were treated to the delights of the touring minstrels unless on pass back to the base sections. But Joe E. Brown was a singular exception. He went to the fighting men, performing in the rain and the mud for highly appreciative audiences.

These few days of rest and relaxation were welcome ones to the tired infantrymen. Those who could not get passes to Naples stayed behind to make their own divertisement. Someone in D Company, 179th Infantry dug up a football, and before long two teams were splashing around in the mud of a barely defined gridiron. They played for the pure enjoyment of something to do. But Sergeant Ralph Martin of the soldier newspaper *Stars and Stripes* dropped by, noted that one of the players was Lieutenant George Poschner, a former All-American end at the University of Georgia. To the soldiers, their sodden football game was a pleasant pastime, but the next day they read all about it in the *Stars and Stripes*. The game was described in detail; even the stars gained recognition. It seems that there in knee-deep mud they had staged the first in what was to become a series of Spaghetti Bowl football games.

A year later at the big amphitheater at Leghorn with nurses and Wacs in the grandstands, two bruising, specially selected teams would meet each other in the second Spaghetti Bowl contest. The original was merely a mud-splattered lark, the product of a soldier-reporter's imagination.

During those early days of January, 1944, those who could wangle it went to Naples, the Big City. Naples probably was to World War II what Paris was to World War I. Paris in World War II never did live up to expectations, perhaps because its reputation was exaggerated beyond all contrast or because in the second war the city had come under the heels of enemy occupation which might have made the populace sullen. Although it, too, had been occupied by German troops, Naples was different. Naples was a vibrant, pulsating city which seemed to be inhabited only by clowns and shady characters. It was a city affording anything the American soldier might want, but for a price. Naples had fleshpots,

Naples had grand opera. The choice was up to the visiting soldier, and some of the visitors even managed to combine the two. It was not unknown that some of the sopranos on the stage were equally available in the boudoir. Naples had been a seaport for too many centuries, had played host to too many victorious armies. The Fifth Army was merely the latest to invest the city and, in turn, to be invested by it.

The Peninsular Base Section was in full occupation of Italy's number-one city of the south. It took over from the 82nd Airborne Division troops which were garrisoning Naples immediately following the fall of the city. P.B.S., the giant military octopus whose tentacles stretched out to engulf the municipal and provincial governments, the day-to-day existence of the Italian civilian and GI alike, the comings and goings of naval ships and personnel. In short, behind the actual firing line all allegiance was paid to P.B.S. And P.B.S. meant MP's. The rear echelon was swarming with them, and the MP's, facing the constant threat themselves, would in turn pass on the warning that the penalty for any wrongdoing was transfer to the infantry. But for the men already in the infantry, what? Little did the rear echelon realize that a worse punishment for the infantrymen would be transfer to the Peninsular Base Section. So the infantrymen in Naples on a pass, or even without a pass, made their own rules. They turned sections of the sprawling city into a veritable Gomorrah—not that it was difficult, for these sections of the Mediterranean seaport had always been sin pits, only now they were doing better business than usual. The soldier on the town was living for the moment. Anything he wanted was available in Naples, but most of what he wanted lay behind an openly marked "Off Limits" sign. Whole areas of Naples were "Off Limits," but this mattered not to the soldier on the town. He had grown accustomed to taking the things he wanted, and a mere sign wouldn't stop him, nor would the presence of rear echelon MP's. Besides, he could see the activity going on along the waterfront. Other soldiers were boarding boats for still another invasion, and he knew it was only a matter of time before he would be aboard the same boats heading for the same place, back to the foxhole to face the world of anxiety, of frustration, and of death. Little wonder, then, that the soldier on the town for the moment would do exactly as he chose regardless of the limits the rear echelon would like to place on his activities.

Meanwhile, the topside planning went on. At one point, it had been planned to use the troops of the 504th Parachute Infantry Regiment and the 509th Parachute Infantry Battalion in an air drop on Anzio,[16] but this was ruled out for two reasons. Their drop would have alerted the Germans to the impending operation, pinpointing the area to be invaded. Further, their primary objective was relatively the same as that of the British 1st Division. In the end, both parachute units were attached to the 3rd Division and boarded boats the same as infantrymen.

Anzio, it should be pointed out, was a collection point for a conglomeration of irregular formations, and here again the Prime Minister was at work. Throughout World War II, Churchill entertained some rather bizarre notions concerning the conduct of the war, constantly favoring and promoting unorthodox military formations over the regulation units. Anzio bore witness to this. In addition to the British 1st and American 3rd divisions, there were Rangers, Commandos, Special Service forces, paratroopers, and what not, each trained for a particular task, none of which they were called on to perform in establishing the new beachhead. Rather, they were utilized as regular infantry companies, battalions, and regiments. And it was as regular infantry units that the Rangers, Commandos, and paratroopers clambered aboard the invasion craft at Naples on January 19 and 20 in time to set sail for the new mission.

At four minutes past midnight, January 22, Admiral Lowry's armada of more than 250 ships reached the transport area off

[16] Bowditch, *op. cit.*, 6.

Anzio. The sea was calm, the night was black. H hour was set for two o'clock in the morning. Almost two hours to wait. Two hours for the final check of equipment, final plans, and instructions to the men in the squads, the last chance for any changes to be made.

There were none.

Far to the north, a small but purposefully noisy Allied naval force staged a mock invasion along the coast in the vicinity of Civitavecchia, shelling the shoreline and carrying out dummy landings.[17] It was timed to coincide with the actual landings at Anzio, also to lend credence to the reports the Germans had received about a landing at Civitavecchia.

As for Anzio itself, no preliminary shelling of the waterfront and immediate inland areas by the escorting warships was ordered.[18] To gain surprise, only two of the newly developed British rocket craft would be used to soften up the beach defenses. At H hour minus ten minutes, these especially fitted LCT's were to unleash thousands of five-inch rockets on the beaches to destroy enemy defenses and rout any German units which might be lying in wait.

Aboard the command ship *Biscayne* as H hour approached, the Army and Navy commanders of the operation learned by radio some of the details of the diversionary action going on in the south. They learned that things were not going too well, especially for the 36th Division in its attempt to cross the Rapido. Just how badly things were going, they would not learn until days later.

Aboard the other vessels, the infantrymen of the first waves were brought up out of the hot holds. The cool night air brushed their sweating faces, filled their lungs, and helped dispel some of the anxiety welled up within them. No matter how many invasions a soldier has behind him, there is always a moment of fear that is built up in the closeness of the cramped quarters below decks. The open bravado is purely synthetic, designed to over-

[17] Linklater, *op. cit.*, 188.   [18] Bowditch, *op. cit.*, 14.

come the uncertainty that develops immediately before battle.

Beach-identification groups already were aboard their landing craft, preceding the first wave onto the beaches to locate the landing sites and designate them with colored lights pointing out to sea; red beach, yellow beach, green beach, traditional of all amphibious operations.

The usual loading confusion was apparent on the decks of the personnel carriers. Over the ships' public address systems could be heard the commands: "Boat team 11, take your stations."

The usual scuffling of rubber-soled shoes (the British boots with their hobnails were noisier) on the steel decks, the inevitable voice above the hubbub: "Bob. Where's Bob?" And the captain who misplaced his map case, the sergeant counting off his squad, and the private whose chocolate D rations are missing, obviously pilfered by some sweet-toothed friend below decks.

To the wary it all sounds louder than it is. To the command it is all unnecessary. Tensions mount, tempers are triggered. And finally they are over the side and down the nets and into the landing boats. Then the endless circling of the craft, the interminable waiting. It is dark and clammy, and the spray from the boats' bobbing wets faces and hands but, worst of all, equipment. The worry about wet equipment disperses all other worries.

Suddenly the night lights up and a deafening roar pierces the eardrums. It is ten minutes to two, and the rocket-firing LCT's have opened up. The entire sky is aflame with the fiery rockets as the salvo grows in intensity. Off in the distance the shoreline is ablaze and the rumble of the rockets' impact is like an echo.

Just as suddenly as it started, it stops.

The blackness of the moonless night once again engulfs the shore and the sea and the boats. Eardrums still pulsating from the racket of the rockets make it impossible to distinguish the noise of the tiny flotilla's engines as the boats, now in their wedge-shaped formations, surge in toward the beach.

At exactly two o'clock in the morning, January 22, 1944, the invasion craft thumped against the sand, lowered their ramps, and the infantrymen scrambled across the beach and up into the tall grass and on.

The first wave was ashore.

The invasion of Anzio was underway.

CHAPTER FOUR

Case Richard

T HE Roman Plain at Anzio stretches inland some twenty miles, rising slowly from the sea as it spreads across almost flat farmlands and reclaimed marshes to the now extinct volcanic heights of the *Colli Laziali* and the Lepini Mountains, both of which rise abruptly to forbidding summits of some three thousand feet. Here and there are patches of woodland, dense in some places.

Three roads lead out of Anzio, one to the northwest and hugging the coastline—the *Via Severiana*, it continues on up to the mouth of the Tiber then turns inland to Rome. The middle road heads due north out of Anzio for more than ten miles, then cuts northwest to join Highway 7 (the *Via Appia*) near Albano at the foot of the *Colli Laziali*. A third road heads east from Anzio, passes

57

through Nettuno, then turns northeastward to cut Highway 7 at Cisterna.

The latter two were the main roads within the beachhead.

One led directly toward the immediate military objective of the *Colli Laziali*. The other provided an approach to the south and around that objective. Both were to be the scenes of fierce fighting in the months to come.

Few other roads at Anzio were paved. Most were dirt lanes suitable for little more than oxcart paths and were used for that purpose by the farmers of Latium, as the entire area is known.

For some four or five miles behind Anzio a pine forest spreads inland. Known as the Padiglione Woods, it would provide excellent cover for supply dumps and troop assembly points. A more thickly wooded area, dense with underbrush, lay to the west on the other side of the Anzio-Albano road. On the maps it is listed as the *Selva di Nettuno* (the Nettuno Wilds), and wild land it is from the road westward to the sea, as the veterans of the British 1st Division were to discover. It was also "wadi" country, a term left over from the African campaign alluding to the many deep ravines and narrow gullies carved into the volcanic loam that formed the Roman Plain by centuries of rainwater draining toward the sea. Many were fifty feet deep, barely six feet wide, and had absolutely perpendicular sides. These wadis were dry most of the year, but during the rainy season the water in their bottoms would be almost hip deep.

What was to become the Anzio beachhead had been one of Benito Mussolini's prized public works projects only a few years earlier. He had instituted a giant reclamation program which turned the otherwise useless bogs into arable, fertile, and valuable farmland stretching for scores of miles southeastward from Rome over the Pontine Marshes. Huge drainage ditches were constructed, modern villages emerged from the swamps, and hundreds of *"podere"* studded the region. These, too, were to figure in the ultimate fighting, for, as the Allied soldier would readily admit, the Italian stone-mason was a master at constructing formidable,

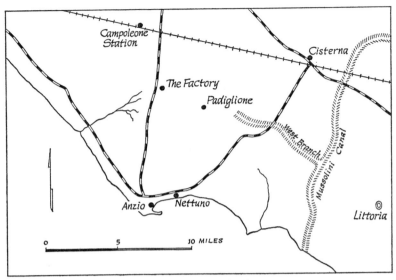

Roads out of Anzio

thick-walled farmhouses that could be turned into veritable fortresses easily defended by a handful of men with little more than rifles and a light machine gun. Each of these *podere* would, in its turn, hold up an entire company of infantry and would take a direct assault by tanks or tank destroyers to overcome a squad of enemy holed up inside. Usually painted a bilious blue, these square two-storied *podere* were of a uniform visual monotony typical of a governmental housing project. Each had emblazoned above its entryway the year of its construction, the year numbered not in *Anno Domini* but in *Anno Mussolini*. There for all to see was the evidence that these houses were built in the twelfth year of the Fascist regime.

Other mementos of the *Duce's* beneficence were scattered throughout the region. The huge drainage ditch into which all others flowed was named appropriately for this latter-day Caesar, the Mussolini Canal.

The canal at its widest had a breadth of sixty yards, and through it drained the waters of the marshes, a man-made river often sixteen feet in depth.[1] In addition to its original purpose, the Mussolini Canal was to provide a convenient and redoubtable tank trap, an admirable defensive position as well as a source of fresh water for the invaders.

Water at Anzio, however, was more of a problem because of its abundance than because of its scarcity. Over wide, low-lying areas of the beachhead, surface water was seldom more than two feet below the ground, which made the digging of foxholes an impossible task.

In the early hours of January 22, 1944, the first waves of the assault forces splashed ashore at three separated points.[2] The British 9th and 43rd Commandos struggled onto Peter Beach, some six miles northwest of Anzio, opposed only by those natural barriers—the sand bars—of which the Navy had warned. To the Commandos' left, the 2nd Brigade Group of the British 1st Division waded the final hundred yards past the sand bars and onto Peter Beach. Once ashore, the British struck north and east through the heavily wooded and undulating terrain toward the Moletta River and, to the east, to secure the Anzio-Albano road.

The center beach, X-ray Yellow, immediately adjoined the port of Anzio. The U.S. 6615th Ranger Force (Provisional), consisting of the three Ranger battalions, the 509th Parachute Infantry Battalion, and the 83rd Chemical Battalion, came in over this tiny beach. Their objective was the capture of the port facilities and the elimination of any coastal batteries in the immediate vicinity.

Some four miles farther east, over X-ray's Red and Green beaches, the U.S. 3rd Infantry Division landed three regiments abreast. The 3rd was to push north and east to cut the Anzio-Cisterna road north of Nettuno, establish bridgeheads across the Astura River, and to push on eastward to seize the bridges over the Mussolini Canal. This last task was assigned to the 3rd Provisional Mounted Troop,[3] which was to capture the bridges, pre-

[1] Linklater, op. cit., 186. [2] Truscott, op. cit., 308–309.
[3] Ibid., 309.

pare them for demolition, and await the arrival of the infantry.

The bulk of the British 1st Division would remain aboard ship as a floating reserve.[4] Also to be held in Corps reserve was the 504th Parachute Infantry Regiment, but it was to follow the 3rd Division ashore and assemble a short distance inland. This was the regiment that Churchill had wangled away from its parent 82nd Airborne Division when he still entertained visions of an air drop at Anzio.[5] He had intended to use the British Paratroop Brigade, which was being used as regular infantry along the Eighth Army front, but the lack of available British replacements and the desire to retain still another American unit in the Mediterranean prompted the Prime Minister to implore General Marshall to detach the 504th from the 82nd Airborne Division and keep it in Italy while the remainder of the division sailed for Northern Ireland. In the end, the American paratroopers, too, would be used as regular infantry.

The assault plan assumed the invading forces would meet opposition on the beaches and heavy armored counterattacks within hours after the initial landing, as soon as the Germans realized the extent of the Allied invasion.[6] It was believed that both the 29th and 90th Panzer Grenadier divisions were in the immediate vicinity. Actually, both were committed to battle along the Garigliano River some sixty miles to the south, and only the day before at Kesselring's Army Group C headquarters, Admiral Canaris had expressed the belief that there was no fear of an Allied landing in the near future.[7] This we learned later.

General Lucas' orders placed great emphasis on early entrenchment at initial objectives to repel expected counterattacks. However, the only opposition encountered besides some widely scattered minefields were some sleepy-eyed members of an engineer battalion of the 29th Panzer Grenadier Division. More than

[4] The 3rd Infantry Brigade, the 24th Guards Brigade, the 46th Royal Tank Regiment, the 80th Medium Regiment.

[5] Churchill, *op. cit.*, 443.   [6] Greenfield, *op. cit.*, 252.

[7] Admiral Wilhelm Canaris, chief of Abwehr (espionage and counterespionage of the regular armed forces). See Westphal, *op. cit.*, 240.

two hundred German prisoners were rounded up a short time after H hour,[8] some of them literally dragged out of bed. Pillboxes especially constructed for just such a contingency as the Anzio invasion were not even manned; and explosives, set into the façades of waterfront buildings to be detonated in the event of an enemy landing, thereby toppling the buildings into the streets and hindering the use of the port facilities, were never set off.

By this time, coded signals were flashing to the man responsible for the entire operation. General Alexander sent this message to Prime Minister Churchill: "We appear to have got almost complete surprise. I have stressed the importance of strong-hitting mobile patrols being boldly pushed out to gain contact with the enemy, but so far have not received reports of the activities."[9] On receipt of this, a jubilant Mr. Churchill signaled back his appreciation for the news that the VIth Corps was "pegging out claims rather than digging in beachheads," then immediately radioed Stalin of the success of the landing south of Rome.

But both Alexander and the Prime Minister were overly optimistic. In the first place, "strong-hitting mobile patrols" could get nowhere in the British sector because of the broken terrain. The only mobile patrols that were getting anywhere were those of the 3rd Provisional Mounted Troop, and only one of these patrols had come into contact with the enemy.[10] This, at the southernmost of the bridges across the Mussolini Canal. The members of this group knocked out three German armored cars with bazookas, captured eleven prisoners, and set the remaining Nazi defenders to rout.

By nine o'clock in the morning of D day, an initial phase line three miles deep and twelve miles wide had been established, and forward elements were pushing still farther inland. Along the right flank, Major Robert Crandall's Provisional Mounted Troop was in possession of all the bridges over the canal. To its left, ad-

[8] Bowditch, *op. cit.*, 18.   [9] Churchill, *op. cit.*, 481.
[10] Bowditch, *op. cit.*, 15.

vance detachments of the 30th Infantry Regiment were pushing due north from the invasion beach and by nightfall would reach the west branch of the Mussolini Canal and occupy the bridges from the juncture with the main canal west to Padiglione.

D day at Anzio was a full and rewarding day. We had actually caught the Germans off guard, had landed some 36,000 men and 3,200 vehicles and large quantities of supplies,[11] and had established a threatening position well to the rear of the main German line in the south.

By now the Germans had had time to react. During the night, the three companies of the 71st Panzer Grenadier Regiment of the 29th Panzer Grenadier Division pushed down from Campomorto to retake LeFerriere and blow the bridge across the west bank of the canal. To the east, a battalion of the Hermann Göring Panzer Division attacked the canal juncture from Sessano, capturing among others Major Crandall.[12] Heavy fighting succeeded in pushing the Germans back across the canal at both points.

By the end of D-plus-one, the British had reached the Moletta River on the left flank, and the corps beachhead line was secure.

The British occupied a front of more than seven miles extending from the mouth of the Moletta eastward to the overpass on the Anzio-Albano road. The Americans held a twenty-mile front eastward from the overpass to Padiglione, on along the west branch of the Mussolini Canal, then south along the canal proper to the sea.[13] A semicircular front line deployed around an area fifteen miles wide and seven miles deep, more than enough for the limited number of troops assigned to hold against the expected counterattack, and all along that line they now were in contact with enemy armored patrols.

Back of them, the Allied reserves were building up. The remainder of Major General W. R. C. Penney's British 1st Division had disembarked not over the sand-bar-blocked Peter Beach, but at the port of Anzio. Corps artillery, corps and division transport,

11 *Ibid.,* 18.   12 Truscott, *op. cit.,* 311.   13 *Ibid.*

the 36th Engineer Regiment, and mountains of supplies from the LST's and Liberty ships were being landed.

But the *Luftwaffe* was coming out of hiding.

There were several small air raids on the afternoon of D day during one of which an LCI was sunk, and on the evening of January 23, a flight of German fighters and fighter-bombers came screaming out of the blinding setting sun to stage a heavy raid on the port area. The British destroyer H.M.S. *Janus*, an American Liberty ship, and the hospital ship *St. David* were hit and sunk. A second hospital ship, the *Leinster*, was badly damaged.[14]

While the exulting coded messages were flashing to London and Moscow, a more ominous coded message, "Case Richard," was being flashed the length of Italy and into southern France and Yugoslavia—Kesselring's code for setting his emergency plan into operation. His reconnaissance units, mobile elements, anti-aircraft personnel, rear echelons, all who had been placed on the standby alert to act as his fire brigade were forming up. Some already were on their way to the threatened area; others would roll momentarily to throw up a line of resistance around the new Allied beachhead.[15]

The German Field Marshal correctly judged that a two-division Allied assault, reinforced even as it was, was hardly cause enough to panic along his main line in the south. Further, he had an entire army sitting idly by in northern Italy, one which could be brought into action almost immediately. So, after dispatching his fire brigade to the threatened area, he ordered the 4th Parachute Division and elements of the Hermann Göring Panzer Division to block the roads leading to the Alban Hills, the obvious Allied objective,[16] placed them under the command of the 11th Parachute Corps, and ordered the staff of the 76th Panzer Corps over from the Adriatic front to create a solid operational frame.[17] His next move was to order General Eberhard von Mackensen's Fourteenth Army down from Verona to handle the new Allied

[14] Linklater, *op. cit.*, 189. [15] Kesselring, *op. cit.*, 232.
[16] Greenfield, *op. cit.*, 260. [17] Kesselring, *op. cit.*, 233.

threat. Meanwhile, his reports to the O.K.W.[18] in Berlin were being answered with manpower. The 715th Motorized Infantry Division was dispatched to Italy from southern France, the 114th Light (Jaeger) Division from the Balkans, other units amounting to a division from Germany itself, and the 92nd Infantry Division was to be activated in Italy for movement to Anzio.

While all this was going on, Von Vietinghoff's Tenth Army holding the Gustav Line was relatively undisturbed. If anything, it was being bolstered.

Kesselring's emergency plan was working perfectly. By nightfall of D day he had more than 20,000 troops either already deployed or well on their way to the troubled zone. By January 25, when Von Mackensen's Fourteenth Army assumed control of the defenses, there were elements of eight divisions opposing the attackers and five additional divisions with many supporting units en route to the Anzio area from the north.[19] Within the next few days, Von Mackensen's army would number more than 70,000 troops.

Lucas' corps was growing in numbers, too, but at a less accelerated pace. With the use of the port of Anzio from almost the beginning, Admiral Lowry's Task Force 81 was able to unload 90 per cent of its cargo and personnel by the end of the first day. Thus the ships could get back that much sooner to Naples to bring up the 45th Infantry Division and half the 1st Armored Division. The 45th was being brought up one regimental combat team at a time but would be brought to Anzio *in toto*. The 1st Armored, on the other hand, was being split in two. Its Combat Command A would be assigned to Anzio; Combat Command B would remain in the south to be used in the event of a Fifth Army breakthrough into the Liri Valley.

In addition to these front-line troops, three more battalions of 155-mm. field rifles were being added to VIth Corps.

[18] O.K.W., *Oberkommando Wehrmacht*, equivalent to our combined chiefs of staff.
[19] Bowditch, *op. cit.*, 21.

While awaiting reinforcements, VIth Corps dug in and Lucas ordered extensive patrolling, especially along the roads leading to Campoleone and Cisterna, his immediate objectives.

On January 24, British General Penney launched a strong mobile patrol up the Anzio-Albano road. It surprised and overwhelmed a German outpost at Carroceto and continued up the road to a point near Campoleone.[20] By now he had his full division complement under his command; the 24th Guards Brigade had been replaced in corps reserve by the 179th Infantry Regiment of the 45th Division. Penney dispatched this brigade, one squadron of the 46th Royal Tanks, and the bulk of his division artillery up the road toward Campoleone to expand the gap forced by the mobile patrol. These three battalions of the 24th Guards (1st Scots, 1st Irish, and 5th Grenadier Guards) pushed their way through a mine field east of the road and drove a battalion of the defending 3rd Panzer Grenadier Division out of the model modern village of Aprilia, northeast of Carroceto.

Because of the geometric layout of the village and the design and shape of the buildings, the Allied soldiers consistently referred to the town as "The Factory" rather than by its proper name of Aprilia.[21]

Taking 111 prisoners and leaving the 5th Grenadier Guards in possession of the strong point, the brigade continued northward to expand the salient.

The next morning the Germans, sensitive to the loss of this important position along the main road, mounted a combined tank-infantry attack to regain the position. This was beaten off, and the Germans lost four tanks, a self-propelled gun, and forty-

[20] *Ibid.*, 23.

[21] Built originally as a collection point for the farm produce of the area, it was a cluster of low, red brick buildings several hundred yards beyond the old town of Carroceto. Aprilia consisted of a Fascist party headquarters building, a town hall, a wine shop, a string of buildings in which farm produce was stored and made ready for market, and a church. The only thing resembling a factory was a small government-operated cigarette shop in which tobacco was rolled and fashioned and packaged. Nevertheless, Aprilia was henceforth known solely to GI and Tommy alike as "The Factory."

six more prisoners, but they continued to press along the flank of the British salient.

Far to the east and simultaneous with the British attack, the U.S. 3rd Division began to probe toward Cisterna. Four companies of the 15th and 30th Infantry regiments made some headway along the roads and across the muddy fields but were stopped by enemy mobile units. The following morning (January 25) General Truscott ordered an attack in force with the 1st Battalion 30th Infantry driving up the Campomorto-Cisterna road, the 2nd Battalion 15th Infantry attacking to the right along the Conca-Cisterna road.[22]

Lieutenant Colonel Lionel C. McGarr's 30th Infantry pushed beyond the canal, across the flat, treeless farmlands for some two miles before running into the fire of a well-entrenched unit of the Hermann Göring Panzer Division, which was dug in around the road junction below Ponte Rotto.

The 15th Infantry ran into similar heavy resistance after gaining about a mile and a half across the open fields toward Isola Bella. German machine gunners set up in several farmhouses pinned down the advancing Americans, and an enemy self-propelled gun knocked out four of the accompanying tanks of the 751st Tank Battalion. Before additional armor could be brought up, German infantry advanced down the hidden stream bed from Isola Bella and drove back the outposts along the 15th's right flank. Intermittent fire fights continued throughout the remainder of the day across the 3rd Division front.

Meanwhile, the 504th Parachute Infantry Regiment, which had taken over much of the right flank of the beachhead along the Mussolini Canal, had launched a diversionary attack aimed at the capture of Littoria. Aided by the heavy guns of the U.S.S. *Brooklyn* and several destroyers offshore, the paratroopers crossed the canal to take the villages of Borgo Sabotino, Borgo Piave, and Sessano. Halfway along the road eastward from Borgo Piave to Littoria, D Company, 504th was ambushed and cut off

[22] Bowditch, *op. cit.*, 21.

by a strong German counterattack. The company suffered heavily, but many of the paratroopers managed to infiltrate back to the regiment.

During the night of January 25–26, the paratroopers withdrew from their exposed positions in the open fields. And the following morning the 3rd Division resumed its attack in the direction of Cisterna. The 30th Infantry succeeded in driving the enemy from their entrenchments at the road junction below Ponte Rotto while the 15th Infantry, to the right, advanced to the northeast to cut the main road from Cisterna to Littoria. Supporting the twin-pronged attack was the heaviest concentration of artillery the division could muster, but the Germans hung on to their main defenses around Cisterna. Each additional unit that arrived in the area was brought into the line immediately to keep the Americans from breaching Highway 7.[23]

By January 27, still some three miles from Cisterna, it was evident that the 3rd Division attack had bogged down and that a more powerful, concentrated drive would be necessary to reach the objective. Truscott halted the advance and began to regroup.

With the British 1st Division halted a mile and a half above The Factory and the U.S. 3rd Division regrouping short of its objective, it was time to dig in and await reinforcements.

As Mark Clark reported the action up to that point:

> It was considered wise to make only limited advances the first few days in order to consolidate positions about seven miles deep and 15 miles long around Anzio pending the arrival of reinforcements. This schedule was designed to prevent the enemy from cutting off our forward elements, as he might have done.
>
> Later there was criticism of our failure to advance deeply inland in the beginning, but in my opinion we most certainly would have suffered far more heavily, if not fatally, had our lines been further extended against the reinforcements the enemy was able to move in rapidly.[24]

But VIth Corps was growing. Some forty LST's were leap-

[23] Kesselring, *op. cit.*, 233.   [24] Clark, *op. cit.*, 290.

frogging each other between Naples and Anzio bringing up supplies, ammunition, and most of all, men. Well offshore, the Liberty ships coming up from the North African supply bases were emptying their cargoes into LCT's and Ducks to be ferried ashore. The port of Anzio was too small, the waters too shallow to permit the deep-draft Liberties to get closer than a mile offshore.[25] This, too, had its benefits, since the huge floating targets would remain beyond German artillery range and the relatively tiny LCT's and Ducks posed little attraction for the enemy observers.

By January 29, VIth Corps had built up some 27,000 tons in its supply dumps, 60 per cent of it ammunition. Moreover, the corps numbered more than 60,000 in strength with more than 500 artillery pieces and almost 250 tanks. The relatively good weather for five of those first seven days,[26] combined with a tremendous amount of energy, facilitated the establishment and quick buildup of the beachhead, but the spell of mild winter weather also provided Kesselring with the opportunity to speed his defensive forces into position,[27] and the *Luftwaffe*, which was now on hand in large numbers,[28] was afforded the chance of striking hard against the operations of the Allied beach parties.

Our Air forces were flying thousands of sorties a day over the new beachhead, but from bases far removed from the combat area. Because our fighters and bombers had to take off and land during daylight, there was an hour or more just after sunrise and just

25 Bowditch, *op. cit.*, 24.

26 High winds and heavy surf on January 24 and 26 prevented unloading operations, particularly of the Liberty ships, which had to transfer their cargoes to the small LCT's and Ducks. Winds of gale proportions on January 26 beached one LST and thirteen other smaller landing craft as well as destroying the pontoon causeways in the Anzio harbor.

27 Kesselring, *op. cit.*, 233.

28 As part of "Case Richard," two medium-bomber squadrons were hastily flown from their air bases in Greece to the *Luftwaffe* fields around Rome. Also several squadrons of torpedo and glider bombers were brought down from airfields in southern France. The *Luftwaffe* was putting up its biggest show of strength since Sicily.

before sunset when the beachhead was uncovered from the air—this, to permit our fliers to arrive from and return to their bases far to the south. The *Luftwaffe*, on the other hand, had the advantage of operating from bases around Rome and could therefore spend a longer period of time over the beachhead and less in transit to and from their bases.

Their two heaviest air attacks were staged at sundown and near midnight January 29 with more than one hundred German bombers pulverizing the waterfront around Anzio, sinking the British cruiser H.M.S. *Spartan* and a Liberty ship.[29]

Colonel Edgar W. King's 68th AAA Regiment of 40-mm. and 90-mm. anti-aircraft guns by this time were well installed and, combined with the ack-ack guns on the ships offshore, had run up a score of almost one hundred enemy planes downed over the beachhead in those first few days. To discourage the enemy pilots further, barrage balloons were run up, and the chemical smoke battalions were screening the beach area with a thick, acrid, oily haze billowing out of their mobile smudge pots.

Also, an attempt was made to establish an air base of our own just east of Nettuno. The 307th Fighter Squadron moved their P-40's to the improvised strip,[30] and British Beaufighters and night-flying Spitfires were assigned to beachhead patrols during the hours that Anzio had hitherto been uncovered from the air. Our beachhead air base, however, was short lived. With the entire Allied position within easy artillery range of the enemy, it did not take long for the Germans to make sitting ducks of our planes on the ground. By February 5, the strip was abandoned and would be used only for emergency landings. The night fighters, however, remained in action and offered at least a partial air umbrella during the off hours.

The Allied position plus their necessarily slower rate of build-up demonstrated to Kesselring that the time was ripe for him to launch an attack in an effort to wipe out the beachhead.[31] The Allied weakness was apparent. Penned in as Allied forces were and

[29] Bowditch, *op. cit.*, 24. [30] *Ibid.*, 26. [31] Kesselring, *op. cit.*, 235.

under complete observation, there was no room for maneuver, nor was there room for Lucas to set up a defense in depth. Further, a directive from Hitler ordered the elimination of "this abscess south of Rome."

What was obvious to Kesselring was equally so to Lucas. His position was precarious, and despite the fact that his corps was mounting in numbers he was still outnumbered by the enemy and daily becoming more so.[32] Lucas reasoned that it was imperative that he push out from the restricted limits of his beachhead line, and that he do it before the Germans became too strong for him even to try. As it was, the hurried Nazi buildup left little opportunity to set up more than a series of strong points dotting the area, a string of road blocks before the obvious Allied objectives, and a handful of hastily installed mine fields. Von Mackensen appeared to be setting up his first line of defense behind the railroad bed between Cisterna and Campoleone. His main line would be, it was believed, high in the mountains from Cori to Velletri.

In both camps, the advantage remained still with the attacker. He could select the point at which he would strike with everything available to him, whereas the defender had to content himself with holding a thinly-manned defense line and keeping his reserves in position to meet what obviously had to be the unexpected.

At this point, several factors came into play.

In London, Churchill was thrashing about and registering complaints to virtually anyone who would listen, and he had a veritable army of listeners. He was especially irate over the absence of some Napoleonic gesture on Lucas' part. In a typical Churchillian statement, one fully expressing his ire while sugarcoating it with a touch of humor, he noted: "I had hoped we were hurling a wildcat on the shore, but all we got was a stranded whale."[33]

[32] VIth Corps G–1 recorded corps strength as of January 30, 1944, at 61,332; VIth Corps G–2 estimates of enemy strength on the same date, 71,500.
[33] Churchill, *op. cit.*, 488.

Mark Clark, too, held the belief that "the beachhead progress was lagging unnecessarily,"[34] and he made a special trip to Anzio aboard a Navy PT boat to spur on his corps commander.

Meanwhile, on the other side of the line, it was evident that the Neapolitan underground was hard at work again. General von Mackensen received word direct from Berlin that a second Allied landing would be attempted north of the Tiber in the vicinity of Civitavecchia, and that he was to dispatch some troops from Anzio to meet the threat.[35] This he did on January 28, the very day he had planned to launch his big attack to wipe out the Allied beachhead at Anzio. Now it was necessary to postpone the attack until February 1, when additional reinforcements would be available to him.

In the deep wine cellars carved into the soft strata of sandstone that served as VIth Corps headquarters, Lucas called a meeting of his staff and divisional commanders at which he delineated an all-out attack to get underway on January 29. His plan called for the 3rd Division to take Cisterna, then swing northwest along Highway 7 toward Velletri. The British 1st Division was to push up the Albano Road through Campoleone and capture the slopes above Albano and Genzano on the *Colli Laziali*, while Combat Command A of the 1st Armored Division would trundle along in support of the British, then swing to the west to take the high ground above Marino along the western flank of the *Colli Laziali*.[36]

For the next two days, Lucas reorganized his front, moving the 36th Engineer Regiment into the British positions along the Moletta River on the left of the beachhead perimeter. On the other extreme, the 179th Infantry Regiment of the 45th Division took over the 504th Paratroopers' positions along the Mussolini Canal. The British 1st Reconnaissance (Recce) Regiment was moved into the relatively quiet center of the beachhead line.

Lucas was ready to strike on January 29.

[34] Clark, *op. cit.*, 292.   [35] Bowditch, *op. cit.*, 27.   [36] *Ibid.*

But the British divisional commander, General Penney, begged off for another day to permit General Ernest Harmon's 1st Armored Division tanks, which were still arriving on the beachhead, time to jockey into position to bolster his drive up the Albano Road.

The extra day's delay was especially deleterious to the plans of the 3rd Division,[37] for during the night the German 26th Panzer Grenadier Division, brought over from the quiet Eighth Army front, had taken over the area west of Cisterna from the thinly spread Hermann Göring Panzer Division. Truscott had based his planning on the fact that the Göring Division was stretched out over such a wide front that it had to organize its defense in a series of strong points supported by mobile armored units, and he planned to infiltrate two battalions of his attached Rangers through these German strong points under the cover of darkness to enter Cisterna. His regular infantry supported by tanks and tank destroyers would overpower the strong points and pound their way into the town behind the Rangers. The arrival of the 26th Panzer Grenadier Division and the consolidation of the Hermann Göring Panzer Division was to forestall Truscott's plans.

Further complicating an Allied breakthrough to the *Colli Laziali* was Von Mackensen's own planned offensive set for February 1.

As Lucas was juggling his units in the line, so, too, was his opposite. To launch his offensive, Von Mackensen was dividing his forces into three combat groups with his main thrust down the Albano Road spearheaded by his most powerful force—Combat Group Graeser—consisting of seventeen infantry battalions heavily supported by artillery.[38] The other two combat groups, less powerful than that in the center, were to launch simultaneous attacks against Anzio from the northwest and the northeast.

In effect, the same routes were to be used by both sides. A glance at the map will explain how both Lucas and Von Macken-

[37] Truscott, *op. cit.*, 313.   [38] Bowditch, *op. cit.*, 26.

sen reached the same conclusion. None other was possible with only two main roads leading out of or into Anzio.

The two armies were about to meet head on, but Lucas got the jump on his opponent.

At one o'clock in the morning of January 30, VI Corps jumped off.

CHAPTER FIVE

The Campoleone Salient

IN an effort to divert German attention away from the two-pronged assault at Anzio and possibly draw off some of the *Wehrmacht* units there, the Fifth Army along the main front before Cassino mustered what strength it could for renewed activities. But its strength was fairly well sapped by the earlier attacks along the Garigliano and Rapido.[1]

The British Xth Corps was busy consolidating its bridgehead across the Garigliano. On its right, the American IInd Corps already had resumed its offensive against Cassino following the debacle of the 36th Division in its attempt to force the Rapido.

---

[1] "The southern front," I noted in my diary on January 30, "is like two boxers in the ring, both about to collapse. I have committed my last reserve and I am sure the *Boche* has done the same."—Clark, *op. cit.*, 276.

Farther east, the French Expeditionary Corps was continuing its slow movement into the mountain mass above Venafro.

Along the Eighth Army front, extreme winter weather combined with rugged terrain made any forward progress an impossibility. The new Eighth Army commander, Lieutenant General Sir Oliver Leese,[2] was also losing troops to the Fifth Army front, where the ground still permitted large offensive operations. The British 1st Division already had been diverted from the Eighth Army to participate in the Anzio invasion; the British 5th Division was under orders to follow over to the Fifth Army front, as were the New Zealand Corps and the 4th Indian Division.[3] Leese's attempt to cut Highway 5 west of Pescara at Chieti was forestalled when the Canadian attack along the Adriatic petered out, and further attempts to continue northward were frustrated by the lack of available troops.

Only in the center was there any effective diversionary action to draw German attention away from Anzio. There, the U.S. 34th Infantry Division under IInd Corps was doggedly pushing its way into the headlands above Cassino following its successful crossing of the Rapido, and Juin's French Corps was seriously threatening an envelopment of Cassino from the north with his Algerian and Moroccan divisions moving in quick and vicious spurts across the mountaintops of the southern shoulder of the Abruzzi.[4]

This renewed Allied threat against Cassino, kingpin of the Gustav Line, brought German reinforcements to the area, but they came not from Anzio, rather from the quiescent Eighth Army front. Except for those troops dispatched to Civitavecchia on a wild goose chase, Von Mackensen's Fourteenth Army remained poised, awaiting the arrival of additional forces from the north before launching its scheduled attack February 1. In all,

[2] Lieutenant General Sir Oliver W. H. Leese was named commander of the British Eighth Army on December 30, 1943, following General Montgomery's departure for England, where he took over the Twenty-First Army Group to prepare for the Normandy invasion.

[3] Linklater, *op. cit.*, 135.   [4] Kesselring, *op. cit.*, 233.

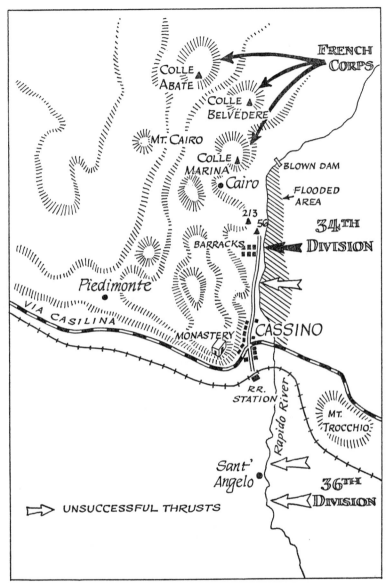

Fifth Army Diversion on Southern Front, January–February, 1944

Von Mackensen had thirty infantry battalions, plus six more in reserve, supported by tanks and artillery, lined up against the very routes along which Lucas was to attack.[5]

At one o'clock in the morning, January 30, the 1st and 3rd Ranger battalions moved silently out into the night from their positions south of the west branch of the Mussolini Canal.[6] Each man had two bandoleers of .30 caliber ammunition slung over his shoulders, grenades stuffed in every pocket and hanging from his pack harness. In columns they moved stealthily along the Pantano Ditch to the east of the Conca-Cisterna road. The ditch cuts under the road less than half a mile from Cisterna. Close to the ground and hugging the sides of the narrow ditch, the long, noiseless column crept forward, sometimes within feet of German sentries patrolling the area. But the dark of the moonless night and their own stealth kept their presence unknown to the enemy. They were to emerge at daybreak where the ditch cuts the Conca-Cisterna road, a scant eight hundred yards from their goal—the village of Cisterna.

An hour after the two Ranger battalions moved out, the 4th Ranger Battalion and the 3rd Battalion, 15th Infantry started up the road itself with the 4th Rangers in the lead supported by tanks. To their left, Colonel Harry Sherman's 7th Infantry pushed north along LeMole creek and the gravel-topped Crocetta-Cisterna road. The 1st Battalion, along the creek, was to reach Highway 7 north of Cisterna before dawn. Both battalions were passing through the division's 30th Infantry positions.

The right flank of the attack was launched by two battalions of the 504th Parachute Infantry moving along the main Mussolini Canal to the northeast. Their mission was to destroy the bridges over the canal and cut Highway 7 southeast of Cisterna.

The paratroopers pushed up the canal, and after a stiff fight, the 1st Battalion, 504th, succeeded in reaching the two bridges

[5] Bowditch, *op. cit.*, 27.

[6] *Ibid.*, 28–30. See also Truscott, *op. cit.*, 313, and James Altieri, *The Spearheaders*, 308.

that crossed it only to discover that they had been blown up by the retreating Germans. The battalion captured a large number of prisoners from the Hermann Göring Panzer Division and the 356th Reconnaissance Battalion. The 1st Battalion 504th remained to consolidate their positions while the 2nd Battalion pushed on to continue the drive toward Highway 7. However, they got only as far as the Cisterna Creek. The Germans had blown the bridges here, too, to prevent the Americans from getting their armor across, and without armor the paratroopers could not advance across the open fields.

That afternoon, the 7th *Luftwaffe* Jaeger Battalion crossed the Mussolini Canal south of the paratroopers and attacked them from the rear.[7] Heavy and lengthy shelling by the 69th Armored Field Artillery Battalion finally drove off the marauding *Luftwaffe* Jaegers, but by nightfall the paratroopers were still on their side of the Cisterna Creek, unable to get their supporting armor across and unable to move forward without it.

The main attack against Cisterna by the 3rd Division itself got off to a bad start.[8] The 30th Infantry was still fighting for the ground the 7th Infantry was to use as a line of departure, thereby eliminating the possibility of any advance reconnaissance of the route of attack. Instead, the 7th had to rely on air photographs, which provide skimpy information at best. For example, what appeared from the air to be hedgerows crossing the advance route of the 1st Battalion, 7th Infantry, were, in reality, drainage ditches overgrown with briars. In the pitch black of a moonless night, these were to pose impossible barriers especially for the accompanying tanks, which were unable to cross them in the dark. As result, the battalion had to advance without the support of its armor. It had gotten no more than a mile and a half across the fields before it was caught in a burst of German flares that com-

[7] The 7th *Luftwaffe* Jaeger Battalion, made up of hardened disciplinary cases who chose combat service rather than prison sentences. In essence, they were highly expendable shock troops but, because of their psychological attitudes, were extremely dangerous antagonists.

[8] Truscott, *op. cit.*, 314.

pletely exposed the advancing infantrymen.[9] The only cover available was the runoff ditches into the creek, but it seemed that every one of these was under the direct fire of a German machine gun. As dawn broke, the 1st Battalion, 7th Infantry, was not astride Highway 7 as had been planned, but was rather effectively caught in a pocket, surrounded on three sides by enemy gunners, and that after covering only a short distance from its starting point. The heavy weapons of D Company were set up and the riflemen deployed against the commanding knoll to their right rear, which they succeeded in overrunning. By this time, the tanks had managed their way across the briar-covered ditches and came up in support, but the battalion had suffered heavily and was scattered. At best it could only hold the knoll it had wrested from the enemy and dig in against increasing German artillery and mortar fire. Major Frank Sinsel assumed command after Lieutenant Colonel Frank Izenour had been wounded,[10] and did his best to reorganize the battered battalion while awaiting reinforcements.

The 2nd Battalion, 7th Infantry, got off to an even worse start. It was delayed in jumping off when its own supporting artillery fire fell far short of its intended mark; and when the battalion finally moved up the road, it ran head on into the prepared positions of a unit of the Nazi 1st Parachute Division around the road junction south of Ponte Rotto. Sherman committed his reserve 3rd Battalion and brought up his tanks to eliminate this enemy strong point that afternoon.

By dawn of January 31, the 7th Infantry was only halfway to its objectives.

In the center of the drive against Cisterna, the infiltrating Rangers emerged from the Pantano Ditch at dawn on schedule, out onto the road leading into Cisterna. They were discovered immediately by the German defenders, who moved three self-propelled guns and a strong force of infantry down the road to intercept them. The Rangers deployed and quickly knocked out the three guns with bazookas, but the Germans set up machine

[9] Bowditch, *op. cit.*, 31.   [10] *Ibid.*, 32.

guns, mortars, and snipers in farmhouses and haystacks and deployed along the high ground around them. Soon the two battalions of Rangers were trapped in a sea of enfilading fire.

To the south, along the Conca-Cisterna road, the 4th Ranger Battalion and the 15th Infantry renewed their attack against stiff opposition in a desperate effort to reach their trapped comrades. Throughout the morning, a violent battle raged along the road with the enveloped Rangers calling for artillery fire literally on their own heads in an effort to extricate themselves from the trap, and with their fellow Rangers and the 15th Infantry making every determined effort to reach them.

Colonel William O. Darby, the commander of the Ranger force, was maintaining radio contact with his trapped battalions, directing the supporting artillery, and prodding the relief battalions on to superhuman efforts along the Conca-Cisterna road. A platoon of the 3rd Reconnaissance Troop managed to break through the German defenses and race up the road to cover the rear of the beleaguered Rangers, but the Germans closed the gap and they were the only ones to get through. The 4th Rangers and 15th Infantry were halted short of Isola Bella, little more than half a mile from the trapped Rangers.[11]

Shortly after noon on January 30, Colonel Darby received his last radio signal from his two surrounded battalions. His old sergeant major from the original Rangers, First Sergeant Robert Ehalt,[12] told of German tanks coming down from Highway 7 and churning up and down through the Ranger positions, firing at will and forcing them out into the open and splitting them into small groups. Without antitank guns and heavy weapons, the Rangers were at the mercy of the German tanks. Only ten men were left around First Sergeant Ehalt when he radioed his last message back to Colonel Darby: "They're closing in on us, Colonel. We're out of ammo—but they won't get us cheap."[13]

It was only a matter of time before it was all over for the 1st

11 Truscott, *op. cit.*, 314.   12 Bowditch, *op. cit.*, 30.
13 Altieri, *op. cit.*, 312.

and 3rd Ranger battalions. Intermittent firing continued on into the afternoon, then faded away.

Of the 767 men who advanced along the Pantano Ditch the night before, only six escaped.[14] And of the 43 men in the platoon of the 3rd Reconnaisance Troop who fought their way to join the Rangers, only one man returned.[15]

Total loss—803 men in one day at one point along one road at Anzio.

It was an ironic fate for the Rangers after their earlier successes in Africa, Sicily, and southern Italy; even more so since they were under the direct command of the two men individually responsible for the formation and training of the Rangers in the first place —Truscott and Darby.

That was back on May 26, 1942, when the brand-new Brigadier General Truscott (he had just received his star that day) dispatched a memorandum to the War Department in Washington. Truscott had been sent to Britain in the vanguard of those early-arriving Americans to acquaint himself with British Army methods and to gain experience in combined operations.[16] Truscott was especially impressed with the formation, training, and purpose of the British Commandos, and in his memorandum suggested the creation of similar American units to enable them to get actual combat experience by staging raids as the Commandos were doing along the French coast. Two days later he received the necessary approval from General Marshall and proceeded to set up his first experimental battalion. At the time he was prevailed upon by General Eisenhower to select a name for this group other than "Commandos." Eisenhower felt that the term rightly belonged to the British.

Many names were submitted, but Truscott decided on "Rangers" because of its purely American historical connotations.

The only American ground troops in the United Kingdom that early in the war were the 34th Infantry Division, which had

[14] Clark, *op. cit.*, 296. [15] Bowditch, *op. cit.*, 30.
[16] Truscott, *op. cit.*, 39.

arrived in northern Ireland the preceding January, and the advance elements of the 1st Armored Division, which were just arriving.

Assigned as a guide to Truscott in these early days was a young major who had been an aide to Major General Russell P. Hartle, the commander of the U.S. Army forces in northern Ireland. Major William O. Darby, West Point class of 1933, had graduated in artillery. He had impressed Truscott in their daily contact, and when Hartle recommended his young aide for assignment to the Rangers, Truscott was happy to receive him. In fact, he appointed him the commander of the 1st Ranger Battalion, which was built around almost five hundred personally selected officers and men who had volunteered for the hazardous training and duty.

It was a sad day almost two years later when Truscott and Darby saw only six men out of the two Ranger battalions return from the slaughter along the road to Cisterna, sadder still when the remainder of the Rangers were withdrawn from Anzio a few weeks later and returned to the United States.[17] Mark Clark was fearful of the unfavorable publicity surrounding the loss of the Rangers at Anzio,[18] and implied that they were unsuitable for the mission to which they had been assigned. The Nazi propaganda mill was broadcasting to the world the announcement of the annihilation of the elite of the American Army, and there were pictures showing the captured Rangers being marched through the streets of Rome before jeering crowds lining the sidewalks.

The loss of the Rangers was a serious blow to the VIth Corps's attempt to seize the pivotal base of Cisterna in its two-pronged

[17] Of the 4th Ranger Battalion, 199 of the original members were returned to the United States by mid-March to become instructors at various infantry-replacement training centers. The remainder of the battalion—some 250, who had joined the Rangers as replacements in Sicily and southern Italy—were transferred to the 1st Special Service Force, itself badly in need of replacements at the time. It might be noted that the 2nd and 5th Ranger battalions, still training in Britain at the time, played exemplary roles in the Normandy invasion. The 6th Ranger Battalion served with distinction in the Philippines.

[18] Truscott, *op. cit.*, 314.

attack toward the *Colli Laziali*. In the face of increasingly strong opposition and mounting casualties and with no reserves to draw upon, Truscott temporarily halted his 3rd Division along the Ponte Rotto–Isola Bella–Cisterna Creek line. He knew now that he was facing more than just the thinly spread Hermann Göring Panzer Division. In fact, the Germans had the equivalent of three divisions manning the defenses before Cisterna and guarding that portion of Highway 7. Further, Truscott's forces had suffered more than three thousand battle casualties since landing at Anzio and had lost more than one-third of their tanks and tank destroyers. After three bitter days of hard fighting, the 3rd Division got no closer to Cisterna than about one mile. By the afternoon of February 1, still another German unit appeared on the scene, the 71st Infantry Division.[19] Its presence forecast the inevitable counterattack, and Truscott withdrew to more easily defensible ground than the open fields before Cisterna. The 3rd Division went on the defensive behind hastily sown mine fields, barbed wire, and strategically placed antitank guns.

While Truscott's attack on the right was brought to a halt by determined enemy forces superior in numbers, the main VIth Corps effort up the Albano Road was about to meet the same fate. A little before midnight on January 29, the 24th Guards Brigade moved into position north of The Factory and, with the 1st Scots and 1st Irish Guards leading the way, launched an attack to seize the crossroads a little more than one mile south of the Campoleone railroad station. This was to be used as a line of departure for the British 1st Division's fresh 3rd Infantry Brigade, which was to push through the Guards and continue the attack up the road. But the Guards ran into trouble almost as soon as they started out. The 1st Scots, on the right, suffered heavily at a mined and barbed-wire road block but fought through to their objective.[20] To their left, the Irish Guards ran into even heavier initial resistance and by morning were forced to retire to positions south of the Scots. British and American tanks were brought up to reduce

---

[19] Bowditch, *op. cit.*, 34.   [20] Linklater, *op. cit.*, 193.

the German opposition, and by midday the Guards were firmly entrenched at the crossroads, with the 3rd Infantry Brigade only then moving toward their line of departure. It was not until three o'clock in the afternoon of January 30 that the King's Shropshire Light Infantry and the Duke of Wellington Regiment began their attack up the Albano Road, more than twelve hours behind schedule. By nightfall, however, both units had overcome scattered resistance and covered more than two thousand yards to reach the railroad embankment south of Campoleone. The 46th Royal Tanks hotly engaged in a slugfest with enemy armor and antitank guns beyond the embankment, but the fight was a stand-off. Both sides dug in for the night, a night of continuous artillery dueling.

The next morning, the 2nd Battalion of the Sherwood Foresters supported by tanks resumed the attack and managed to cross the embankment, but they ran into such devastating enemy fire from the Germans barricaded in the farmhouses beyond the embankment that they had to retire to their original positions of the night before. And there they stayed.

The U.S. 1st Armored Division's Combat Command A, meanwhile, was set to strike to the left of the British, but found the land unsuitable for the use of heavy vehicles since it was marshy and cut by deep gullies. General Harmon decided to use the abandoned railroad bed that runs northwest from Carroceto as his avenue of attack, and he ordered Colonel Kent Lambert to clear the area west of the Albano Road and north of the Moletta River.[21] Lambert chose to move his vehicles along the single-track rail line immediately west of and paralleling the Albano Road so as not to interfere with the high-priority traffic along the road itself. His leading armored cars ran into sniper and machine-gun fire from enemy positions on the Buonriposo Ridge, and, unable to cross the deep ravine of the Moletta River, they hugged the south bank and pushed on toward the old railroad bed. Here they were stopped by a mine field and by heavy enemy fire, and, once

[21] Bowditch, *op. cit.*, 37.

stopped, the monstrous vehicles sank to their underbellies in the soft ground. They were forced to stay there for the night, until the remainder of Combat Command A could be brought up to reinforce the stranded group and help dig out the mired vehicles. The following day, five tank companies with the 6th Armored Infantry crossed the Moletta ravine and engaged the enemy on the northern ridge. Most of the tanks once again sank into the soft earth but suffered little more than embarrassment, since the enemy artillerists were bracketing the area with air bursts that merely showered the buttoned-up tanks in a hail of harmless shell splinters that bounced off the heavily armored vehicles. The accompanying 6th Armored Infantry had managed to push on to the gravel road beyond the ridge, where they were stopped by a mine field and antitank guns set up at the intersection of the road and the old railroad bed. Combat Command A was halted, its infantry dug in, its tanks mired and unable to continue.

At this point, General Lucas revised his plan. Since the heavy vehicles could not traverse the sector assigned them, he decided to hold them back until the British had captured the road junction at Osteriaccia, one mile north of the railroad crossing on the Albano Road. The new plan called for the 1st Armored Regiment, with the 3rd Battalion, 504th attached, to push through the British at Osteriaccia and continue up the Albano Road.[22] The 6th Armored Infantry would drive along the old railroad bed to the west until it reached the Ardea road, then swing north to join the left flank of the main attack.

The renewed assault got underway at 10:30 in the morning of January 31 with the 2nd Foresters and 46th Royal Tanks again crossing the railroad embankment and striking out for Osteriaccia, but they ran into the same situation all over again,[23] being halted immediately by the withering fire from the well-entrenched Germans and from the tanks and self-propelled guns that had been rammed through the rear of the farmhouses to fire through the windows against the approaching British. Brigadier

[22] *Ibid.*   [23] Linklater, *op. cit.,* 193.

86

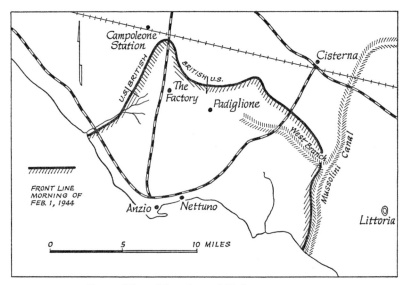

Front Line, Morning of February 1, 1944

J. R. James of the 3rd Infantry Brigade ordered the withdrawal of his infantry while his armor and artillery attempted to soften up the avenue of approach. The tanks of the 1st Armored's Combat Command A once again fanned out to the west of the Albano Road to take the ridge south of the Campoleone station, but they were unable to cross over the railroad before nightfall, and they retired behind the ridge.

To their left and below them, the 6th Armored Infantry was able to gain only five hundred yards up the abandoned railroad bed before being stopped by mine fields and stiffening enemy opposition.

That was all for the 1st Armored. During the night it was re-placed by the 24th Guards Brigade, and it went back into Corps reserve.

It had become apparent in this sector, too, that the unexpected strength of the enemy, along with the advantages of the natural terrain in their favor, was too great to be overcome by the Allied forces pitted against them. The combined Anglo-American attack had succeeded in pushing a salient deep into the enemy lines and had opened a two-mile-wide gap in the center between the 3rd Panzer Grenadier Division and the 65th Infantry Division,[24] but reaching the Nazi first line of resistance was as far as they went. Lucas reasoned it would take a stronger force to penetrate that line, and he called a halt to await reinforcements.[25] Further, it appeared that the Germans were in a position to launch a full-scale counterattack.

Despite continued Allied air attacks against the German front line as well as behind the lines during the big VIth Corps offensive and the great number of casualties inflicted, especially by the heavy Allied artillery bombardments, the German Fourteenth Army held its line surrounding the Anzio beachhead. It did so only by committing all of its units laboriously built up for its own scheduled offensive, units comprising some 110,000 troops.[26] The truth is that the VIth Corps had come dangerously close to breaking through the German line at Campoleone station and with a bit more effort might have succeeded.

Now both sides settled back to lick their wounds. Von Mackensen was of the opinion that Lucas would continue the attack to push his salient deeper along the Albano Road, but such an attack failed to materialize. Lucas was aware of his limitations, aware that he was attacking a force larger than his own in numbers, although less well supplied, especially in vital artillery. He would wait and gird himself against the counterattack he knew was coming.

The Germans made a half-hearted attempt to recover some of their lost ground south of Cisterna, but their attacks were easily beaten off by artillery concentrations. A reluctant attempt was made against the bulge south of Campoleone, but this also came to naught.

Both Generals Clark and Alexander made a quick inspection trip to the beachhead on February 1. The following day a radio

---

[24] Bowditch, *op. cit.*, 40.   [25] Truscott, *op. cit.*, 315.
[26] Bowditch, *op. cit.*, 41.

message from Fifteenth Army Group headquarters instructed Lucas to dig in behind mine fields and barbed wire, hold his front with a minimum number of troops, and prepare reserve positions in expectation of a large-scale enemy attack.[27]

Strangely, on the same date, Alexander cabled a full report of his visit to Anzio to Prime Minister Churchill, explaining the increased enemy resistance before both Cisterna and Campoleone, but adding:

> We shall presently be in a position to carry out a properly coordinated thrust in full strength to achieve our objective of cutting the enemy's main line of supply, for which I have ordered plans to be prepared.[28]

All of this only added to the frustration of the Prime Minister, who already was voicing his disappointment that the situation was not living up to his great expectations. While Alexander was instructing Lucas to form up highly mobile reserve forces behind his defensive line, Churchill was disparaging the VIth Corps commander for having on hand some eighteen thousand vehicles on so tiny a strip of land and alluding to the number of personnel necessary to drive and maintain these conveyances. To General Sir Henry Maitland Wilson, the remote Allied commander-in-chief in the Mediterranean, he cabled: "We seem to have a great superiority of chauffeurs. I am shocked that the enemy have more infantry than we."[29] The last part of his statement was quite true. The enemy indeed had more infantry; they had more troops, some ten thousand more, and still others were arriving.

On February 3, two days after putting the VIth Corps on the defensive, General Alexander prodded Clark to alert the 3rd Division to resume the attack in an all-out effort to take Cisterna.[30]

[27] Allied Central Mediterranean Forces, Operations Instruction #37, dated 2 Feb. 1944. (The name of the Fifteenth Army Group had been officially changed to Allied Central Mediterranean Forces, but continued to be known as Fifteenth Army Group.)

[28] Churchill, *op. cit.*, 485. [29] *Ibid.*, 488. [30] Clark, *op. cit.*, 298–99.

Then, from his headquarters late that same night, he called Clark to advise him that Fifteenth Army Group Intelligence had received word that the Germans were preparing a strong counterattack at Anzio. Alexander's Intelligence was right but a little late. The Germans actually had begun their counteroffensive at Anzio that very day.

CHAPTER SIX

Soldiers' Battle

T HE beginning of what was to become the greatest "soldiers' battle" of World War II was insignificant enough. February 3 dawned cold and
cloudy and dour, and VIth Corps busied itself digging in to hold
those positions it had wrested from a determined enemy, an
enemy more powerful and under orders from Hitler himself to
eradicate this "abscess" south of Rome.[1] The weather did nothing
to alleviate the growing feeling of futility among the Allied defenders. Going on the defensive was something new for these
troops conditioned only for the attack. Laying mine fields, string-
ing barbed wire, digging connecting trenches and waiting for the
enemy to come to them, all this is debilitating to an army used to

[1] Clark, *op. cit.*, 299.

bringing the war to the enemy. But VIth Corps was to learn the tactics of the defense, learn them the hard way.

The German attack started simply. A small-scale probe, involving hardly more than a company, was launched in the mid-afternoon against the tip of the British salient south of Campoleone. It was easily repulsed.

The Campoleone salient was a finger some four miles deep and a mile and a half wide jutting into the German lines, and it denied them the use of the all-important Factory-Carroceto area which commanded the approaches to Anzio. The Germans needed the high ground for observation, the buildings of the Factory behind which to assemble their forces, the road hub around Carroceto to bring up tanks, heavy equipment, and supplies.

An hour before midnight, the German artillery opened up in earnest, this time concentrating on both sides of the base of the British salient, and German infantry followed up the rolling barrage, pouring out of their positions to attack both sides of the salient. From the west they infiltrated along the deep gullies that knife the area west of the Albano road, slipping between and around and in back of the British strong points and posing the definite threat of cutting the vital roadway. From the east they attacked over the flat farmlands in a frontal assault bolstered by extremely heavy artillery concentrations. It was obvious that the enemy meant to pinch off the dangerous salient and to cut off the entire British 3rd Brigade at its point.

Throughout the night and well into the next day, the German onslaught continued, now reinforced with heavy Panther tanks. Every unit of the 3rd Brigade was under attack, but the Irish Guards on the left and the 6th Gordons on the right were receiving the heaviest blows.

Fighting under heavy skies and intermittent rain, without air support, outgunned and outmanned, the British fought valiantly, falling back slowly and making the Germans pay heavily for the gains they were making. But by noon of February 4, the situation was critical enough to force General Penney to throw in troops of the 168th Brigade, reinforcements from the south still debarking from LST's at Anzio.[2]

By midafternoon a battalion of the 168th Brigade staged a counterattack to seal a breach that had been forced in the British lines, a serious gap between the 3rd Brigade out at the point of the salient and the 24th Guards Brigade, which was holding the flank. The newly arrived battalion, the 1st London Scottish, supported by the Sherman tanks of the 46th Royal Tank Regiment and with the help of the tank-destroyers of the U.S. 894th Tank-Destroyer Battalion plus heavy artillery support, forced the Germans to retire and reunited the two separated brigades by four o'clock in the afternoon.

When the German attack began to show signs of weakening, the VIth Corps commander decided to pull back the overexposed forward elements of the British 1st Division and to straighten his line. Most of the units staged an orderly withdrawal to more defensible positions, but the 1st Battalion, Duke of Wellington's, under more direct enemy fire, had to wait until after dark to carry out its withdrawal. By this time, the Germans were aware of the Allied maneuver and the 1st Duke of Wellington's Regiment suffered heavily. One company was completely cut off and captured; the rest of the battalion was forced to leave behind its heavy equipment, including its antitank guns.

By midnight the British lines again were intact, but they had

---

[2] This brigade, part of the 56th Division, had been taking part in the heavy fighting along the Garigliano River when it was hastily withdrawn from that front and put aboard boats for Anzio. At Anzio it was ordered directly from the boats into the line without even stopping at an assembly area en route. The remaining two brigades and headquarters of the British 56th Division would follow within a week, being equally as hastily withdrawn from the struggle to gain Monte Maio—the Germans' commanding position overlooking the Garigliano River— in the Xth Corps' attempt to obtain a foothold in the Aurunci Mountains to the west of Cassino. The British 5th Division was spread thinly to its right to cover the front that had been held by the 167th and 169th brigades, but this drastic reduction in strength brought the Xth Corps' offensive abruptly to an end.

lost their salient and counted some fourteen hundred in killed, wounded, and missing.[3] The Germans had suffered correspondingly higher casualties with an estimated three-fifths of their attacking force either wiped out or captured.[4]

Of those captured, many were willing enough to talk with Allied interrogators, especially the older ones and the disillusioned who had seen action in Russia and then had been sent to what they had been told was the less grueling Italian front. The German 71st Division had been all but obliterated at Stalingrad, then was reconstituted and sent to Anzio only to find that aside from the weather, the fighting itself was even more severe. They complained in particular about our artillery. Still others would tell of recent furloughs home, or show letters they were receiving from their homefolks describing the nightly holocausts, the desolation caused by our heavy bombers. Many of the letters would tell of entire families killed, or maimed, or ruined, but would end on the pathetic hope that "you are still young and if you come through this, you can make a new life for yourself."

There were the young and cocky and surly paratroopers who would not talk or, when they did, would launch into lengthy political tirades. They would demand to know why we were fighting the Germans at all when the Russians were our real enemies.

And there were the elders who had no illusions left. One actually boasted, "I was a good prisoner in the last war, too."

From these prisoner interrogations could be pieced together the picture on the other side of the line. It showed that Von Mackensen's counteroffensive was hurriedly organized, not fully reconnoitered in advance, and that some units had arrived at the front only after long forced marches and then were thrown immediately into battle.[5]

[3] Bowditch, *op. cit.,* 46.

[4] The 1st London Scottish Battalion alone accounted for more than three hundred prisoners in their afternoon counterattack.

[5] Bowditch, *op. cit.,* 46.

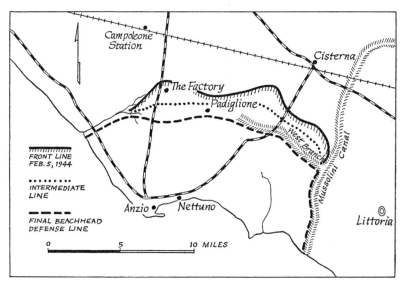

Battle Lines, February 5, 1944

But the picture was also plain that Von Mackensen was successful in the opening round of his three-phase counteroffensive —the withdrawal of the British salient at Campoleone. His attempt to cut off and capture the British 3rd Brigade, however, was largely unsuccessful. Further, he had paid a heavy price in both men and equipment, and he was still not in possession of the vital Factory-Carroceto area.

More important than what these talkative prisoners had to say was the discovery on one of them of a copy of the *Journal* of the German Fourteenth Army, dated February 3, 1944.[6] It listed in detail Von Mackensen's plans for eliminating the new Allied beachhead.

The *Journal* explained that Von Mackensen had hurriedly gathered his forces to contain the initial Allied landing and pointed out that many of his units were merely remnants of larger organizations incapable of consolidation into a strong assault force

[6] A summary of the translation of the *Journal* may be found in Bowditch, *op. cit.*, 43.

95

by themselves. For the moment, he planned a series of limited attacks in an effort to weaken the Allied defenses, then he would deliver the all-out blow. But to do this he would need additional troops. This, he put in the form of a request to Kesselring.

The *Journal* further explained the reorganization of the Fourteenth Army virtually on the eve of launching its initial attack down the Albano road to eliminate the British salient. The 1st Parachute Corps, which had been commanding the entire Anzio front, now was charged only with the western half from the Albano road westward along the Moletta River to the sea. Under its command were two divisions, the 4th Parachute along the coast and the 65th Infantry inland. The 76th Panzer Corps, newly arrived from the static Eighth Army front, was given command of the central and eastern sectors at Anzio. It consisted of five divisions. The 3rd Panzer Grenadier occupied the sector immediately east of the Albano road, and continuing eastward were the 715th Infantry, the 71st Infantry, and the Hermann Göring Panzer divisions, with the 26th Panzer Division in reserve.

The *Wehrmacht's* assault tactics were unlike those of the British or the Americans. Rather than assigning entire divisions to an attack, it was common practice to preselect various units within an army and form them into a combat group with specific assignments to spearhead an all-out assault.[7] The remainder of the army would follow up behind the combat group.

It was thus that Combat Group Graeser was formed. Under the command of Major General Fritz H. Graeser, the combat group was given the assignment of smashing through the center

---

[7] The *Schwerpunkt*, "point of main attack." Our armies would form task forces in much the same manner that the Germans created combat groups, but the missions of a task force would be of much less importance. For the most part, our task forces were makeshift affairs designed to fill a gap. For carrying out a large-scale breakthrough of an enemy position, the U.S. Army would assign a strong, proven division heavily reinforced with attached armor and corps and army artillery. Later in the war, such assignments were given to both the 3rd and 45th Infantry divisions by the U.S. Seventh Army in France and Germany.

of the Allied beachhead perimeter, then to continue down the Albano road to the sea to knife the VIth Corps in two.

While Combat Group Graeser concentrated on cracking the center of the line, another German thrust was to be made from Cisterna in hopes of at least pushing the defenders back to the West Branch of the Mussolini Canal, if not all the way to Nettuno. This was the assignment of Combat Group Berger.

As Von Mackensen envisioned it in his *Journal*, Graeser would pinch off the British Campoleone salient and capture the Factory by February 10, then push all the way to Anzio and cut the Allied beachhead in two by February 20. There would be nothing left to do but to mop up the remaining forces, this by the beginning of March.

By the afternoon of February 5, VIth Corps defenses had been re-established along a line running approximately one mile north of the Factory. The 168th Brigade replaced the worn and weary 3rd Brigade in the center of the British line, and the situation appeared to be stabilized at least for the moment. But the Corps was braced for the inevitable. Disaster stared it in the face.

The months of preparation and procedure, the great energies expended, the lives lost, and the great soaring hopes—all these had reached their apex and were plummeting.

Anzio was a failure.

On paper, it was about to be wiped out.

True were the warnings voiced at Marrakech that it would not, within seven days, link up with the advancing forces from the south, that plans had to be made to sustain it for a greater length of time, that it could not live up to the grandiose desires of a prime minister whose imagination turned back the pages of history to the days of Napoleon.

Deep in the wine cellars that served as headquarters for the VIth Corps under the hill behind Anzio, a pall of gloom settled over the planners; desperation was setting in, slowly at first, finally overwhelmingly. Orders were issued to hold. Then, frantic orders not only to hold but to establish a secondary line on which to fall back. Still later, orders to begin construction of a third and final Beachhead Defense Line.[8] And all the while to stand and hold.

There were few enough troops to stand and hold on the initial line in the face of the enemy's superiority, let alone assigning part of these to the construction of additional lines of defense, but such was the attitude at Corps headquarters. The orders went out, and the construction got underway. The front was thinned out, and anyone in the rear who could be assigned to wield a shovel was given that task.

Regimental and division headquarters forward echelons were combed for personnel not actually performing absolutely essential chores. The paperwork could pile up while the clerks pitched in with shovels. Everyone would eat K rations while the cooks and KP's lent a hand to the construction of the defense lines. And when the sun went down and the shovels were put aside, these same cooks and clerks were put an guard duty against possible German parachutists. These were anxious times at Anzio. All avenues of attack had to be covered and all at once.

It was still a paper-thin front line the Germans ran into the night of February 5 when they renewed their offensive, this time in the Cisterna sector. Sometime after sunset the sky brightened again and became alive as artillery and tanks opened up against the front of the 3rd Division west of Ponte Rotto. It appeared to be an all-out assault with the point of the attack coming against the 2nd Battalion, 7th Infantry. Enemy artillery, tanks, mortars, and machine pistols, all created a hellish racket, and flares lit up the battlefield. By ten o'clock the battalion commander, a Major Elterich, was on the phone to regimental headquarters seeking permission to withdraw to the secondary line of defense which everyone knew was being constructed some distance to the rear.[9] He spelled out a hopeless picture. His battalion was overextended, had suffered heavily, was in danger of being surrounded, could not hold out. Regiment got to division, and General Truscott ap-

<hr>

[8] Truscott, *op. cit.*, 315.   [9] *Ibid.*, 316.

proved the withdrawal. But this meant similar withdrawals by the units on either side of 2nd Battalion, 7th Infantry. And the battle had just got underway.

All across the 3rd Division front, the platoon-sized outposts began withdrawing to that inviting secondary line. From Carano across the flatlands to Ponte Rotto, the 3rd Division was giving up almost a mile and a half of territory, and all without a fight. If this were what going on the defensive meant, Truscott would have no part of it. Shortly after midnight and after frustratingly watching his G–3 map men working frantically with their grease pencils on the acetate overlays marking in the new positions of unit after unit, Truscott called his regimental commanders together. He had had time to study the situation more thoroughly and decided he had made a mistake in authorizing the wholesale withdrawals. Now he ordered a counterattack in the 30th Infantry sector to set the stage for a general attack to regain the positions so hastily given up.

K Company, 30th Infantry, supported by tanks and tank-destroyers, led the attack up the gravel road to Ponte Rotto, meeting only light artillery and mortar fire. For the next two and one-half hours, the 3rd Division maneuvered and fought minor skirmishes. By daybreak it was back on its original line, and, with the exception of the 2nd Battalion, 7th Infantry, which suffered some casualties in the opening engagement, only the somewhat autocratic feelings of the Regular Army had been damaged.

But the 3rd Division had learned a lesson. It could not do three things at once—hold the main front while attending to the construction of two more lines of defense behind it. Further, it learned that a resourceful enemy with the clever psychological use of concentrated firepower and flares could trick it into the belief that it faced a much heavier attack than was actually underway.[10]

The 3rd Division was not to be fooled a second time.

They wired in their front, planted mine fields, moved up tanks

[10] Bowditch, *op. cit.*, 50.

99

and tank-destroyers, and dug them in where they could provide direct fire against any further enemy attempt to dislodge the 3rd Division. At first, the tankers objected to what they believed was a needless proximity to enemy guns,[11] but Truscott pointed out that their mere presence was a stimulus to the men in the foxholes to show that the front line was to be the main line of resistance regardless of the previous preoccupation with the construction of additional lines farther back. In time the tankers themselves came around to agree with the General.

Also, Truscott relieved his fighting men of the pick-and-shovel work of setting up those extra defense lines. They were returned to their individual companies, which brought the regiments in the line up to full strength along the front. Only the 7th Infantry, in division reserve, was concerned with construction problems, and with the help of the division's 10th Engineer Battalion and VIth Corps' 39th Engineer Regiment, work went on to firm up defensive positions along the West Branch of the Mussolini Canal. If needed, this would be the Beachhead Final Defense Line, but its construction would not now pose any problems to those units assigned to holding the front.

The division turned next to its artillery. It had what amounted to seven full battalions of its own and VIth Corps' field guns assigned to it, and fire patterns were worked out whereby the mass of the division's artillery power could be brought to bear on any point along the division front, with or without forward observation. In the event communication lines were knocked out at any given point, the division's guns would fire predetermined concentrations at repeated intervals until communications were restored. On paper it was simple, but it was a tremendous task the artillerymen set up for themselves. Ultimately it proved to be rewarding not only for the 3rd Division but for every other division on the Anzio beachhead.

The VIth Corps was outmanned but not really outgunned at this stage of the operation. In effect, the Allies had fewer guns

[11] Truscott, *op. cit.*, 317.

and those of smaller caliber than did the Germans. We had nothing to compare with their 170-mm. heavy guns or their 210-mm. and 240-mm. railroad guns, which could lob shells from comparative safety onto any spot within the Allied beachhead. Against these we had the guns of the heavy cruisers far offshore and the bombs of the Air Corps, which was extremely limited by the Italian winter weather. Our own artillery—105's and 155's—were far outranged by the German heavy guns. What we did have was a seemingly endless supply of ammunition. Our howitzers and field rifles could and would belch out high explosives in a ratio of twenty to one in any artillery slugfest. This gave us the tactical edge. A not-so-simple matter of logistics. Those all-important LST's had built the stockpile.

A momentary lull engulfed the beachhead after the 3rd Division had re-established its positions. The VIth Corps was feverishly preparing its lines of defense and building up for the inevitable resumption of the German attack which, it had been warned, would get underway the following morning.[12] The word had come from our underground sources in Rome, which, with Italy officially out of the war, were now considerable. The Office of Strategic Services was set up in force in the Italian capital, and the network of intelligence agents, Italian, British, and American, had access to a wide range of German activity. Their report warned of a new attack to begin at four o'clock in the morning of February 7 against the front of the 3rd Division.

Just before midnight, some four hours early, the Germans unleashed a monstrous artillery barrage, but at the other end of the front—against the 2nd Battalion, 157th Infantry, which was dug in along the Moletta River. Following up the barrage, a strong enemy force attempted to drive a wedge into the Allied line at this point. Little more than an hour later, however, the fight was over, and the Germans were thrown back with heavy losses.

The dawn of February 7 broke over Anzio, and, although there were heavy exchanges of artillery fire, the awaited German

[12] Bowditch, *op. cit.,* 53–54.

offensive failed to materialize. The *Luftwaffe* was out in force concentrating on the port area and ammunition and supply dumps. In one fifteen-plane raid along the waterfront shortly before noon, ME 109's and FW 190's bombed and strafed the Allied emplacements accounting for thirty dead and forty wounded.

Later that afternoon, a lone German plane, in a desperate attempt to elude a Spitfire right on its tail, released its bombs in an effort to gain altitude. Flying at almost four hundred miles an hour, it would have been impossible for the German pilot to realize where he was at that particular instant, but his sticks of bombs landed in the midst of the 95th Evacuation Hospital, almost centering on the surgery tents. That one twist of fate resulted in twenty-eight deaths and injuries to sixty-four others. Among the dead, three nurses—First Lieutenant Blanche Sigman, the head nurse, from East Akron, Ohio, First Lieutenant Carrie Sheetz, of Camp Hill, Pennsylvania, and Second Lieutenant Marjorie Morrow, of Audubon, Iowa.

Ironically, the German pilot was shot down by the pursuing Spitfire and delivered as a prisoner-patient to the very hospital he had just bombed. There he received the regular treatment accorded the wounded and was ultimately evacuated from the beachhead aboard an LST. But his one moment of panic, one flick of his finger, added twenty-eight new grave markers to the growing military cemetery on the hill behind Nettuno, the bodies of twenty-eight noncombatants, including three American women.

In so tiny and congested an area it was not possible to separate the combatants from the noncombatants, the military emplacements from the hospital installations. The large red crosses painted on the canvas tents were readily visible to the German observers high up in the hills of the Lepini Mountains or atop the water tower in Littoria, but equally visible was the emergency airfield just a few hundred yards beyond the hospital confine, also the Long Tom gun emplacements that ringed the area, and the ration and gasoline dumps surrounding the hospital. An artillery shell carrying too far or falling short of its intended target easily enough could fall into the loosely drawn hospital area. Unfortunately, too many did.

The front-line medic with his white brassard and red cross was respected by the enemy. Rarely was one deliberately fired upon. But the tent city that was mushrooming in size each day was another matter, despite its medical insignia designed to point out its humanitarian role. Its merely being at Anzio at all made it an impossibility that it would remain unscathed. Everything at Anzio was under fire, deliberate or innocent. No one was wholly safe. It was only at Anzio that American nurses were constantly exposed to artillery fire and daily bombings for so long a period of time. Elsewhere during World War II, hospital areas were occasionally bombed or strafed, or even surrounded and captured. But at Anzio it was constant, daily, for four full months.

The number of times that the 95th Evac came under enemy fire contributed to its earning the rather uncomplimentary GI nickname "Hell's Half Acre." In many instances, a soldier with a superficial wound would prefer to remain in a dugout at the front and take his chances with tetanus rather than take his chances in the open and unprotected hospital area at Anzio.

Along the front, February 7 was a relatively quiet day. There had been a brief flareup around the Factory, and the British picked up several prisoners who claimed they were deserting rather than have to take part in what they had been told would be a big attack. They described the preparations going on behind the German lines for a heavy assault against the Factory-Carroceto strongpoint. Their stories of a renewed German offensive down the Albano road made more tactical sense than did the Rome underground report of a push toward Anzio from Cisterna.[13] Further, they agreed with the plan spelled out in the captured documents of the Fourteenth Army.

Reports from the Roman underground to the contrary, Von Mackensen stuck to his original plans and opened his attack in

[13] Truscott, *op. cit.*, 318.

just the manner described by the German deserters. Heavy artillery concentrations were laid down on both flanks of the British 1st Division beginning at ten o'clock that night. Fifteen minutes later, German infantry was hammering against the division's left flank along the Buonriposo Ridge. The full force of the German 65th Infantry Division was turned loose on the worn and depleted 24th Guards Brigade. Taking advantage of a dark night and the deep gullies that cut through the region, the Germans infiltrated the British positions and in a series of hand-to-hand encounters soon overran or cut off the Guards' strong points along the ridge. In the resulting confusion and having lost radio contact with the rear, the confused and overwhelmed Guards began making their way back as best they could to the secondary positions held by the 1st Irish Guards and the 3rd Battalion, 504th Parachute Infantry, before Carroceto and the Factory. Groping their way along the old railroad bed leading back to Carroceto were the remnants of the 5th Grenadier Guards Battalion. One of their lorries was set up as a mobile battalion headquarters around which the straggling battalion could regroup. It was parked on the embankment above Carroceto Creek where a side stream empties into it from almost right angles. Spread out around the lorry in a defense perimeter was the battalion Support Company under Major W. P. Sidney; their task—to cover the withdrawal and regrouping of the battalion and to prevent any German breakthrough at this point. With mortars and Bren guns set up at strategic places overlooking the wide gully of Carroceto Creek, the Support Company was spread thin when the enemy struck. The whole area came alive, the Bren guns and mortars of the Grenadiers and the light machine guns and Tommy guns of the American paratroopers on their right tore into the onrushing enemy, but still they came, hundreds of them teeming down the slopes of the Buonriposo Ridge, slithering down the embankment of the creek, and thrashing about in the brambles that lined the creek bottom. Once across and up the other side, there was nothing between them and possession of the coveted Carroceto-Factory area—nothing but the Support

Company of the 5th Grenadiers and Major Sidney stood in their path to the Albano road. The full force of the point of the German attack suddenly was concentrated there on the far bank of the Carroceto Creek. The Major, with Tommy gun and hand grenades, held them at bay as they stumbled about the bramble-covered creek bottom groping for a crossing place. Supported now by a pair of Grenadiers, one to either side of him, and a mortar section, this tiny knot of determined Grenadier Guards blunted the edge of the German attack until still more arrived on the scene to drive the enemy back. Sidney was wounded in the thigh during the engagement but continued to lead the defensive buildup until the battalion's position again was secure. His citation for the Victoria Cross reads:

> Barely able to walk, he allowed his leg to be bandaged, and all the next day, when contact with the enemy was so close that he could not yet be taken to hospital, his high spirit gave encouragement to those about him.

But the German attack had been slowed, halted at this point by a relative handful of men who rose to the occasion to follow one man—Major Sidney.[14]

To the left of the Guards Brigade, the 3rd Battalion, 157th Infantry, radioed back to regiment that enemy tanks and infantry were operating to its rear. Also, British stragglers out of contact with their units and out of ammunition were coming in to the American lines. One British major asked if he might share the dugout of Pfc. Blair London of Niagara Falls, New York, until the situation cleared and he could get back to his unit. He was more than welcome, especially since he had brought along the better part of a full bottle of rum.[15]

---

[14] Major W. P. Sidney, now the Lord de l'Isle and Dudley, living in Penshurst Place, Kent. The Major is a direct descendant of Sir Philip Sidney, hero of the Battle of Zutphen in 1586. The encyclopedia describes Sir Philip as "one of the chief ornaments of Queen Elizabeth's court," but it would appear his role was more than ornamental.

[15] The British liquor ration was long the envy of the Americans. Midway in World War II, the Pentagon relented in a small way to permit officers to buy a

Not so fortunate were the members of the second platoon of K Company, 157th Infantry. They were assigned the task of flushing out some German snipers along the right flank of the company's sector. Technical Sergeant Erwin W. Vanderpool of Montrose, Colorado, led the platoon along one of the numerous gullies and up onto the level ground. Instead of snipers, they ran head on into the spitting cross-fire of three German machine guns only seventy feet away. In the brisk action that followed, one of the Germans scampered back toward a haystack, and from the stack erupted an armored car. It rolled out into the open, its machine guns blazing, its cannon tracking a target. Vanderpool fired clip after clip with his M–1, aiming at the driver's position. He must have scored a hit, for the *flakwagen* rolled down the hill, crashed into a rock wall, and burst into flames. Vanderpool's platoon in the meantime was leveling Browning Automatic Rifle fire and rifle grenades against three enemy machine gun positions. They counted twenty-three German dead before they returned to their company positions.

They got back in time to accompany the rest of the battalion to new positions south of the Buonriposo Ridge. The 3rd Battalion, 157th Infantry, with its right flank wide open, had been ordered to withdraw to form a new line. And it was from these new positions that T/Sgt. Vanderpool left to go to the hospital. Malaria.

As the sun came up on February 8, the Germans were in full possession of Buonriposo Ridge and in position to continue the attack toward the Factory and Carroceto. Their attack along the eastern flank of the British 1st Division was not nearly so successful. It was slower in getting started, and the flatness of the terrain prevented a rapid breakthrough. Combat Group Graeser employed two regiments—the 29th Panzer Grenadiers in the fore-

certain amount of American whisky and enlisted men bottled beer. This probably was done in an effort to obviate their purchases of the putrid (and in some cases, blinding) locally manufactured alcoholic beverages. By the closing days of the war, the Army had gotten around to a regular liquor ration for everyone. The liquor was for sale at a reasonable price, and it was authentic.

front, the 725th Infantry immediately behind—against the battalion front of the 10th Royal Berkshires.[16] During the night they scored some slight gains as the "Berks" slowly withdrew in the face of the onslaught. One group of the 29th Panzer Grenadiers got as far as the eastern end of the Factory, where it came in contact with three tank-destroyers of the U.S. 894th Tank-Destroyer Battalion. The lead vehicle, under the command of First Lieutenant Bernard Schaefer, opened fire with its .50-caliber machine gun against the house in which the Germans had sought shelter while the tank-destroyers' three-inch gun was trained on the building. Of the seventy Germans holed up inside, more than half were killed. The rest surrendered.

Throughout the remainder of the day, hard fighting ensued with the Germans continuing their drives against both flanks of the British 1st Division's front. General Penney ordered the 3rd Battalion 504th, from their secondary positions into the line southwest of Carroceto to support the Guards Brigade. Their two tank-supported counterattacks failed to gain ground, although they materially aided in slowing down the German advance.

In the afternoon, Penney committed his reserve brigade in an effort to gain the lost positions atop Buonriposo Ridge, but it made little headway against the well-dug-in enemy. For the rest of the afternoon and well into the night, the tired and battered British 1st Division, which had borne the full fury of two all-out German offensives and was seriously weakened, contented itself with consolidating its positions and regrouping its forces. Many units had been so depleted in the fighting for the Campoleone salient and now for the Factory, that they existed more on paper than in reality. The 2nd North Staffordshire Battalion had been reduced to only 17 officers and 364 enlisted men.[17] The 6th Gordons had to be reorganized into a mere two companies. Sappers and members of beach details were pressed into service to fill out that battalion.

Shortly after midnight, the Germans renewed their twin as-

---

[16] Bowditch, *op. cit.,* 56–57.   [17] *Ibid.,* 57.

saults against the Factory-Carroceto objective, using the same tactics as the night before, heavy artillery and mortar fire followed by infantry infiltration at the weakest points. Elements of the German 65th Infantry Division drove what was left of the Guards Brigade back to the single-track railway line paralleling the Albano road, while on their left the King's Shropshire Light Infantry and the 2nd Foresters were forced still farther south of the Buonriposo Ridge.

But this time, the main German attack was directed against the British right flank. There, Combat Group Graeser pounded against the 168th Brigade still holding the Factory and the road leading east toward Carano. Graeser threw four infantry regiments plus what tanks and self-propelled guns he could muster mainly along that lateral road. By daylight they had broken through at several points, and by midday were in possession of the Factory and that vital lateral road along which supplies, reinforcements and, more important—armor—could be brought in.

The next objective—the road junction and high ground of Carroceto.

While the German armor was maneuvering into position, ours was brought into play. Harmon's Combat Command A launched a counterattack west of the Albano road aimed at retaking the lost positions along the Buonriposo Ridge. It got off to a good start, then petered out as the heavy tanks bogged down as soon as they left the road and became easy prey for the quickly installed German antitank guns. With the initial loss of seven tanks, Harmon dropped the Buonriposo Ridge objective and turned the tanks against the Germans in possession of the Factory. Here, too, they were stopped short, this time by mine fields as well as a large number of antitank guns. But they had momentarily set the Germans on the defensive.

Despite the weather and a wind of near-gale force, our artillery and naval guns continued to deluge the attacking Germans in a rain of high explosives, and from the skies more than two hundred Allied bombers struck against enemy assembly areas around Campoleone with amazing accuracy.

As dusk began to settle in, the fighting died away. Both sides had suffered serious losses and were near exhaustion. Only around Carroceto did the fighting continue. Sometime after midnight, more than a dozen enemy tanks ventured out of their haven at the Factory to strike against the 1st Scots Guards. Artillery fire and tank-destroyers of B Company, 894th Tank-Destroyer Battalion drove them off.

The remainder of the night was quiet enough until just before dawn, when the Guards Brigade and the 3rd Battalion, 504th Paratroopers, came under attack from three sides. The 5th Grenadier Guards and the American Paratroopers put up a determined stand, but the 1st Scots to the north of Carroceto suffered heavily. Their two forward companies were isolated, and the rest of the battalion, with the tank-destroyers of B Company, 894th, covering their withdrawal, fought their way back to join the Grenadiers. The American tank-destroyers that night appeared to be everywhere at once, performing every imaginable deed in addition to their normal roles, and warranted the sobriquet the Scots handed them after that—"the fighting tank busters."[18]

But the tide of battle was plain enough to see. Shortly after five o'clock in the morning, General Penney sent a message to VIth Corps that his command, now operating at less than half its effective strength, could no longer hold out unless fresh troops were to take over more than half of his front.

Until now, General Lucas had retained most of the 45th Infantry Division in Corps reserve, temporarily committing a regiment to holding an inactive portion of the beachhead perimeter. The 179th Infantry had been assigned to the beachhead's right flank along the Mussolini Canal until the 1st Special Service Force arrived to relieve it of that duty. And since the night of January 31, the 157th Infantry had been committed to holding the left

[18] *Ibid.,* 62.

flank of the beachhead along the Moletta River. Lucas ordered the division's third regiment—the 180th Infantry—into the line to replace the depleted British 2nd Brigade, and during the night of February 10–11, the 179th Regimental Combat Team took over the positions of the British 168th Brigade, which, by this time, was down to less than one-third its normal strength.[19] The realignment, however, left Lucas without any fresh infantry units in his corps reserve, so he replaced two battalions of the 157th Infantry along the Moletta River with the 36th Engineer Regiment. The engineers had been taught the rudiments of infantry battle during their basic training, and in the weeks to come they were to prove that they had retained that knowledge as they put down their shovels and picked up rifles to cover an important although static sector of the front.

With fresh troops in the center of his line, Lucas was now able to order a counterattack in an effort to retake the Factory. This assignment went to the 179th Infantry. Major General William W. Eagles, commander of the 45th Division, ordered the 1st Battalion, 179th, with the support of companies A and B, 191st Tank Battalion, to push through the positions of the 3rd Battalion, 179th, and move against the Factory from two directions, from the southwest and from the southeast. The attack was to begin at six-thirty on the morning of February 11.[20]

Lieutenant Colonel Wayne L. Johnson's 1st Battalion, 179th, jumped off on schedule following a brief but intense artillery barrage. A Company followed the tanks up the Albano road to approach the Factory from the southwest. B Company went up the gravel road to the east and parallel with the hard-topped Albano road. The tanks and infantry fought their way to the lateral road

19 *Ibid.*

20 This move was later criticized by General Truscott, who believed Eagles should have assigned the entire 179th Infantry Regiment to the task, but prisoner interrogation indicated that the attack would have taken the Germans completely by surprise had it not been for a freak interception of a radio message just before the attack began. Thus warned, General Graeser was able to move in reinforcements in time to meet the attack against his newly won strong point.

immediately south of the Factory shortly after ten o'clock in the morning and clung to their positions until forced to retire for more ammunition. By one o'clock in the afternoon, they were back along the southern ditch of that road, and, with the support of direct fire from the guns of the 27th Armored Field Artillery Battalion (1st Armored Division), the riflemen of B Company moved into the buildings at the southeast corner of the Factory. At this, German infantry emerged from the cellars to engage the Americans in stiff hand-to-hand fighting.

By late afternoon, the outnumbered Americans were driven back to the ditch along the lateral road. Still later, they retired farther back to reorganize for another assault.

At two o'clock in the morning of February 12, Colonel Johnson pushed against the Factory again, this time with three rifle companies and a company of tanks. The tanks were stopped short of the objective by a mine field, but the infantrymen of companies B and C were back inside the German positions shortly after four o'clock in the morning. At dawn, the Germans mounted a strong counterattack and forced the Americans back to their original positions some five hundred yards south of the Factory. There the battle ended, except for a brief period later the next day when the 1st Battalion, 179th, and the British battalion to its left withdrew temporarily to permit the dive-bombing of the German positions northwest of Carroceto.

Although it had come close to succeeding, the double assault upon the Factory by the 1st Battalion, 179th, was not without serious loss. A Company, for example, which took part in only the initial attack, was reduced to three officers and forty enlisted men. The 191st Tank Battalion counted eight of its tanks completely lost and several others badly damaged.[21] And at least two artillerymen suffered a loss of face.

Corporal Max Stallcup of Chickasha, Oklahoma, and Private Richard Gould of Pittsburgh, Pennsylvania, at the height of the artillery preparation for the attack against the Factory, were

---

21 Bowditch, *op. cit.,* 65.

working their 155-mm. howitzer as fast as the 189th Field Artillery Battalion fire direction center was calling for fire. Several officers from corps artillery on an inspection tour were standing by witnessing the performance. Given an audience, the gun section began to speed up their activities until at one point the lanyard was pulled, there was the customary roar, but instead of the muzzle blast, a huge streak of flame erupted from the mouth of the howitzer, arced out for some seventy-five yards, came to earth, and flared even brighter. Their battery mates and visiting inspectors sought out anything that would provide cover until it was pointed out that the great ball of fire was simply the powder charges. In their haste, the two artillerymen had failed to load the gun with a projectile.

At that, the more than four hundred Allied artillery pieces, most of them concentrating on the center of the beachhead line, inflicted tremendous casualties against the enemy. Allied artillery was spewing out an average of 25,000 rounds a day.

We are given no accurate account of German casualties suffered up to this point in the battle for Anzio, but some indication may be gleaned from the size and numbers of additional German units arriving to reinforce Von Mackensen's Fourteenth Army:

From Germany—the Infantry Lehr Regiment,[22] along with the 1027th and 1028th Panzer Grenadier regiments. From northern Italy—the 362nd Grenadier Division. From Yugoslavia—the 114th Light Division. And from the Gustav Line, Marshal Kesselring dispatched the 29th Panzer Grenadier Division.

Lucas, too, was receiving reinforcements, but far from comparable in numbers. The remaining two brigades of the British 56th Division were coming up from the southern front. The 167th Brigade already was unloading at Anzio, and the 169th Brigade

---

[22] Officially designated the 309th Panzer Grenadier Regiment of the home guard, it was a highly touted élite demonstration unit personally dispatched to Anzio by Hitler himself. Actually, the regiment had never seen battle and was kept in Germany purely for display purposes.

was preparing to embark for the trip up from Naples on the next turn-around of the LST's. And Fifth Army was dispatching still more artillery.

But the battle picture was still foreboding. Von Mackensen was sticking to his schedule as spelled out in that captured *Journal.* He had already pinched off the British salient and was in full possession of the Factory. All this he had planned to do by February 10, and he did it. Our efforts to disrupt that schedule were without success.

His next move was on Carroceto, then down the Albano road to split the Allied beachhead in two.

For the next three days, the fighting at Anzio was limited to extremely active patrolling as the opposing armies reorganized and regrouped. Our patrols were bringing in prisoners, more Germans claiming to be deserters rather than undergo additional pounding by our artillery. In turning himself over to First Lieutenant John McCarthy of Brooklyn, one German's most pressing concern was whether he would be sent ultimately to Canada or Florida. He preferred Florida.

The more talkative prisoners spelled out in detail the changes Von Mackensen was making in his deployment of troops, also what they knew of his plan of attack. But, more important, they gave us the exact date and hour it was to begin.

Six-thirty in the morning of February 16.

CHAPTER SEVEN

Final Beachhead Defense Line

"IT is a great advantage that the enemy should come in strength and fight in South Italy, thus being drawn from other battlefields. Moreover, we have a great need to keep continually engaging them, and even a battle of attrition is better than standing by and watching the Russians fight. We should also learn a good many lessons about how not to do it which will be valuable in Overlord."[1]

By PT boat and by liaison plane, General Clark would pay regular if fleeting visits to Anzio, always accompanied by an entourage of correspondents and photographers both military and civilian. Whether to pass out well-deserved decorations to the

[1] Memorandum from Churchill to Field Marshal Sir John Dill, British representative in Washington on the Combined Operations staff.—Churchill, *op. cit.*, 487.

men or to pose for pictures on the battle-scarred beachhead, the General was there. General Clark and the photographers.

On one occasion, he earned the everlasting disrespect of the fighting man. Although not reported in the press, the incident was spread by word of mouth across the beachhead and throughout the entire Fifth Army. On this occasion, Clark had stopped to share a K ration with a soldier. The two posed for the inevitable pictures, and when Clark moved on, he passed his uneaten K ration to the soldier with merely the words, "Here, son, eat this."

In one unfortunate moment he had created the impression that while K rations were good enough for the men in the line, they were not for him. And he committed this act before an audience which would be prone to repeat it widely.

Yet it was so unlike the man. For all his predilection for personal publicity, Clark did not deserve the remarks being repeated about him by his own army, all for this one momentary lapse, if it were that. In all probability, he genuinely believed that the soldier might appreciate a second K ration for lunch. Clark was no martinet, no George Patton who had aroused the ire and hatred of these same troops in Sicily when they served in his Seventh Army. Unlike Patton, Clark did not employ legions of military police to restrain his troops from the slightest infraction in deportment. He did not have soldiers coming out of the lines arrested and fined for having lost their leggings days or weeks before during the heat of battle, nor would Clark ever be involved in any soldier-slapping incidents at base hospitals. Rather, the terms "generous" and even "considerate" could be applied to Clark. He was especially concerned with the welfare of the men in the line. He had instituted a rotation system during those bleak fall months of virtually static warfare to give a percentage of his fighting men three-day passes to rest camps in Naples, and he continued the system even at Anzio. That the soldier-on-the-town got no physical rest mattered not; Clark was more interested in the fact that the fighting man was given the opportunity to enjoy himself to the fullest, even if it were only for three days.

Clark knew his soldiers, but unfortunately his soldiers did not know him. He was more than aware that the pathway up the military ladder was through the headlines of the newspapers back home, and he maintained an excellent rapport with the war correspondents assigned to his field of operations. But he was less successful in imparting the warmth of his personality to the soldiers under his command. His was not a gregarious nature. For the most part his fighting men saw little of him and, as result, the K ration story could gain wide circulation and credence. He was the remote symbol of the Army and the men hated the Army. There was no passionate dislike for Clark as a person among the troops such as there was for Patton,[2] neither was he particularly highly regarded by the men who served under him.

As a tactician, Clark's ability is debatable.

On the evening before the expected all-out German push to the sea, when Von Mackensen already had wiped out the British Campoleone salient, had taken the Factory, and now was poised to deliver the final blow, Clark astonished virtually every Allied commander at Anzio familiar with the tactical situation that faced them. To their horror, they listened as he outlined his desires for a counteroffensive aimed at smashing through the German defenses around Cisterna.[3]

With what?

But this did not faze the army commander. Rather, he was more concerned over Lucas' trepidations. As he expressed it: "My own feeling was that Johnny Lucas was ill—tired physically

[2] Despite the myth created by the press camp of the Third Army that the flamboyant General George S. Patton, Jr., was the beloved idol of his men, it was far from the truth. Those who served under him in Africa and Sicily particularly resented his penchant for having MP's arrest and fine on the spot any soldier caught in even the slightest infraction of his rather severe code of military deportment. In northern France, after he had acquired the nickname "Blood and Guts," an outsider could get this reaction from most members of the Third Army: "Yeah, *my* blood and *his* guts!" Inside Germany, his rather bizarre interpretation of the "nonfraternization with the enemy" edict hardly developed a large cheering section for him.

[3] Truscott, *op. cit.*, 318.

and mentally—from the long responsibilities of command in battle. I was also inclined to agree with Alexander's viewpoint and had for some time been considering a change."[4]

He gave orders for plans to be drawn up for the Cisterna counteroffensive and with that, Clark headed back for his palace at Caserta.

Exactly on schedule on the morning of February 16, enemy guns opened up all across the VIth Corps front. The bombardment lasted for more than half an hour, when suddenly the German guns began to counterbattery our own artillery, a practice they generally chose to avoid in view of their relatively restricted supply of ammunition. It was soon obvious that the heaviest concentrations of enemy artillery fire were being directed against the area on either side of the Albano road.

Rising out of the pall of smoke and dust, the assault waves of the 3rd Panzer Grenadier and 715th Infantry divisions swept up in a mounting tide against the defensive positions of the 157th and 179th Infantry. Enemy tanks in groups of four and eight emerged from their havens behind the ruined buildings of the Factory and trundled along the network of roads leading from the town right up to the rims of the American foxholes.[5] They would fire at close range against the entrenched infantry, then retire to replenish their supplies. German infantry, working along with the tanks, infiltrated down the gullies that dissected the region.

Throughout the morning the battle raged. All attacks were beaten off with severe losses to the enemy, but still they came, wave after wave of gray-green uniforms, only to be shot down by rifle and machine-gun fire or chewed up by bursting artillery shells. At one point, VIth Corps Fire Control Center directed the massed fire of 224 British and American howitzers and field guns against an enemy regiment attacking south along the Albano road from Carroceto,[6] and within less than an hour these same guns were shifted to four other targets, delivering the same devastat-

[4] Clark, *op. cit.*, 306.   [5] Linklater, *op. cit.*, 201–202.
[6] Bowditch, *op. cit.*, 81.

117

ing results. An indication of the amount of artillery fire being laid down against the onrushing enemy might be gleaned from the rate of fire of just one of these 224 guns. The gun section under Sergeant William R. Hedges of the 189th Field Artillery Battalion was averaging eight rounds of 155-mm. howitzer shells each 45 seconds. This same battalion, under the command of Lieutenant Colonel Hal Muldrow, of Choctaw Indian descent, had literally barrel-sighted its heavy howitzers against the Germans at Salerno. Once again it was having the same telling effects.

The Infantry Lehr Regiment—that supposedly crack unit sent direct from Germany to help eliminate the new Allied beachhead —came under the fire of these guns in the late afternoon of February 16, and despite its *élan*, its high morale, its exemplary role, the Infantry Lehr Regiment broke and ran in complete disorder.[7] Facing this hail of exploding steel splinters and white phosphorous was too much even for this élite unit. But General Graeser drove them on. Now the not-so-élite. Men. Waves of them. There seemed to be no end.

On the other flank of the beachhead front, where Combat Group Berger had launched a simultaneous attack against the 3rd Division positions,[8] the Germans had asked for a momentary truce while they collected their dead and wounded. In front of only one company of the 504th Paratroopers, which was attached to the 3rd Division, they retrieved thirty-eight dead and an equal number of wounded. But no such truce was asked for or granted along the 45th Division front, and the German dead and wounded piled up.[9] It was here that Von Mackensen meant to break through. This was a crisis; there was no time for amenities. The Germans were sacrificing manpower for the prestige of wiping out the beachhead.

Enemy tanks as well as infantry came under the withering

---

[7] Kesselring, *op. cit.*, 235.   [8] Bowditch, *op. cit.*, 74.

[9] One GI who had been taken prisoner, but who had escaped and returned to our lines, told of being marched along the Albano road and seeing the Germans piling the bodies of their dead in stacks of 150 for ultimate mass burial. He estimated he must have seen ten such piles of German corpses.

fire of our artillery, our infantry cannon companies, the three-inch guns of the M–10's of the 645th Tank-Destroyer Battalion, the 75-mm. cannon of the 191st Tank Battalion, the 4.2-inch mortars of the 83rd Chemical Mortar Battalion, the .50-caliber and .30-caliber machine guns chattering on in a seemingly endless spray, bazookas, 60- and 81-mm. mortars, and even the 40- and 90-mm. antiaircraft guns with their barrels leveled and used as antipersonnel weapons. Half-tracks mounting twin .50-caliber anti-aircraft machine guns were moved up onto any available knoll and fired over the heads of the defenders into the unceasing waves of enemy infantry. This was war at its worst, white-hot slaughter.

In the air it was the same story. Messerschmitts and Focke-Wulfs combed the beachhead for any likely target. Heavier German planes concentrated on the docks and dropped mines into the harbor. Our own Air forces flew a total of 468 sorties in support of the VIth Corps that day, with light and medium bombers concentrating on the front immediately before the 45th and British 56th divisions.[10] The heavy bombers worked over the communications and supply lines leading from Rome.

From dawn until dusk, February 16, the land and air battle raged at full fury, but for all their expended efforts the Germans had little to show. Their deepest penetration was in the British 56th Division sector, where the 12th Sturm Regiment overran the 8th and 9th Royal Fusiliers,[11] and two companies of the German 10th Parachute Regiment got as far as the lateral road south of the Moletta River before being wiped out by the tankers of the 46th Royal Tank Regiment. In the center of the 167th Brigade line, the forward companies of the 7th Oxford and Buckinghamshire Light Infantry Battalion also were overrun, but the Germans made no effort to exploit their initial successes in this area. Actually, the lateral road south of the Moletta River formed the Final Beachhead Defense Line. It was apparent now that the attack against the British 56th Division was purely diversionary and that

[10] Bowditch, *op. cit.*, 75.   [11] Linklater, *op. cit.*, 201.

Von Mackensen's maximum effort would continue to be made down the Albano road against the front of the 45th Division. He had wantonly squandered men and machines in what now appeared to be only the opening phase of his big offensive.

Along toward midnight, Combat Group Graeser renewed the attack with one regiment of the 715th Infantry Division infiltrating around and into the positions of the forward company of the 2nd Battalion, 157th Infantry west of the Albano road. During the early morning hours, all but a relative handful of the defending Americans were either killed or captured. The rest were forced back to Captain Felix Sparks's E Company command post and there they set up an island of defense with the aid of four machine gunners from H Company, and three tanks of the 191st Tank Battalion under the command of First Lieutenant Tommy L. Cobb, Jr.[12] Throughout the early morning hours this small group battled furiously against the onrushing enemy, but it was a hopeless situation.

By five o'clock in the morning, the battalion commander— Lieutenant Colonel Laurence C. Brown of Syracuse, New York —ordered Sparks to fight his way out of the trap and rejoin the battalion. Under a screen of smoke shells laid down by the 158th Field Artillery Battalion and the protective fire of the three-inch cannon and .50-caliber machine guns of the three tanks, Sparks got back to the battalion command post with only fourteen of his own men plus the machine gunners of H Company, and the tankers. But the withdrawal opened a gap between the 157th and the 179th Infantry to its right, and it was opened at exactly the point Von Mackensen had been aiming. He had separated the forces at the Albano road.

As dawn broke on the morning of February 17, an armada of Nazi fighter-bombers peeled off all along the 45th Division front, bombing and strafing. In a matter of moments, three regiments of enemy infantry supported by tanks unleashed their full might against the 2nd and 3rd battalions, 179th, east of the Albano road.

12 Bowditch, *op. cit.*, 75, 77.

Two separate German tank-infantry forces moved down along the road itself from the Factory, through the positions previously held by E Company, 157th Infantry, in a flanking movement against the 2nd Battalion, 179th. The frightful speed of the German attack and the lack of our own air support, because of the early hour and the distance from the southern air bases, caused hurried countermeasures on the part of the 179th's regimental commander. Determined to cover his left flank, Colonel Malcolm R. Kammerer ordered a withdrawal to the stream line one thousand yards to the rear under the cover of an artillery smoke screen. In doing so, Kammerer sacrificed his forward company, Company G.[13] Then, rather than halting at the stream line of the west branch of Carroceto Creek, the two battalions were forced back still another thousand yards before they could establish a new line of resistance at the Dead End road. This, less than a mile from the Final Beachhead Defense Line.

General Eagles earlier had visited the 179th's sector, conferred with Kammerer, and told him to get out all regimental headquarters personnel, including staff, to halt the withdrawing troops and assist in firming up the positions along the stream line of Carroceto Creek. Eagles later was to learn that little had been done to carry out these orders, and that, in fact, Colonel Kammerer had dispatched his most able staff officer to the rear to select a new regimental command post.[14]

This lack of decision and leadership at a most critical moment was to cost Colonel Kammerer his command.

Along the eastern shoulder of the new German salient, the 2nd Battalion, 180th Infantry was forced to extend its lines to keep in contact with the withdrawing 179th. G Company, 180th, exposed and under constant enemy pressure, nevertheless held its ground, and the Germans were unable to widen their salient.

Meanwhile, virtually everything that flew was assigned to the

---

[13] *Ibid.,* 77.

[14] From personal conversations and correspondence between the author and General Eagles.

defense of Anzio. Regardless of the overcast weather, the XIIth Air Support Command threw more than seven hundred bombers of various assortments against the attacking Germans that day.[15] All other missions had to be scrapped, the planes assigned to the critical situation at Anzio. It was to date the greatest number of bombers and the largest bomb tonnage allotted to direct support of ground troops. Ranging from Campoleone to the Factory, the bombers zeroed-in on enemy assembly points and troop concentration areas up and down those three miles of the Albano road until darkness set in. But they were not unopposed. The Germans had mounted the heaviest concentrations of anti-aircraft fire ever encountered by the fliers in the Mediterranean Theater.

Second Lieutenant Thomas Judge of Boston was piloting a brand new B–17 Flying Fortress on its initial combat flight that day. The plane was hit repeatedly by flak, and one chunk of German metal tore through the plane's control cables. It was seen wobbling through the air southward toward its base, both wing tanks ablaze. The Lieutenant landed his stricken craft safely back at base only after the cables were hastily spliced and other emergency repairs were made in flight, but the ground crew stopped counting the holes in the riddled fuselage when they reached five hundred. That B–17 was beyond repair and had to be scrapped. And this had been its first mission.

On the ground, the Germans had mounted a total of fourteen battalions of infantry, and were pouring them in one on top of another in an effort to keep up the momentum of the assault against the 45th Division front, with their main effort concentrated against the 2nd and 3rd battalions, 179th.[16] Enemy tanks and infantry continued to flow down the Albano road, and two Mark IV's got as far as the First Overpass before being knocked out. The remainder gathered at the junction of the Albano and Dead End roads, where they found concealment behind a small knot of farmhouses, and the German infantry dug in around them.

[15] Bowditch, *op. cit.*, 77. [16] Linklater, *op. cit.*, 202.

Just south of Dead End road, the two battalions of the 179th were setting up their new defense line.

To the west, on the other side of the Albano road, the 2nd Battalion, 157th Infantry was cut off and virtually surrounded by small German units infiltrating along the gullies between it and the British 167th Brigade to its left. And throughout the afternoon, Harmon's tanks operated up the Albano road from the First Overpass to Dead End road to hold off the advancing German armor.

During the night, Lucas moved his Corps reserve up along the Final Beachhead Defense Line—the east-west road which crosses the Albano road at the First Overpass—and added depth to the 45th Division positions astride the Albano road one mile to the north.[17] Also, Eagles ordered a combined counterattack by the seriously weakened 2nd and 3rd battalions, 179th, and the 3rd Battalion, 157th. It was to start an hour before midnight. Its objective, the stream line of the west branch of Carroceto Creek—an advance of more than one thousand yards. The 3rd Battalion, 157th, was to reach a parallel position west of the Albano road to link up with the isolated 2nd Battalion, 157th.

The two depleted battalions of the 179th jumped off on schedule, but the 3rd Battalion, 157th, was an hour and a half late in getting underway. The battalion commander, Captain Merle Mitchell, had been wounded in the stomach and shoulder, but would not allow the medics to evacuate him until he had received reconnaissance reports on the route of advance and had personally directed the jump-off. The German defense was so strong, however, that Captain Mitchell's battalion got no farther than the junction of the Albano and Dead End roads.[18]

With his left flank wide open, Lieutenant Colonel Charles Wiegand's 2nd Battalion, 179th, came under withering fire from enemy tanks and infantry which had been brought up aboard half-tracks, and he was forced to retire. To his right, Major Mer-

[17] The British 1st Division (less the 3rd Brigade) plus the 2nd Battalion, 6th Armored Infantry.
[18] Bowditch, *op. cit.*, 79.

lin Tryon's 3rd Battalion, 179th, which had been reduced to 274 men but had A Company, 179th, attached to it, reached the stream line; but K Company was virtually in a trap, and the remainder of the battalion was in a highly exposed position. Enemy artillery had knocked out communications, and the situation seemed even more fluid than it was. After several hours of confused fighting in the darkness and the rain, it had to be admitted that the counterattack had failed. Worse, the enemy was moving up fresh troops and infiltrating behind American positions along both shoulders of the new German salient.[19]

At VIth Corps headquarters, the apprehension was oppressive. The situation maps showed the Germans had penetrated to a depth of almost four miles over a four-mile front in the center of the beachhead perimeter,[20] and that at the crucial point they were literally pounding against the Final Beachhead Defense Line. The equivalent of six enemy divisions was pitted against four sorely tried and depleted American battalions. The maps showed the definite probability of an iminent enemy breakthrough.

The anxiety was not limited to the cave dwellers at the VIth Corps.

In Washington, Secretary of War Henry L. Stimson called a hurried press conference to plead with the American public to abandon its pessimism concerning Anzio. Newspaper reports of the preceding days could not help but reflect some of the official alarm. Now the Secretary of War was attempting to quiet the mounting public fear. "The situation in Italy," the Secretary stated at the news conference, "is an example of the old American saying, 'Keep your shirt on.' "

For the benefit of the British public whose newspapers were carrying accounts of impending calamity at Anzio, General Alexander announced from his Fifteenth Army Group headquarters:

> There is absolutely no Dunkerque here—there's no basis for pessimistic rubbish.

[19] Linklater, *op. cit.*, 203.   [20] Truscott, *op. cit.*, 322.

I assure you the Germans opposite us are a very unhappy party. The Germans realize they've lost the battle, though events have not gone as swiftly as we ourselves hoped. Had everything gone perfectly we might have gone straight through to Rome in the first round.

As it is, we are near the end of the second round and we are winning it.

Don't compare this situation to Dunkerque or Salerno.

This was heady talk designed for home consumption as well as for the propaganda effect it might have on the Germans, but it was heady talk coming from men far removed from the Final Beachhead Defense Line. There, it was another matter, with the British and American troops absorbing the worst punishment the Nazi war machine could mete out. General Lucas more than ever was being blistered by the "Salerno Complex" pinned on him by Churchill.[21] Alexander, always too ready to agree with his prime minister, had been discreetly suggesting that Clark remove the Corps commander. No official order, merely repeated expressions of general dissatisfaction. It was no secret that the British could not get along with Lucas and that Lucas returned their displeasure in kind,[22] and that their mutual lack of confidence would ultimately lead to Lucas' removal.

On February 17, the situation at Anzio was so critical that Clark's hand was forced. In deference to an old friend, Clark could not abruptly dismiss Lucas. Instead, he assigned Truscott as Lucas' deputy with the intention that Truscott would take over the Corps within a matter of days and Lucas would be reassigned as one of Clark's deputies on the Fifth Army staff.[23] Brigadier General John W. O'Daniel, better known to the infantrymen as "Iron Mike," was moved up to full command of the 3rd Division, and Colonel Harry Sherman would replace him as assistant division commander. The Rangers' Colonel William O. Darby would assume command of Sherman's 7th Infantry Regiment.

[21] Churchill, *op. cit.,* 487.   [22] Truscott, *op. cit.,* 320, 329.
[23] Clark, *op. cit.,* 309.

An insight into VIth Corps' anxiety might be gathered from General Truscott's own report concerning his departure from command of the 3rd Division:

> Just before I left the Third Division CP, General Keiser, the Corps chief-of-staff, had telephoned to ask when I was going to report. He had terminated the conversation with the observation that he did not know whether or not there would be any Corps Headquarters by the following morning for they would probably be driven into the sea.[24]

Truscott arrived at Corps headquarters at half-past one on the afternoon of February 17, and his first reaction was that the situation was considerably worse than he had been led to believe over at his own relatively quiet division command post. But he held to the theory that along the front the situation was rarely as bad as it appeared on the maps at headquarters. His assurances, however, did nothing to dispel the terrible mounting fear in the cellars at VIth Corps headquarters.

Above ground it was another story. It was Truscott's job as deputy corps commander to keep in constant touch with the situation at the front, and the most pressing concern was the front of the 45th Division. There, he met with Generals Eagles and Harmon and found both men thoroughly aware of the gravity of the circumstances confronting them but equally confident that all was not lost. Harmon admitted his armored counterattacks had been a standoff with the German armor, but they had slowed down the momentum of the enemy drive. As for Eagles, he voiced no misgivings about the ability of his division to hold.[25]

On the German side of the line, despite their terrible losses, the night of February 17–18 was the eve of jubilation. They were poised for the final assault, the supreme effort to push on to the sea. Von Mackensen moved five regiments into position to effect the breakthrough—the 721st, the 735th and 741st Infantry, and

---

[24] Truscott, *op. cit.*, 320.   [25] *Ibid.*, 321–22.

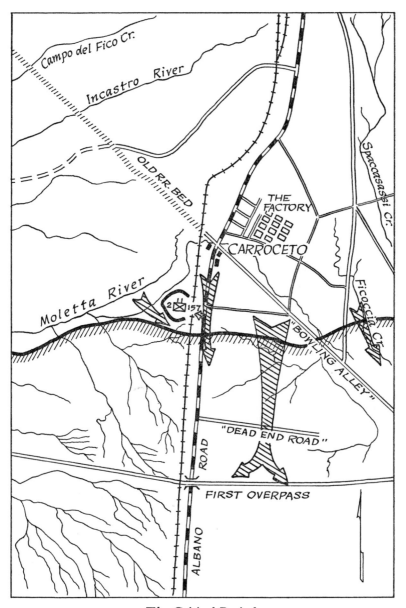

The Critical Period

127

the 29th and 309th Panzer Grenadier regiments—each supported by tanks.[26]

Throughout the night of February 17, small units of German infantry took advantage of the confusion along the two-battalion front of the 179th to infiltrate the positions, and as dawn came up on February 18, the full strength of the German attack was loosed on the battered American battalions. From eight in the morning until eight at night, the Germans pounded at the Allied positions; yet the staying power of the American infantrymen kept the enemy at bay, and the deluge of GI artillery shells frustrated every German attempt to break through. All along the lateral road, from the First Overpass to Padiglione, fierce hand-to-hand battles developed. At one point, Colonel Darby, who in a last-minute change was assigned to replace Kammerer as commander of the 179th,[27] proposed falling back to the Padiglione Woods, where a reorganization would be possible, but Eagles would not permit another thousand-yard withdrawal. Darby was told to hold the Final Beachhead Defense Line at all costs.

With only Lieutenant Colonel Johnson's 1st Battalion still

---

[26] The 309th Panzer Grenadiers, otherwise known as the Infantry Lehr Regiment, was speedily reorganized and thrown back into the battle despite its poor showing in the field on the afternoon of February 16. The Germans were feeling the pinch of their losses in manpower as well as materiel. An order (copy) from the commander of the 29th Panzer Grenadier Regiment made a special note of the losses in equipment and criticized officers and soldiers for their inadequate efforts to salvage weapons and parts. The document read: "The problem of replacing materiel is growing more and more difficult and even unsolvable in some cases. This leads to an insufferable weakening in our combat efficiency.

"I am not willing to allow the reputation of the regiment to be torn down by such losses in weapons."

The Germans were finding it increasingly difficult to keep the mountains of supplies flowing toward the beachhead from the supply dumps around Rome. With the slackening of the winter rains, our bombers were seriously disrupting the enemy supply lines, and the Germans were forced to conscript Italian labor to move supplies and ammunition from Rome to Anzio by horse and donkey carts. Admittedly, this was a much slower means of supply than truck convoy or railroad, but it did keep the Germans supplied in addition to frustrating our bomber efforts by minimizing the targets.

[27] Truscott, *op. cit.*, 323.

capable of organized resistance, Darby assigned it to the center of the 179th's line. Lieutenant Colonel Wiegand's 2nd Battalion was to take over the right side with what troops he had and whatever additional he could find. And Major Tryon was ordered to pick up all stragglers and rear echelon troops as a reserve. Eagles was determined to hold the line, and Darby was doing his utmost to carry out these orders.

Along both shoulders of the German salient, the attack was equally furious. The 2nd Battalion, 157th Infantry, west of the Albano road, was ringed by German infantry but still holding out behind its wired-in positions. It was the second day of fighting off fanatical attacks for the isolated Americans, and the German dead and wounded continued to pile up before them. One German, wounded early in the attack, was hung across the barbed wire entanglement. At regular intervals he would cry out in English, "My name is Müller, I am wounded." Over and over again, hour after hour, "My name is Müller, I am wounded." But neither side made any attempt to dislodge him, and the battle went on despite his cries. And there were other cries. Preceding each new attack, the Germans would shout dire threats. The gutteral warnings could be heard: "Watch out Company F." Or, "Here we come again."

And they would come, with everything they had, only to add to the dead and wounded, only to join Müller on the barbed wire out in front. Then the fighting would die off and the artillery would open up and the voice would cry, "My name is Müller, I am wounded." And the fury would start all over again.

During the early morning hours, a patrol fought its way through to bring up a supply of ammunition to the surrounded battalion, but they brought no food or water, and there was no way of getting the wounded back. They had to be left in soggy slit trenches, tended as best they could be by the hard-pressed medics. Still the battalion fought on, repulsing one enemy assault after another. And still the never ending plea from the man on the wire: "My name is Müller, I am wounded."

Müller's pain-wracked chant finally became too much for one man of the 2nd Battalion, 157th. Late in the afternoon of the second day of listening to the imploring voice of the wounded enemy out on the wire, a pin was pulled, the grenade lobbed out toward the barbed wire, and the almost silent mutter: "What's your name now, you son of a . . . ."

The question trailed off and was accentuated by the explosion of the hand grenade. For a brief moment there was silence.

Then the battle resumed around the isolated American battalion.[28]

Dug in to watery foxholes and into niches carved into the loamy slopes of the maze of ravines along which trickled the waters that fed the Moletta River and flowed eventually to the sea, the battalion fought on in what was to become known as "The Battle of The Caves."[29] Possession of this strategic point, which denied the German armor the use of a network of dirt roads leading south to the Final Beachhead Defense Line, was imperative to the safety of the entire Allied position at Anzio. Enemy tanks rumbling down the Albano road repeatedly rolled up the right flank of the battalion; and German infantry, infiltrating along the many gullies, successfully worked around behind the position to cut off the battalion's supply lines. But the battalion clung tenaciously to its string of caves and foxholes, at times calling for the 105-mm. howitzers of Lieutenant Colonel R. D. Funk's 158th Field Artilley Battalion to fire directly upon their own positions. Some of the men of 2nd Battalion, 157th, were killed by their own supporting artillery fire, but the attacking Germans, bunched up as they were in strong waves, suffered fearfully. And the crossfire of the heavy machine guns assigned to First Lieutenant Joseph Robertson's G Company, which was set up atop the ridge

[28] Related to the author by Captain Felix Sparks immediately following his return to the 157th regimental command post after the "Battle of the Caves."

[29] Caves of Pozzolana, sheepherders' caverns dug into the shale of a ridge, a series of connecting tunnels running underground for several hundred yards. The largest of the caverns served as the battalion's command post.

into which the caves were dug, cut down the advancing waves of enemy in incredible numbers. Still they came, forcing finally the remnants of G Company to abandon their positions atop the ridge and seek refuge in the caves below. Armored patrols of the 2nd Battalion, 6th Armored Infantry, occasionally fought their way up to the isolated battalion with supplies and, when possible, would bring back wounded, but the 2nd Battalion, 157th, remained for the most part cut off from the rest of the VIth Corps. Holding their positions not only frustrated the German attack, it also provided an anchor for the left flank of the Allied line. They had been told to hold, and hold they did despite desperate enemy efforts to dislodge them.

Fighting from inside the caves was a nightmare. Each rifle shot echoed and re-echoed off the walls and ceilings and floors of the chambers and connecting passages and sounded more like the report of a cannon than of a .30-caliber M–1, and German machine-pistol fire and exploding potato mashers kept the defenders well back from the mouths of the caves, adding to the cacophonous racket inside. In the lulls between enemy attacks, the men busied themselves refilling M–1 clips by stripping now useless machine-gun belts, and they listened to the chatter of the German prisoners huddled in the corner of one of the larger caves, where they were out of the line of fire.

At the same time along the opposite shoulder of the German salient, some three miles to the east, the 2nd Battalion, 180th Infantry was under attack along the three roads leading southeast from the Factory toward Padiglione and Carano. A strong force of enemy tanks trundled down the "Bowling Alley"—that part of the old railroad bed that had been converted into a vehicular road-way—and German infantry moved along the defiles of the Car-roceto, Ficoccia, and Spaccasassi creeks to force the attack against the overextended American battalion. The 645th tank-destroyers had fourteen of their M–10's knocked out on February 17 alone. Those that remained in action had to be dug in to the marshy ground for protection and soon became mired and virtually impossible to free. Many had to be abandoned when the defending infantry companies were forced to fall back.

They fell back reluctantly and in a much more orderly fashion than did the two battalions of the 179th on their left. Colonel Robert L. Dulaney, a more forceful and able commander than Kammerer,[30] pivoted the battalion on the strong point held by Captain Ellis B. Ritchie's E Company, north of Padiglione. Dulaney ordered the remainder of the battalion to swing southeastward to the point where it regained contact on the left with the 3rd Battalion, 179th, thereby shortening his lines as well as re-establishing the division's defense line. It meant giving up more than a mile at the westernmost point along the Bowling Alley. Of necessity, because communication lines were disrupted by enemy artillery and dive-bombings, orders to withdraw were dispatched by company runners. G Company, however, had been cut off from the remainder of the battalion north of the Carroceto Creek by the Germans who had infiltrated that creek to its rear, and withdrawal orders never reached the company commander.[31] First Lieutenant Benjamin Blackmer of South Dorset, Vermont, had assumed command of the company only the day before. He had been transferred from another line company of the 180th after G Company had lost all but one of its officers, but none of its fighting spirit.

By noon of February 18, Blackmer's new command consisted of barely fifty men. It was completely encircled, and ammunition was down to ten rounds per man with one box per machine gun. Eleven rounds of mortar shells were left. No grenades.

By two-thirty that afternoon, Blackmer attempted to extricate what was left of the company from what was developing into a hopeless situation. In its isolation, G Company was being subjected to as much Allied artillery fire as German. Blackmer

[30] After Anzio, Colonel Dulaney was given his first star and left the 45th Division to become an assistant commander of another division in Italy. When the 45th was called up to active duty for the Korean War, General Dulaney was the division commander.

[31] Bowditch, *op. cit.*, 82.

ordered his men to move down Carroceto Creek some three hundred yards in hopes of getting out of the intense shellfire and possibly linking up with the remainder of the battalion. The wounded had to be left behind. One of these was Pfc. William J. Johnston of Colchester, Connecticut, a machine gunner who had been hit in the chest by a shell splinter. In the earlier fighting to hold the position, Johnston had performed prodigious feats with both his machine gun and a rifle. Now he had to be left behind. The company medic said he was dying.

"It's okay, fellows," he said as his buddies crept past him headed for the rear. "Those guys paid for it, and they'll pay more. So long."

The last noncom to leave saw Johnston crawling toward his machine gun with his last bit of strength. The sergeant helped him to the gun, made him comfortable, then left.

G Company moved slowly down the creek, hugging the sides of its vertical embankment, and an hour or so later met the company runner head-on coming up the creek. Pfc. Robert Keefe had managed to slip through and around German strong points with the message from battalion headquarters. It instructed Blackmer to fight his way back.[32]

Throughout the afternoon, the men of G Company could hear the stutter of machine-gun fire from the position they had left—an American machine gun. Each burst, they figured, would be the last. And finally, the last burst was fired. The men kept listening, but Johnston's gun was silent. After dark, the remnants of the company waded through waist-deep water and fought their way through German entrenchments for more than a mile. They rejoined the battalion. Dulaney was notified, "Blackmer came through smiling."

That night as the 45th Division made the most of a temporary lull to strengthen its positions. Eagles threw his last reserves into the most seriously threatened sector. He assigned the 1st Battalion, 157th, to the 179th Infantry. A strong patrol of the 6th Armored

[32] *Ibid.,* 83.

Infantry again broke through with supplies for the isolated 2nd Battalion, 157th. And that night Pfc. William J. Johnston was officially listed K.I.A.—killed in action.

That night headquarters personnel of each division on the beachhead—the clerks, drivers, dispatchers, cooks, the orderlies, and off-duty telephone operators—all were herded together and set to work digging in each division headquarters as possible islands of defense in the event of an enemy breakthrough. This was the last possible moment, and every desperate effort had to be made even if it appeared fruitless. This was the supreme moment at Anzio. In the morning the Germans would renew the attack; everyone knew that.

And that night in his trailer at Nettuno, the indefatigable Truscott was poring over the day's battle reports and fretting over the situation along the 45th Division front. Only a day and a half away from command of his 3rd Division, he held the belief that his old Regular Army men of the 3rd would have halted the German attack and handled the situation much better than the Colorado and Oklahoma National Guardsmen of the 45th. This, despite the fact that Truscott himself was an Oklahoman. He was proud of the Regular Army, especially of the 3rd Division which he had commanded in battle for almost a year. Thumbing through the pages before him, he hit upon what he believed to be the answer in the day's ammunition expenditure reports. They showed that only one battalion of the 3rd Division's artillery, covering a comparatively inactive front, had fired more rounds than had all four battalions of the 45th Division's artillery which was pitted against the major German offensive.[33] This, he believed, dated back to those intricate fire patterns worked out less than two weeks before by the 3rd Division's artillerymen.

By ten o'clock that night, Truscott was closeted in the wine cellars of VIth Corps headquarters with the Corps artillery officer, General Baehr, and the 3rd Division's artillery fire-control co-ordinator (S–3), Major Walter T. "Dutch" Kerwin. The sit-

[33] Truscott, *op. cit.*, 325.

uation was explained to both men, and Kerwin was ordered to set up the same system of emergency fire patterns as those of the 3rd Division throughout every other division's artillery battalions on the beachhead. Baehr was instructed to see to it that the young Major's orders were carried out. Truscott explained that he did not have time to go through the routine channels.

Just before daybreak, Truscott was informed that his orders had been carried out.[34]

And just as day was breaking over Anzio, February 19, an outpost of one company of the 180th Infantry spotted a lone figure working his way toward the American lines. He would walk a few steps, crawl a short distance, stop and rest, then take a few more steps and fall. He kept it up till he got close enough to identify himself as a GI, and two men crawled out to him and brought him back. He could barely talk. He was badly wounded in the chest and was shoeless. He explained the Germans had come upon him and a German medic had bandaged his wounds, but that the medic did not call for a stretcher-bearer because he believed he was too far gone. One enemy soldier took off his shoes, and they left him to die on the battlefield. Then, haltingly, the wounded GI gave accurate information on the location of enemy gun positions he had noted on his arduous trip back. And he identified himself: Pfc. William J. Johnston of G Company, 180th Infantry.

Moments later, the guns he had seen and every other enemy

[34] British military accounts of the Anzio campaign make no reference to Major Kerwin's instructions to their artillery units, and from personal conversations between the author and Generals Eagles and McLain, the artillery commander of the 45th Division, no such instructions were passed on to them. Lieutenant Colonel R. D. Funk, commanding officer of the 158th Field Artillery Battalion at the time, recalls no such nocturnal visit by the Major. Nevertheless, General Truscott maintains that Major Kerwin's emergency fire patterns were standardized among the artillery battalions across the beachhead. In essence, they consisted of extravagant and sometimes effective map firing in contrast to the much more effective and, in terms of rounds expended, much less costly practice of observed firing. It should be noted that Truscott was a cavalryman, not an artillerist.

gun within reach opened a tremendous bombardment in preparation for the final thrust against the Allied line. Its aim—the port of
Anzio. Von Mackensen so far had kept to his schedule. Now, one
last powerful lunge would smash the Allied defenses, and victory
would be his. And the name Eberhard von Mackensen would go
down in German military annals alongside that of his father, Field
Marshal August von Mackensen.[35] Another Von Mackensen and
another war, and the son was seeking his place among his nation's
most honored men.

After ten minutes of the heaviest artillery concentration yet
delivered, the German infantry rose up out of their lines to strike
anew against the 45th Division front, and the heaviest blows were
directed against the 1st Battalion, 179th, and the 1st Loyals, on
either side of the Albano road. With lightning speed, two battalions of the 15th Panzer Grenadier Regiment supported by
three Mark IV tanks quickly overran one company of the Loyals
and got as far as the lateral road.[36] But this was the only point at
which they were able to crack the line, and this group came under
the heavy fire of F Company, 1st Armored Regiment, and was
forced to withdraw by eight o'clock in the morning. The 179th
and the remainder of the 1st Loyals stood firm in the face of repeated enemy armored thrusts down the Albano road. Before
noon the M–10's of the 701st Tank-Destroyer Battalion had
knocked out two enemy Tiger tanks and five Mark IV's, and the
remainder of the attackers were coming under the increased artillery fire. The guns of the 45th and those of the supporting Corps
artillery were firing prepared defensive concentrations for extended periods of time, firing by map only and not knowing the
effect of their salvos. Thousands of rounds were belched out of
the muzzles of these guns throughout the morning and on into the
afternoon. Only occasionally would the guns be trained upon an

[35] The infamous "Death's Head" of World War I, scourge of the Eastern
Front, occupier of Serbia, and military commander of Romania, the elder Von
Mackensen had risen from a lowly start as a history teacher—but history teacher to
a youngster who one day would become Kaiser Wilhelm II.

[36] Bowditch, *op. cit.*, 84.

observed target, but the horrendous hail of splintering steel from more than two hundred howitzers and Long Toms stopped short each new enemy attack as soon as it got underway. And the big guns of the cruisers offshore added their weight and distance to the intense Allied artillery sweep.

By early afternoon, it was evident that the German attack had failed.[37] The Albano road had a dead end so far as Von Mackensen's hopes and desires were concerned. This was the turning point for the VIth Corps, the moment to strike back.

Truscott was first to note that the German Fourteenth Army had reached the end of its tether, but there was little with which to strike back. Corps reserve consisted of the 6th Armored Infantry and its tanks and the 30th Infantry. The British 56th Division's 169th Brigade was just arriving at Anzio but was delayed in unloading because of mines dropped in the harbor by German planes.[38] Nevertheless, with Lucas' approval, Truscott set up two task forces. Force H under Harmon would consist of his armor and the 30th Infantry and would attack astride the Bowling Alley; Force T under Templer would consist of the 169th Brigade and would attack up the Albano road from the First Overpass. The two forces were to start out simultaneously, but the difficulty in unloading the British brigade in the mine-clogged harbor necessitated a change in plan. The propitious moment no longer could be postponed, so only Harmon's force was turned loose.[39] It caught the Germans, so thoroughly engrossed in their own attack down the Albano road some three miles to the west, completely by surprise.

The tanks and infantry of Task Force H barreled up the Bowling Alley, and in less than two hours had gained more than one mile before meeting stiffening resistance. At the same time, the 1st Armored Regiment, covering the right flank of the attack, had rumbled out of Padiglione and was stopped only momentarily by a blown bridge over Spaccasassi Creek, then continued on up the

---

[37] Linklater, *op. cit.*, 204.   [38] Truscott, *op. cit.*, 324.
[39] Bowditch, *op. cit.*, 86.

road and so completely confused the Germans that they were surrendering in droves. The bag of prisoners got so big that the tankers had to call on the 180th Infantry to dispose of them.

By four-thirty that afternoon, Harmon called a halt to his limited attack, withdrew his main assault force, and left two battalions of infantry as a covering force.[40] They remained throughout the night and on into the next day before being ordered to withdraw. In all, Task Force H had collected more than two hundred prisoners and had done it with comparative ease. One tank platoon leader, Second Lieutenant Rexford Neal, of Arcadia, Ohio, gave particular praise to the supporting artillery.

"Those Germans are coming out of their lines trembling and shaking," he said. "Every so often the Germans, who have good observation only a thousand yards away, were mortaring and even machine gunning their own men because they were surrendering so fast."

This much can be said for the Germans who were surrendering: They had been thoroughly misled by falsehoods deliberately fed them. They had been told that this was a glorious expedition to which they had been assigned, that the Allied forces at Anzio had been badly beaten and that their task would be merely a mopping up exercise, and that in fact the Allies already had begun evacuating the beachhead.[41]

This last was partially true. Just that morning, operations had begun to evacuate the 18,000 Italian civilians from their homes and shelters within the Allied beachhead. They were to be taken by boat to Naples and quartered in a huge relocation center. Officially, they were to be removed "from within the range of bombardment." Actually, they were in the way and had to be taken out of there. Too, not all the Italian civilians at Anzio were reliable. Most, we must remember, were the beneficiaries of Facism. They owed everything to the land-reclamation program set up by Mussolini, and their proximity to the enemy was a danger we no

[40] Truscott, *op. cit.*, 326.   [41] Clark, *op. cit.*, 310.

longer could afford to ignore. On at least one occasion an Italian shepherd maneuvered his flock to point out likely artillery targets to the distant German observers. Once the flock moved on, enemy artillery pulverized the area. But the ruse was short lived; the shepherd was caught, thoroughly pummelled, and turned over to the military police barely in condition to give further testimony concerning his acts. As for his sheep, well, even mutton tastes good after a long diet of K rations.

The German prisoners were another matter. More than seven hundred were captured on February 19 alone. They told of frightening horrors endured during our artillery bombardments and of the effectiveness of our bombers. They told, too, of serious disorganization among Von Mackensen's army. They told of attacks starting out in battalion strength being whittled down to less than the size of a platoon by our artillery before reaching our forward positions.[42] Still others told of disrupted communications, of whole regiments attacking as much as a day late because orders failed to reach them in time. And they told of the employment of the last of the reserve divisions intended to be withheld for the exploitation of the expected breakthrough. But that breakthrough was never to come.

At this point, late in the afternoon of February 19, the back of the German army had been broken. First at Stalingrad, now at the plains south of Rome.

With ten divisions strongly supported by armor, artillery, and the largest number of planes the *Luftwaffe* could muster since the fighting in Sicily, Von Mackensen's Fourteenth Army began the attack with all the initial advantages save one—the determined staying power, high morale, and lasting resilience of the British Tommy and American GI. That plus the huge quantities of artillery ammunition built up on the beachhead by General Lucas, for which he was so bitterly criticized by Winston Churchill. Von Mackensen's army was still a formidable force, still not de-

---

[42] Bowditch, *op. cit.,* 87.

feated, but it had been met and stopped. No longer did it pose the threat of annihilation. A Saturday afternoon at Anzio finally brought to an end the German offensive potential.

VIth Corps had proved it was not the "stranded whale" that had been tossed up on the beach.

CHAPTER EIGHT

"The Other Fellow Will Quit First"

IN one of the many ironies of the war, the world would little note the heroic stand at Anzio made by American and British infantrymen in the face of tremendous odds. The great wave of public concern of only a few days before had been washed away in an ocean of controversy and consternation. The climactic three-day battle at Anzio was far overshadowed now by public argument over the massive Allied bombing of the abbey at Monte Cassino on February 15.

The bombing of the religious shrine—although preceded by weeks of public debate on the advisability and military necessity of destroying the abbey—surprised and shocked the world when it was actually carried out. Spurred by the incessant demands of the New Zealand Corps commander—Lieutenant General Sir Bernard Freyberg,[1] whose New Zealand, Indian, and South African troops took over from the U.S. IInd Corps the Fifth Army assignment of breaking through the Gustav Line at Cassino and pushing into the Liri Valley—the orders to bomb the hilltop monastery were passed on to Clark by Alexander. From the airfields in southern Italy, Sicily, and as far away as North Africa, heavy and medium bombers took off to converge on a pinpoint target. At nine-thirty on the morning of February 15, the first bombs fell within the courtyard of the ancient monastery. By late afternoon, a total of 576 tons of explosives had been dropped on the sacred edifice, and when the bombing ceased, the artillery opened up.[2]

After the smoke and dust had settled, the New Zealand Corps, which had so doggedly persisted in calling for the destruction of the historical shrine, was to learn that the piles of rubble of the ruined monastery and the town beneath it only added to the impregnability of the German defenses as well as providing the enemy with a legitimate excuse to move in and man those ruins. Heretofore, there were grave doubts that the Germans were actually occupying the abbey, although Freyberg and Major General Sir Howard Kippenberger, commander of the 2nd New Zealand Division, insisted they were. And the commander of the U.S. Air Corps in Italy, Lieutenant General Ira C. Eaker, had flown at low altitude in a Piper Cub over the monastery and reported seeing German soldiers and a radio antenna within the cloister. He was accompanied on that flight by Lieutenant General Jacob L. Devers, the deputy theater commander, but Devers would neither confirm nor deny the report.[3]

[1] Clark, *op. cit.*, 315–18.

[2] Official announcement by Allied Air Command, Mediterranean Theater, dated February 15, 1944, stated that 142 B-17 "Flying Fortresses" and 112 medium bombers had dropped 576 tons of bombs on Monte Cassino. It should be noted that not all fell on the monastery. Some were dropped as far away as Venafro, which from the air had similar contours, although there was no monastery atop the mountain behind Venafro. Allied troops suffered heavily from the stray bombs that fell behind our own lines.

[3] Majdalany, *op. cit.*, 116.

Just a few hours before the first bombs were dropped, however, the elderly Abbot-Bishop of Monte Cassino had signed an official document attesting to the fact that the only German soldiers ever stationed within the walls of the monastery were three military policemen, and that they were there only briefly to assure the neutrality of the religious building.[4]

Even after all these years, during which time the monastery has been rebuilt, the dispute over the righteousness of the bombing still has not been settled, and it is a strange quirk of fate that of all those who still argue that the bombing was both wanton and criminal, the name of the man who set the act in motion should be among the foremost—Mark Clark. He contends it was not only a military mistake but "an unnecessary psychological mistake in the propaganda field."[5]

For their part, the Germans were quick to make propaganda capital out of the Allied air attack, and they were aided considerably by the natural revulsion on the part of virtually everyone not immediately involved at the destruction and desecration of the religious site. The arguments that followed went on for days in the press and completely obscured the momentous events that were taking place some sixty miles to the northwest on a tiny strip of land where the Anglo-American forces were accomplishing the near impossible.

Even in Rome, so close to the Anzio battlefield, the storm of debate over the Cassino bombing obliterated the tantalizing prospect of liberation by the invading forces at Anzio. Now, every-

---

[4] Leaning on the altar of the Chapel of the Pietà in the early morning hours of February 15, 1944, the eighty-year-old Abbot Gregorio Diamare signed the following document at the request of a German lieutenant: "I certify to the truth that inside the enclosure of the sacred monastery of Cassino there never were any German soldiers; that there were for a certain period only three military police for the sole purpose of enforcing respect for the neutral zone which was established around the monastery, but they were withdrawn about twenty days ago." And Field Marshal Kesselring writes in his memoirs (*op. cit.*, 234): "Once and for all I wish to establish the fact that the monastery was not occupied as part of the line; it was closed against unauthorized entry by military police."

[5] Clark, *op. cit.*, 312.

thing was dominated by the reports of the destruction of the Monte Cassino abbey, and Anzio was being overlooked. Placards and posters went up all over the city showing photographs of the ruins of Monte Cassino with the monks and refugee civilians cowering in corners. And reproductions of the signed statement by Monsignor Diamare, the abbot-bishop, were plastered on walls all over the Holy City.

While the controversy raged, the military men on both sides were well aware that the bombing of the monastery was of little practical consequence.[6] It neither enabled the New Zealand Corps to crack the Gustav Line nor alleviated enemy pressure against the Anzio beachhead. Its propaganda value in the long run was minimal as propaganda usually is, and the following air attacks against the abbey would go virtually ignored.

The war went on. The stalemate continued along the southern front, and when no further alarming word came from Anzio, the American and British public settled back in complacent reassurance that both the Secretary of War's and General Alexander's appraisals of the situation on the beachhead were correct. Anzio was of secondary importance. Unrecognized, unreported, and unappreciated was the fact that the VIth Corps had cracked the backbone of the German offensive power.

Von Mackensen's army was still intact and still outnumbered the Allied forces at Anzio, but it had lost its determination in the face of overwhelming firepower. It could continue to go through the motions, but the *Blitzkrieg* had in itself been blitzed in a series of soldiers' battles in which the Germans had come up against better soldiers than themselves.

Years later, Kesselring was to reflect on the battles at Anzio. In his words, "Anzio was the enemy's 'Epic of Bravery.' " He described the Allied troops there as *"Ausgezeichnet"*—distinguished. "We felt we were opposed by equals," he said. "Our enemy was of the highest quality."[7]

[6] *Ibid.* Kesselring, *op. cit.*, 234.
[7] On the eve of his transfer to Venice to stand trial before a British war

General Eberhard von Mackensen (left)
and Field Marshal Albert Kesselring.

Corporal Roderick R. Loop (right), of the 191st Tank Battalion, bids good-bye to his son, Private William R. Loop, also of the 191st, at Anzio. The pair enlisted together at Binghamton, N. Y., took basic training together, and fought together. Following the big battle of mid-February, the elder Loop, a veteran of World War I, was reassigned to the States.

Signal Corps

The Mussolini Canal, long the front line at Anzio, with GI's dug
into the reverse slope of the dike. Note the flatness of the land
and the *podere* studding the area.

Signal Corps

Bombing of the Abbey of Monte Cassino, February 15, 1944.

Major General Lucian K. Truscott, Jr.,
at his desk at VIth Corps Headquarters at Anzio.

Signal Corps

Major General Vyvyan Eveleigh, assistant to the beachhead
commander, assigned to Anzio by Alexander to re-establish
cordial relations between the American
and British commanders at the beachhead.

Imperial War Museum

Self-propelled 105-mm. howitzers in position
to fight off the big German assault of mid-February.

Signal Corps

An anti-aircraft gun dug in for camouflage.

Signal Corps

But this was on reflection. At the time, the German Fourteenth Army was charged, by Hitler himself, with making still another assault against the defending Allies. Von Mackensen, however, was realist enough to recognize that he had been bested in his frontal assault, and that another would only warrant him further losses in men and materiel and would not accomplish the objective of wiping out the Allied beachhead. In the preceding three-day battle, his 65th Grenadier Division had been whittled down to an effective force of little more than 900 officers and enlisted men, his 735th Infantry Regiment stood at 185 officers and men.[8] And so it went with other units that had been thrown into the all-out attack down the Albano road; they existed more on paper than in reality. In the end, Von Mackensen decided to concentrate his attention along the western shoulder of the salient he had driven into the Allied line, where the 2nd Battalion, 157th, was still holding its isolated position in the caves.

While Von Mackensen drew up his battle orders, so too did Lucas. The VIth Corps commander regrouped his forces. His most pressing problem still was the front of the 45th Division, and, on February 22, the 3rd Division took over about a mile of the 45th's eastern front, and control of its western flank was assumed by the British 1st and 56th divisions.[9] These moves cut by two-thirds the front to be covered by the severely pounded 45th, but

crimes court for his role in the Ardeatine Massacre—the reprisal slayings of 235 Italian hostages for the ambush killing of 32 German soldiers by Italian partisans in a side street in Rome on March 23, 1944—Kesselring was interviewed by Associated Press correspondent Daniel DeLuce in Marburg, Germany, January 22, 1947. The Field Marshal recounted his bitter failure to drive the American and British forces from the Anzio beachhead. Kesselring was lavish in his expressed admiration for those Allied troops that opposed him at Anzio.

At his trial, incidentally, the Field Marshal testified that the orders for the reprisals had been issued by Hitler, who called for killings at the rate of twenty to one. Kesselring modified the *Führer's* orders as much as he dared, but willingly assumed full responsibility, as commanding officer in the area, for carrying them out. He was sentenced to death. The sentence later was commuted to life imprisonment, still later to twenty years. In 1952, suffering from cancer of the throat, he was given full release.

[8] Bowditch, *op. cit.*, 91.   [9] Linklater, *op. cit.*, 205.

there was still the matter of relieving the isolated American battalion hanging onto the dominant terrain west of the Albano road. These troops—the men of the 2nd Battalion, 157th—were under almost continuous fire, their own as well as enemy, since the Germans launched their opening drive from the Factory. At one point, in one company area, an estimated total of six hundred rounds of enemy artillery churned up the ground around them during a forty-minute period—one shell every four seconds—but the company had been so well entrenched it suffered only one dead and eight wounded in this, the most intense artillery fire.

For more than a week the fighting had been extreme in that heavily wooded, harshly broken ground studded with ravines. The fiercest fighting took place at night, with patrols from both sides scouring the region inch by inch. Sergeant Alvin Biggers, of Mountain Home, Arkansas, told of one eight-man patrol he was leading along a path at night when the Germans, "perched in trees like monkeys, came hurtling down on our backs and jumped up from the bushes on each side of us. There must have been about twenty. We had terrific hand-to-hand fighting, and finally we killed at least ten and took four or five prisoners."

He added, "They aren't so tough when they get into good, hard fighting." Sergeant Biggers' summation more than anything else was indicative of the growing morale of the Allied soldiers during this most desperate period on the beachhead. As the days went on, despite the miserable weather, the savage fighting, and the terrible losses, the individual British and American soldier could sense a feeling of mounting self-assurance as he held his position in the face of an apparently irresistible force. The longer he held out, the more confident he became that his was the role to be reckoned with, that he was the dominant force merely by his continued presence in the enemy's path. To the men of the 45th, it was an old proverb bearing fruit: "If you want to hold a position, you can do it; the other fellow will quit first."

Hold it they did, this 2nd Battalion, 157th, until finally relieved by the 2/7 Queens of the British 56th Division.[10] Major General Gerald Templer, commanding his own 56th Division as well as the British 1st Division following the wounding of General Penney, dispatched the 2/7 Queens to the relief of the Americans in the caves at the same moment Von Mackensen renewed his attack against the western shoulder of the salient he had driven into the Allied lines.[11] As result, the British battalion, fighting its way up to the isolated Americans, was subjected to an inordinate amount of shellfire and was bombed by German night fighters. Its supply train and carrying parties were unable to bring up heavy weapons and ammunition, so the relief battalion arrived virtually empty-handed. But it arrived in time to join in with the Americans in battling off still another enemy attack, this time with only small arms and what heavier weapons the Americans had available. An attempt the following day to bring up the needed supplies and heavy weapons failed, as did the attempt to send tanks and anti-tank guns up the Albano road to reach the isolated defenders of the caves. Throughout the day, the guns of the 158th Field Artillery Battalion were trained on the ravines around the caves, and barrage after barrage filled the draws with dead and wounded Germans, and Von Mackensen's newest attack was broken up.

By nightfall of February 22, radio instructions to the 2nd Battalion, 157th, ordered them to turn over their heavy weapons to the British and fight their way back to the main line. Sometime after midnight, the beleaguered Americans started out in a column of companies led by Colonel Brown. Stumbling through the pitch-black night and the rain, the remnants of the 2nd Battalion, 157th, headed south to rejoin the main forces. The wounded, unfortunately, had to be left behind, and the battalion surgeon—Captain Peter Graffagnino, of New Orleans—and his aid men

[10] The tradition-bound British Army designated its units according to historical connotation rather than by arithmetical progression; so it was that the 2/7 Queens was organized as the second unit bearing the designation "7 Battalion, the Queen's Royal Regiment (West Surrey)."

[11] Bowditch, *op. cit.*, 93.

chose to remain with them. About halfway back, the column was ambushed by Germans secreted in a small knot of stone houses, opening up on the Americans with intense automatic and small-arms fire. The battalion sought out what cover it could find and fought back, but without its automatic and heavy weapons it was easy prey for the well-placed German machine gunners. The enemy succeeded in splitting the column and the smoke shells laid down on the area by the guns of the 158th Field Artillery Battalion made a reorganization of the battalion even more difficult. The first half of the column, under the direction of Colonel Brown, finally snaked its way back to the main lines; the rest became scattered. Throughout the remainder of the day, small numbers of men managed to filter back, but it was apparent that the battalion had suffered seriously, not only from its nine-day isolation but also in fighting its way back.

Captain Sparks and Sergeant Leon Siehr were the only members of E Company to survive, and it was two days later that Siehr turned up. He had joined a nearby British unit and continued fighting. Captain George D. Kessler, of Craig, Colorado, the battalion S-3, also brought back a handful of men with him. But of the entire battalion of more than 800 men, only 225 returned from the Battle of the Caves, and 90 of these were hospitalized immediately.[12] Many had temporarily lost their hearing from the intensive artillery fire and the horrendous echoing inside the caves. A large number were suffering so badly from trench foot that it was feared they would have to undergo amputation. But that any returned from the nightmare in the caves is a supreme tribute to the determination of the American infantryman.

For the British who relieved them, it was another story. The 2/7 Queens suffered misfortune from the outset, first in merely getting to the scene, then in attempting to hold the position. Cut off in its turn, the British battalion fought off one German attack after another until two companies were overrun and the third was

[12] *Ibid.*, 94.

forced into the caves with the battalion headquarters. After dark, February 23, their first full day in the new positions, the 2/7 Queens split up into small units and attempted to make their way to neighboring outfits. Less than half succeeded.[13] The Germans finally were in possession of a small shell-scarred knoll which had frustrated their drive to the sea, but it would do them no good now. They had spent themselves in their headlong attack down the Albano road; they had come to a complete stop.

Simultaneously with his attack against the western shoulder of the salient, Von Mackensen also had collected the remnants of five of his battalions to throw against the eastern shoulder, which was covered by the 180th Infantry. The relatively small size of the German force plus its hodge-podge makeup indicated that the attack was purely diversionary, but it was accompanied by the heaviest concentration of artillery the Germans had yet delivered on the beachhead, and at Anzio the Allies had run into the greatest amount experienced so far in the war.[14]

Late in the afternoon of February 20, enemy infantry attempted to infiltrate between the 2nd and 3rd battalions, 180th, along the beds of the Spaccasassi and Ficoccia creeks, but the move was broken up by artillery and mortar fire. Enemy tanks followed the infantry, and the tanks of two companies of the 1st Armored Regiment engaged them in a fierce duel before the Germans retired from the scene. Both sides suffered heavily in lost vehicles.

The following day the attack was resumed, this time accompanied by dive-bombers as well as air bursts from lowered flak guns. Two Mark VI tanks supported the attack, which was concentrated against L Company, 180th, but again the enemy was repulsed by heavy artillery and mortar fire. The Germans tried a third time the next day, but were beaten off.

The slackening of the battle along the center of the beachhead front gave rise to speculation that Von Mackensen was regroup-

[13] Truscott, *op. cit.*, 327.   [14] Bowditch, *op. cit.*, 95.

ing for an attack elsewhere.[15] He was still under orders to eliminate "this abscess south of Rome."

Meanwhile, the man responsible for the abscess—the British
Prime Minister—reported to Parliament on February 22:

> There has been in the last week more severe and continuous
> engagements. Up to the present moment the enemy has sustained
> very heavy losses but has not shaken the resistance of the bridge-
> head army. These forces are well matched, though we are definitely
> stronger in artillery and armor and, of course, when weather is
> favorable our air power plays an immense part.
>
> General Alexander has probably seen more fighting against the
> Germans than any living British commander, unless it be General
> Freyberg, who is also in the fray. Alexander says the bitterness and
> fierceness of the fighting now going on both in the bridgehead and
> on the Cassino front surpasses all his previous experience. He even
> uses in one message to me the one word "terrific."
>
> I can say no more than what I have said, for I would not attempt
> to venture any overconfident predictions, but their leaders are con-
> fident and the troops are in the highest spirit of offensive vigor.[16]

The Prime Minister deliberately avoided mentioning our own
losses, which were considerable. The 3rd Division alone was
2,400 men under strength, and the others were even more so. So
far as manpower was concerned, the British divisions were in the
most serious straits, especially the British 56th Division.[17] Its 168th
Brigade stood exactly at half-strength. Its two other brigades—the
167th and 169th—had been reduced to one-third of their numbers.
The British 1st Division's 24th Guards Brigade was at half-
strength. Since the British were alloted only seven hundred replacements a week, they were forced to impress their B Echelon—
clerks, cooks, mechanics, and drivers—as well as engineers and
anti-aircraft gunners as riflemen.[18] These were poor substitutes
for trained infantry replacements.

The 24th Guards Brigade was another matter. This brigade

[15] Truscott, *op. cit.*, 344.   [16] *The New York Times*, February 23, 1944.
[17] Linklater, *op. cit.*, 205.   [18] Truscott, *op. cit.*, 332.

could only accept replacements from its own replacement pool. The traditions of the British Army were strictly adhered to throughout the war regardless of the strain on military operations, and this was one of them. The Guards, although they received the usual amount of basic training, were given it in much more intense form. Also, the enlisted men of the Guards were recruited from among the less desirable elements of Britain's manhood—juvenile delinquents, petty thieves, those who had served jail sentences—but they were also instilled with a tremendous pride in organization during their Guards training. If morally they were inferior, physically they were above average, and they were a highly effective fighting force. At half-strength, however, they lost most of their effectiveness.

The supply of American replacements in numbers was adequate if not exceptional. But with the American units the problem was one of assimilation. Absorbing new men while a company was in the line was most difficult and led to a significant lowering of battle efficiency. The replacements would get over their initial fright soon enough, but then would develop a natural reluctance to fire their weapons lest they give away their positions and attract enemy attention. This was a problem for the squad leaders and platoon sergeants, who quickly learned that the most direct method of dealing with it was also the best. The sergeant soon would discover that the new man was not firing his rifle. He would make his way to the nonshooter, take the weapon away from him, fire a quick clip, then hand the rifle back to the man.

"There," the sergeant would say. "See, it shoots. Now they know you're here, so go ahead and shoot it all you like. They're not going to tell us when we can fire and when we can't. We'll damn well shoot whenever we please."

One lecture along these lines usually was all it took. Not only did it overcome the new man's reluctance to fire his rifle, it also placed him in a compromising position with the rest of the men around him, and he would make certain to do the most firing at the next opportunity.

The biggest problem facing the individual newcomer was the terrible feeling of loneliness, of being the new one in a group of old-timers, of not belonging. The front lines offer little opportunity for socializing, and the squad leaders and platoon sergeants had enough to do without conducting introductions all around. The new man would be placed in position, told his assignment, then left completely on his own. The more gregarious would become acquainted readily; for most it would take weeks. Those whose companies were in secondary positions were more easily assimilated; those in reserve, still more easily.

But for those companies that had suffered most heavily—especially those in the 157th and 179th, which had sustained the full force of the German drive down the Albano road—a complete reorganization was necessary. They were withdrawn from the line, and the 180th Infantry, which had been less heavily hit, was literally cannibalized for seasoned officers and noncoms around whom to rebuild the two sister regiments. Whole companies and battalions were actually reconstituted within gunshot of the enemy. It was basic training all over again with forced marches and field problems and all the annoying rudiments of soldiering right under the eyes of the Germans. This time the infiltration course was for real, as enemy artillery regularly dispersed the training groups. But it was necessary to rebuild the division. Since it was being done solely for the benefit of the new men, the oldsters bore a natural resentment. Fortunately, this did not last long.

The underlying principle of absorbing large numbers of replacements was to get the new men and the old men to know one another and to work together. To do this in the shortest period of time was a herculean task and one that had to be faced, especially by General Eagles, whose 45th Division was receiving the largest number of replacements. A sensitive, practical man with a soldier's insight, Eagles adopted a policy to the point of obsession. He would say, "If you're going to fight together, you've got to know one another." And he drove home that point over and over again on his many inspection trips around the division. He made a ritual of demanding names as he would inspect each company, not individual soldier's names but rather an inquiry of each soldier about the names of others in his squad or platoon.

Of the replacement, he would ask, "Who's your sergeant?" And the man would point, not knowing his sergeant's name, explaining he had only been with the company a few days. In turn, the General would ask, "Is this your company commander?" pointing to the accompanying officer at his elbow. "What's his name?"

Inversely, it embarrassed the captain rather than the soldier and insured that in future the company commander would make certain that every replacement arriving in his company would get to know his name first off.

The most seriously depleted regiment of the 45th Division was the 179th Infantry. It had suffered most heavily, had been reeled back to the Final Beachhead Defense Line, had lost most of its morale and a large part of its discipline, and had had its regimental commander replaced. In its new commander, however, it not only had an excellent combat leader but a good showman as well. Colonel William O. Darby tackled almost with zest what to another commander would be an insurmountable perplexity. In addition to rebuilding two of his three battalions and restoring morale and efficiency, Darby also was charged with disciplining a large number of stragglers and malingerers. Since he had come from command of the well-trained, almost fanatic Rangers, the matter of handling low morale and lack of discipline was something new to Darby, but his sense of showmanship held him in good stead. The most serious cases of malingering he sent back to the stockade, but the majority he assigned to the worst, most menial, and unpleasant tasks, and as close to the front as was possible—burying dead animals, policing the areas around secondary positions, which meant picking up empty cartridge casings, and worse, collecting human excrement that had been scooped into empty K-ration boxes and tossed out of foxholes days or weeks before. They were assigned to perform the most indelicate tasks right before the eyes of their friends and comrades. Further, Darby instituted a check list whereby each man's name would be called out not once, but three times, and loudly enough for every man in the immediate area to hear. In addition, the officer conducting the roll call would make grand, sweeping gestures as he checked each name off the list. When this was over, Darby himself would make a ceremony of instructing the collected stragglers and shirkers: "You are not to leave your position regardless of what anybody tells you unless you get the word from me, personally. Do you understand that?" And again each name was called out loudly, and each man was called on individually to confirm that he understood the regimental commander's order. And another sweeping check-mark.

It was downright embarrassment, but Darby's showmanship paid off. He quickly brought the regiment back to fighting effectiveness and high morale.

During the critical period at Anzio when the front was most fluid, every unit on the beachhead was troubled by stragglers and malingerers. The former were easily explained. They had become separated from their companies in the constant fluctuation of the battle line, or had found themselves isolated, or the man in the next foxhole had crawled over with an improbable rumor. "I heard the company has received orders to withdraw. We'd better start now while we have a good chance." Or, "You and I are the only ones left. We'd better get out of here."

And they would lose themselves in some rear area, more often than not worrying over a possible court-martial that awaited them for having run away in the face of the enemy. Their consciences soon would get the better of them, and they would make their way back to their outfits.

The malingerers, on the other hand, called for direct action. The VIth Corps instituted a mess-check system whereby each mess sergeant was instructed not to feed anyone not on his own company roster. This would starve them out.

It starved out one man in particular, a young soldier from New York City. He was of Italian extraction and spoke the language fluently, which aided him in composing his alibi. He told of having been captured, escaping, and hiding out behind the lines with the natives before making his way back. His story was accepted by the company commander. Division G–2, however, naturally was interested in getting information from anyone who had been behind the enemy lines. Where he had been, what he had seen, which roads the enemy was using to bring up supplies, the disposition of artillery pieces—all this was of importance to the intelligence section. And so the man was questioned.

Invariably, the returned soldier was enthusiastic and loquacious in recounting his experiences, and more often than not the story was embellished to the point of incredibility. In this case, however, the returned soldier was extremely close-mouthed. He volunteered no information, and would answer simply "yes" or "no" to questions about blown bridges in the areas he claimed to have been in, or about whether enemy guns were placed behind this knoll or that. His story lacked an authoritative ring, and he was questioned further. Finally, he admitted the truth. He had run out on his company and had hid out in the rear areas.

He was court-martialed and sentenced to five years. It was generally thought that the punishment should have been much more severe in view of his attempt to pass along false information, information that could have resulted in serious damage to the Allied effort and even death to his own comrades.

He was one man among few, however. Most who claimed to have been captured and to have escaped were telling the truth, and only their profuse enthusiasm was open to doubt.

Typical of the returned soldier was Corporal Lloyd Greer of Lindsay, Oklahoma, a mortar man who had run out of ammunition during the big February battle. He had sent his ammunition-bearer for more, but when the man did not return, Greer set out after him. The Germans had overrun the ammunition dump, and Greer was captured as he walked into the trap.

"For you the war is finished," Greer said a German colonel told him. "In three days, the others will be swimming in the sea."

Greer was kept at a sub-prison for four days to work on road repairs while most of the other men taken prisoner were sent farther to the rear. Finally, he managed to escape, kept dodging German patrols, and wound up in Rome, where he hid out for eight more days. Back on the road once again, he took to the countryside and finally made his way back to the Allied lines.

Greer had little of tactical value to offer the G–2 inquisitors, but he painted a realistic picture of the time he spent in German hands. The food was awful, he said. Breakfast consisted of colored water which the Germans said was tea. Lunch was a mixture of potatoes and sauerkraut. Dinner, one loaf of bread for five men, with an individual pat of margarine. He fared little better after his escape, and had lost thirty pounds in weight by the time he rejoined the division.

Of the German soldiers, he said they were genuinely afraid of our artillery, and that they preferred using burp guns and other automatic weapons to closing in with bayonets. Finally, he said, the Poles pressed into the German Army were much more lenient with American prisoners of war than were the Germans.

Here was a true story, and there were many more like it.

Over-all, however, more time was spent in writing up citations for valor and bravery at Anzio than was spent writing up courts-martial.

Even during the height of battle, the paper work continues, all of it necessary to keep up the flow of men and materiel in the fight against the enemy. A perusal of some of that paper work can be quite illuminating.

The ammunition expenditure reports of only one division at Anzio, for example, show that during the twenty-nine days of February, 1944, its four artillery battalions fired a total of 129,732 rounds against the Germans.[19] In the four months from Salerno to

[19] 45th Division artillery reports for the month of February, 1944.

the Gustav Line, those same guns fired 167,153 rounds. A comparison indicates the ferocity of the February battle.

Ordnance reports, too, provide an insight into the intensity of the fighting in February. This same division's losses in ordnance ran one-third again as much just during February as over the four-month period on the southern front. A breakdown of the equipment losses makes for meaningful but rather tiresome reading, but the list shows a loss of 88 trucks, 16 trailers, 21 tanks, 17 tank-destroyers, and includes such relatively minor losses as 674 bayonets and 122 wrist watches. These numbers assume added significance when it is taken into consideration that a man was wearing each one of those 122 wrist watches.

Casualty reports are something else. Here we are dealing directly with people. And in the twenty-nine days of February, the division listed a total of 5,251 casualties, almost one-third of its over-all strength. Of the total, there were 241 known dead, 1,405 missing in action, 1,172 wounded, 2,433 sick and injured. Most of the latter were suffering from trench foot, exposure, or combat fatigue. Also included were those men who lost their hearing in the Battle of the Caves.

Paper work of another sort was going on in the cellars of VIth Corps headquarters, the compilation of prisoner interrogation and the identification of enemy units in the various sectors, as well as tracking the readjustments in our own lines. Too, the command of the VIth Corps had been turned over to General Truscott on February 23, and Alexander also had dispatched British Major General Vyvyan Eveleigh, the commander of the British 78th Division, to the beachhead with the nebulous title of "assistant to the beachhead commander," but with the specific assignment of restoring rapport between the British and American command there.[20] Relations between the higher echelons of the British and American commands had been strained to the breaking point mostly on account of the almost constant bickering between

[20] Truscott, *op. cit.,* 332.

Lucas and the British staffs. In Lucas' defense it must be stated that he was suffering harangues not only from the British divisional commanders at Anzio but from as high up as Prime Minister Winston Churchill, and that despite the criticism lashed out against him from 10 Downing Street, his caution and demand for a buildup of supplies were more than justified when the Germans finally opened their series of counterattacks. Too, Lucas was not alone in his inability to get along well with his opposite numbers in the Royal Army. Mark Clark was known to have become testy in his dealings with British officers, especially those who had had more soldiering experience than he.[21]

But the combination of Eveleigh and Truscott, who was an Anglophile to begin with, restored the friendly relations among the higher-ups of the two armies, at least at Anzio. Lucas departed with bitterness, blaming his relief on British influences,[22] which was correct. He headed for a short rest at Sorrento and eventually returned to the United States, where he took over command of the Fourth Army.

Truscott cut a more dashing figure than his predecessor, with his leather jacket, calvary breeches, tanker's boots, and white scarf. Only one thing marred the picture. The General had a small head and a short face which somehow didn't set right under a steel helmet. There was no denying, however, that he was the man for the job. He was young, vigorous, imaginative, and, when necessary, daring. Further, he was acceptable to the British Prime Minister.[23]

His first days in full command were hectic ones, days of frantic activity as the VIth Corps prepared to meet the new German attack that obviously was in the making. Intelligence reports indicated that Von Mackensen was shifting his armor and large numbers of his troops away from the center of the beachhead line and over toward the eastern end.[24] The only other obvious avenue of attack open to the enemy was along the network of roads lead-

[21] Majdalany, *op. cit.*, 104–105. [22] Truscott, *op. cit.*, 328.
[23] Churchill, *op. cit.*, 493. [24] Bowditch, *op. cit.*, 96.

ing southwest from Cisterna. But on this relatively inactive front, both the 3rd Division and the Special Service Force had had time to build up their defenses, time to dig in and wire in their positions while the enemy concentrated all his attention to the drive down the Albano road. Also, the arrival of the British 18th Brigade on February 25 afforded the VIth Corps an opportunity to juggle its reserves and move them over to the area of the expected new attack. Further, the British 5th Division was alerted to move up to Anzio to replace the worn and weary 56th Division.[25]

The Germans continued their small-scale attacks along the center of the beachhead in an effort to divert Allied artillery from the Cisterna area and to attempt to camouflage the movement of their stronger divisions eastward. Back into the central sector were thrown the 3rd Panzer Grenadier and the 65th Infantry divisions as well as the Infantry Lehr Regiment. Missing from the area were the more powerful 26th Panzer Division and the 715th Light Division, obviously on the move to the Cisterna sector. Despite the low quality of the German troops involved in the diversionary attacks in the center of the beachhead, the under-strength British forces facing them suffered heavily in beating off the new attacks against them.

On the night of February 28, Corps G–2 Colonel Joseph Langevin received reports of enemy radio intercepts indicating that Von Mackensen had set the following morning for the start of his assault from Cisterna.[26] It should be pointed out that both sides resorted to subterfuge over the airwaves and more often than not would seed their signals with deliberately erroneous information designed to baffle the monitoring enemy. As a result, radio intercepts were far from conclusive proof of the enemy's intentions. It was the job of G–2 to determine which of the intercepted signals were genuine. In this case, Langevin's interpretation was correct.

He estimated that the German attack would get underway at approximately six o'clock in the morning and that it would be

[25] Linklater, *op. cit.,* 209.   [26] Truscott, *op. cit.,* 344.

preceded by the usual artillery preparations. The alert went out to the 3rd Division and to the Special Service Force, which were covering the areas of the expected attack. Also, fire orders were drawn up for every gun within range to be trained on known troop and tank assembly areas, enemy artillery positions, and the roads leading southwest from Cisterna. It was hoped that the deluge of Allied artillery shells would completely disrupt the enemy attack before it even got underway. The cannonading was to begin at four-thirty in the morning and last a full hour, spewing death and destruction in the path of Von Mackensen's newest plans. The 1st Armored Division's two artillery battalions were moved into place to bolster the guns of the 3rd Division as well as those of Corps artillery and the howitzers of the immediately adjacent 45th Division.

That tiny corner of the Italian peninsula erupted in a convulsive roar that was to continue for the alloted sixty minutes, as thousands of rounds of high explosives rent the countryside in a massive display of violent destruction. Then came the lull, the interminable wait to assess the results. The lull was short lived. One by one, the Allied batteries started firing again as the forward observers began to pick out targets in the early morning light. The attack was on; Von Mackensen was not to be denied. Slowly at first, then gaining momentum, the enemy infantry and armor struck southward against the 3rd Division's front through a screen of smoke and dust and shellfire. Then our own artillery came into play against the onrushing enemy.

The main force of the German attack was aimed at the left flank of the 3rd Division's front, which was covered by the attached 509th Parachute Infantry Battalion. Enemy troops of the 1028th Panzer Grenadier Regiment and elements of the 362nd Infantry Division pounded against the paratroopers' defenses northeast of the village of Carano. Aided by engineers who blasted a path through the barbed wire entanglements, the Germans soon overwhelmed the outnumbered paratroopers of B Company and burst into the cemetery on the hill immediately to the northeast of

Carano.[27] The somewhat ornate mausoleum containing the mortal remains of Menotti Garibaldi, son of the famed Italian liberator and himself once a member of the Italian Senate, had been used as a company command post because of its thick walls and ceiling. Fierce hand-to-hand fighting slowed down the enemy advance temporarily, but the paratroopers finally were ordered to fall back on the intermediate defense line some seven hundred yards to the rear. Only twenty-three men of B Company, including one officer, reached that line.

All across the 3rd Division front the fighting was furious, but the deepest enemy penetration was made in the 509th's sector. The artillery (an estimated 66,000 rounds were fired against the Germans that day in the 3rd Division's sector alone) broke up most of the attacks and held the enemy at bay. The next morning, a counterattack by the 30th Infantry restored the lines before the 509th Parachute Infantry Battalion. More than one thousand prisoners were taken, each giving testimony to the devastating effect of our artillery barrages.

An interesting note here and a tribute to the industry of the signalmen: Not only had communication lines been set up from front to rear, but during the comparative lull in the fighting in this sector during mid-February, the industrious wire layers also installed lateral lines of communication so that when the 3rd Division's telephone lines connecting the forward observers with the division's fire control center were knocked out, their firing orders were rerouted laterally through the 45th Division's artillery switchboard, well to the west, with virtually no delay.

The weather also figured greatly in stemming the new German juggernaut. The fact that the ground was still soft and muddy from the incessant winter rains limited the enemy's use of armor to the improved roads in the sector, each of which was interdicted by our artillery. But the skies began to clear toward the end of February, permitting greater use of our Air Corps. Our reconnaissance planes were over the front moments after daybreak and

[27] Bowditch, *op. cit.*, 97.

at midmorning on the opening day of the German onslaught, a flight of more than one hundred medium bombers roared in from the south to pulverize the German troop and tank assembly areas in and around Cisterna.[28] A reported seventy enemy tanks had been gathered within the town seeking shelter behind the buildings, and at least half of this number were destroyed.

The following day, after an all-night rain, the skies were clear again, and the 12th Air Support Command flew more than seven hundred sorties over the beachhead to continue pounding enemy strong points and buildup areas,[29] particularly behind the railroad line running from Cisterna to Campoleone which Von Mackensen was using both as a final defense line and assembly areas from which to launch his attacks. The bombers were out again the next day in equal numbers, but by this time the German offensive had been stopped.

As dawn broke on March 3, a half-hearted last attack was opened against the 7th Infantry southwest of Ponte Rotto. Elements of the 26th Panzer Division managed to dent the line in front of the 3rd Battalion, 7th Infantry, using tanks and armored infantry, but they were soon repulsed. A counterattack late in the afternoon by companies A and B, 7th Infantry, restored the lines to their original positions.

At the same time, at a conference of the German High Command, orders were issued to halt the assaults at Anzio and dig in along present lines, developing defenses along these lines as quickly as possible.[30] For the present, Kesselring planned no further major offensive against the Allied beachhead. But Kesselring was almost two weeks late in discovering a fact that the VIth Corps troops already knew. The German offensive had collapsed, resoundingly broken by sheer tenacity on the part of the individual Allied soldier.

The six weeks of almost continuous total warfare, however, had thoroughly exhausted both sides. It was a victory of sorts for

[28] Truscott, *op. cit.,* 347.　　　　　[29] Bowditch, *op. cit.,* 101.
[30] Kesselring, *op. cit.,* 236.

the VIth Corps, but the original plans for capturing the *Colli Laziali* and linking up with the main Fifth Army troops from the south within seven days of landing at Anzio seemed now more fantastic than when they were first proposed. These were still the objectives, but there would be considerably more bloodletting before that grandiose dream would be fulfilled.

CHAPTER NINE

The Long Wait

THE doldrums set in at Anzio the first week of March as both VIth Corps and the German Fourteenth Army simultaneously went on the defensive. Both sides were equally worn out from weeks of violent offensive and counteroffensive, and time was needed by both for rest, reorganization, and refitting. For the first time in World War II, the fighting took on a semblance of the infamous and debilitating trench warfare of World War I, even down to the appearance of poppies beginning to sprout as the first signs of spring arrived in that part of Italy.

After the first week of March, the front at Anzio was stabilized, and each side limited its activities to constant patrol actions. But even on patrol, men die. However, the daily casualty lists for the next two and one-half months would pale in significance in comparison with those of mid-February, and life on the beachhead could give the casual observer an altogether erroneous impression of apparent unconcern. Everywhere the opportunity arose, the troops at Anzio afforded themselves of whatever recreation was available, from a simple card game to an organized baseball game. Fair skies and warm weather dried up the ground, and huge engineering feats were undertaken without fear of striking surface water.

The biggest of these was digging in the hospital area. By this time there were four evacuation hospitals, several field hospitals and clearing companies of the division medical battalions all clustered together in one sector of the beachhead and all being subjected to regular enemy artillery fire. Hospital tents were dug in some two feet below ground, and sandbags were filled with the offal to build up the sides even higher. Now, nothing but a direct hit would result in casualties among patients or medical personnel.

The fighting troops were also going underground. The closer to the battered towns of Anzio and Nettuno, the more elaborate the underground shelters. The demolished waterfront villas provided wooden beams, doors, and shutters with which to roof over the dugouts and form a base for additional layers of dirt and sandbags. The nightly visits of "Popcorn Pete," with his Butterfly antipersonnel bombs, posed a definite threat to those troops in the middle and rear areas of the beachhead.[1]

Atop the earthen roofs, shelter-halves were spread to protect against the rain, and inside the dugouts, cardboard cartons from the field rations were used as strong and waterproof walls to keep out the field mice and the sifting sands. These rear-area dugouts

[1] "Popcorn Pete" was the nickname given the German night bombers which flew over the beachhead, usually one at a time, dropping their thousand-pound Butterfly bombs. These bombs would fall a short distance then explode in mid-air, dispersing smaller delayed-action grenades which, in turn, would burst just before hitting the ground. The smaller grenades when exploding sounded like a string of Chinese firecrackers going off, hence the nickname "popcorn." But, like another German innovation at Anzio—the "Goliath," a miniature remote-controlled tank loaded with a heavy charge of explosive—the Butterfly bomb was quite ineffective.

became quite elaborate as soldiers, with time on their hands, scoured the ruined buildings for knickknacks and bric-a-brac. Many of the dugouts were festooned with mirrors, candelabra, and commodes, anything that would add to the individual's creature comfort.

Not so comfortable but equally indestructible were the dugouts farther toward the front. The soldiers' ingenuity reclaimed the wooden crates and cardboard tubes in which the 105-mm. artillery shells were packed. Filled with earth and lined crosswise over deep slit trenches, these casings provided safety if not comfort.

During the day the beachhead gave the appearance of casual serenity, but at night the true picture emerged. The *Luftwaffe* would come out of hiding, self-propelled guns would be trundled up to pre-arranged positions, tanks would move up as close to the front as possible, and the defensive war would open up in earnest. One night at Anzio during these seemingly listless months was enough to dispel the deceptive appearance of the daylight hours.

The Germans made the most of the protective cover of nightfall. Our Air Corps was out over the beachhead in great strength during the day, but after sunset it would be back at the southern airfields more than one hundred miles away. Too, the extensive use of self-propelled artillery by the enemy at night was an effective means of avoiding counterbattery fire from our guns. A tank could roll out along a road, quickly fire ten or twelve rounds with its 88-mm. gun, then rumble off to the rear before our fire direction centers could locate it and return the fire. And then, our most efficient means of locating enemy gun positions—the tiny artillery spotter planes—were grounded at night.

Prime targets for the German artillery were the middle and rear areas where the VIth Corps was rebuilding its supply dumps. Ammunition, rations, and gasoline necessarily had to be stored above ground and within plain sight of the German observers up in the hills with their high-powered telescopes. These made choice and easy targets. So, too, did the slow-moving LST's docking two at a time in the port of Anzio, but the port was the sole target of the monstrous 280-mm. railroad guns located on the far side of the *Colli Laziali*. These giants, which were soon dubbed "the Anzio Express," for they sounded for all the world like the rumbling of a subway train as they hurtled overhead in the direction of the port, were carefully hidden away in railroad tunnels and moved into position only for fire missions. But the inordinate amount of time required to set up the huge guns more than offset their success against the LST's, and firing such immense projectiles so long a distance interfered with their accuracy. True, they turned the dock area into one tremendous pile of rubble, but they sank very few ships.

The German artillery was much more effective against the myriad of ration, ammunition, and gasoline dumps scattered about the beachhead, especially those paralleling "Truscott Boulevard." This transverse road, originally little more than an oxcart path, was widened and graded by the industrious engineers to connect the two main arteries on the beachhead—the Albano road and the Anzio-Cisterna road. It was barely a mile behind the front, was unpaved, and was under enemy observation throughout the daylight hours along its entire length. Nevertheless, it was in constant use because of the necessity of bringing up supplies. There was some cover at either end of the jerry-built roadway, defilade along the entrance at the Anzio-Cisterna road, and cover at the other end from the Padiglione Woods. German artillerists gave it considerable attention. Our military police set up a traffic pattern for crossing Truscott Boulevard, allowing only one vehicle at a time to use the roadway and at scattered intervals. Driving across it was a tense and hair-raising experience. Everyone in the vehicle was thoroughly aware that he was under enemy observation, that the vehicle was kicking up clouds of dust, and that at any minute a German shell might come whipping in to destroy the vehicle and everyone in it. As result, drivers adopted their own compensating tactics, varying the speed of their machines while crossing the open stretch to make it less simple for the German gunners to track the moving target.

From the enemy standpoint, anything that moved across Truscott Boulevard was an attractive inducement to fire, since, even if they missed the moving target, chances were the shell would explode in among the ammunition dumps that lined both sides of the road. This inducement was lessened when, with typical GI ingenuity, the engineers of the 1st Armored Division devised a method for attaching a bulldozer blade to the front end of a medium tank and built up earthen revetments around each pile of ammunition.[2] While these revetments did not provide complete protection for the valuable stores, they did confine the damage inflicted by enemy artillery to the individual pile and prevented the fire and explosions from spreading to adjacent stacks. Also, the armored bulldozers would be brought into play to push the dirt from the revetments in on top of a stricken dump to smother the fire.

Like many of the ordnance refinements that came out of World War II, this armored bulldozer was the prototype for a much more effective model manufactured later and distributed throughout the Army. Many such inventions were born of necessity in the midst of battle; for example, the Rube Goldberg–like contraptions for heating mess-kit water in field kitchens—a length of inch-and-a-half pipe bent into a horseshoe and inserted into a GI can filled with water; then a trickle of gasoline was allowed to drip into the pipe and ignited—which eventually were modified and manufactured for the Quartermaster. And there were some bizarre applications of regularly issued items. There was, for instance, the small vial of a popular brand tooth powder readily available to every soldier at Anzio. It was soon discovered that the powder possessed great merits for scouring rifle barrels as well as being a remarkably good substitute for baking powder in whipping up a batch of pancakes. And while radio listeners in the

[2] Truscott, *op. cit.*, 340.

United States were being continually apprised of the fact that "Lucky Strike green has gone to war," it was the red circle on the new white package that actually did go to war. Observing the strictest of blackout precautions, GI's with flashlights soon discovered that the red circle on a pack of Luckies was of the correct translucency and just the right size to fit behind the flashlight lens to provide enough dim light to be useful yet unnoticeable to the enemy.

It was learned, too, that howitzer recoil oil when used as a shortening in preparing French fried potatoes produced an extraordinary cathartic effect.

Life at Anzio was a series of these startling discoveries of which the War Department observers in the field duly took note and forwarded to the Pentagon. To its credit, the Army made the most of these GI improvisations, and the troops who would enter the fighting at a later date benefited greatly from the experiences of those soldiers already on the line. There were, of course, exceptions. The Amphibious Jeep was one. Anyone who had any connection with this monstrosity in the field could compile an unending list of faults; yet, in spite of the wide range and unanimity of derogatory reports, the vehicle continued to be manufactured and issued to troops. And there was the cellophane gas cape, a plastic bag designed to cover a soldier's entire body and protect him against skin burns in the event of an enemy gas attack. The fact that once the soldier encased himself in the plastic bag it was impossible for him to breathe mattered not to the Chemical Warfare Service; the gas capes were general issue. The plastic bags did, however, provide useful service as waterproof wrappings for bedrolls and other articles a soldier might wish to keep for himself and away from the weather.

At Anzio, GI ingenuity moved along other avenues of adventure. One, in particular, involved the innards of shot-down German aircraft. The miles of copper wire and tubing inside a Messerschmitt or a Focke-Wulf were of much more than souvenir value. With the fine copper wire and an empty K ration box and a razor blade, an imaginative soldier could fashion a workable variation of the old crystal radio set, and on it he could pick up the German propaganda radio programs from Rome which featured a renegade American woman, who billed herself as "Sally," and her partner, "George." Their entertainment value was high, their propaganda effect, nil. Operating as a team of disc jockeys, the couple played the latest recordings of American music, which gave rise to the popular sport of speculating on just how they were getting these recordings. The theory held by most GI's at Anzio was that German submarines were venturing close to New York City and surfacing at night in order to record the latest music as it was being broadcast by the big network stations and the name bands. Evolving theories such as this helped pass the time at Anzio.

Hardly a day would go by that Sally and George didn't dedicate the same song to the troops on the beachhead—"Between the Devil and the Deep Blue Sea." But rather than instilling any fear, the song became a standing joke.

Farther to the rear, and with more than copper wire and razor blades available, more powerful receivers were put together on which the B.B.C. and the Armed Forces Network station in Naples could be picked up. Memorable among the British radio entertainers was the music hall comedy team of "Ramsbottom and Enoch." Memorable but unrewarding. The British brand of humor even in those laugh-hungry days went unappreciated.

The copper tubing from the knocked-down German planes was put to a more fascinating use. Those soldiers from the hill country and the dry areas of the United States were quick to set up their own makeshift stills, and when the end came to the supply of wine from the wine cellars at Anzio from which a rather potent variety of brandy could be distilled, these same moonshiners in uniform could turn out an especially virulent brand of raisin-jack. The limited number of German planes shot down within the confines of the beachhead and the length of time it took to distil any sizable amount of the potions, however, kept the demand well ahead of the supply.

The livestock at Anzio was another source of divertisement and relish. Untold numbers of untended cattle "just happened to trip over a mine," when the true cause of their demise was a .30- or .45-caliber slug. But plattersful of hamburgers were unexpected treats for the infantrymen. The sheep on the beachhead suffered to a lesser extent, mostly because of a certain American abhorrence of mutton.

Mules and horses were another matter, but even these had recreational value. It is still being speculated what must have been going through the minds of the German observers in the hills overlooking the beachhead when not one, but two large racing meets were staged on consecutive Saturday afternoons. The "Preakness" and the "Anzio Derby," both the products of the fertile mind of signalman Sergeant Bill Harr, an old Baltimore handicapper. Complete with a public address system and a twelve-piece band, the race course laid out in white engineer's tape, and four pretty nurses from the hospital on hand to congratulate the winners, the Preakness and Anzio Derby were gala events early in May witnessed by hundreds of enthusiastic if only momentary racing fans. It might be noted that neither event added in the slightest to the improvement of the breed. It was all in fun and only contributed to the everlasting bewilderment of the German observers in the hills. In any event, not an enemy gun was trained on either meeting, although the sizable arrays of Allied personnel at the events provided excellent targets.

The usual form of relaxation and entertainment for soldiers in an occupied town with time on their hands was completely missing at Anzio. Had the invasion been staged during the summer months when the more affluent Romans with their girl friends and mistresses thronged to the playland along the Tyrrhenian, the prospect of dalliance might have been a bit brighter. As it was, when the Allies landed late in January, the villas were empty and only a few shopkeepers and their families lived the year round at the summer resort. Farther inland, the hard-working farmers and their families retained the scruples and reticence common to rural people. And then when the civilian population was evacuated from the beachhead, there was no one.

The civilian evacuation posed still another problem, the matter of clean clothes. The glum, taciturn, Fascist-minded farm families might not consort openly with the self-styled liberators, but they were willing for a price to do their laundry. Their departure meant the GI had to do his own. Quartermaster companies set up laundry units for processing the clothing of the front-line troops, but those troops farther to the rear were compelled to fare as best they could. Individual bonfires stewing soiled clothing dotted the area, their smoke adding to the pall deliberately manufactured by the Chemical Warfare Section smudgepots and further helping to camouflage the beachhead. The problem of bathing was solved by each regiment's providing shower facilities for those companies in reserve positions. Everyone else sponged off regularly out of his helmet.

There was a plethora of water at Anzio, but not of towels. Most infantry soldiers had one with them when they landed, if they remembered to stow it in their packs. Many had none. Towels were available at the supply dumps around Naples, also on sale at twenty-five cents apiece at the Base Post Exchange. This, too, was in Naples. But at Anzio, no towels.

One rather enterprising Red Cross field representative stocked up with a large quantity of the twenty-five-cent towels while he was at Naples, brought them up to the beachhead, and offered them openly at the special sale price of three for a dollar. He stood to gain a neat profit, but when the story was reported in the newspapers in the States, the repercussions were quick and stern. The national organization, dependent on public acceptance as well as public monetary contributions, complained bitterly. The complaint was passed on down through channels from Washington to Anzio. The reporter who filed the story was mildly upbraided, but the Red Cross man was hurriedly removed from the beachhead and the organization.[3] The incident, however, did spur the delivery of towels to Anzio.

The role of the Red Cross among front-line divisions in World War II was rather anomalous. Field representatives were attached to all divisions, but their duties were difficult to fathom. Off the line, a fighting division would be doled out free doughnuts and coffee by Red Cross girls from their travelling "Clubmobile." In the big cities that had fallen into Allied hands, the beneficent organization set up gigantic establishments furnishing, in addition to the ubiquitous doughnuts and coffee, cookies, ice cream, soft drinks, and the like, as well as varied entertainment facilities ranging from ping-pong to bridge tournaments. But, under an Army directive, the Red Cross was instructed to make a nominal charge for the food and refreshments. The purpose behind this directive was never fully explained and resulted in considerable animosity against the organization carrying out the directive.

For the most part, the men were left to provide their own entertainment where possible. There were the interminable card games, of course, and the Special Services officers would supply limited amounts of equipment in the sporting-goods line. And there were the regimental bands. These were broken up into small units and traveled about the rear areas at Anzio staging pop concerts. An exchange of bands was worked out between the British and the Americans, and the music of the Scottish bagpipers was enjoyed as much by the Americans as were our jazz combos by the British.

Then, there was the unforgettable "Baron"—Private Roland Ormsby, literally drafted into the Army off the runway of a vaudeville theater in upstate New York. At least, that is where the draft board finally located him. He never laid claim to any place as a home town. Mild-mannered, thoroughly likable, he was never cut out to be a soldier; fortunately the Army discovered

[3] The author was the reporter in question, and the Red Cross man, whose name fortunately has long since been forgotten, was attached to the 179th Infantry Regiment.

early in his military career that he was of more value as an entertainer than as a rifleman, and he was placed on special duty to perform the things he did best. Officially, he was carried on the rolls
of the service company, 157th Infantry, but he literally belonged
to the whole 45th Division—the entire Fifth Army, for that matter. His forte was master of ceremonies and magician. Few people
ever got to know his real name. He was known to everyone simply
as "The Baron."

Dressed in a tuxedo with his Chinese rings, pet duck, and other
paraphernalia of his trade, the Baron would jangle and clatter his
way about the beachhead visiting units on the line as well as off to
stage his one-man show. One particularly quiet evening at Anzio,
the Baron had scheduled a performance at a company command
post set up in the Garibaldi Tomb in the cemetery just outside
Carano. He got to regimental headquarters by jeep, was taken to
battalion headquarters on foot, and the rest of the way was led by
a company runner, traveling mostly on his stomach and all the
way to the accompaniment of the quacking of his duck and the
jangling of his Chinese rings. His other equipment constantly
would get hung up on barbed wire. The noisy trek seemed to
take forever and not without arousing enemy gunners. But he
made it to the tomb and staged a successful performance, bringing
on raucous laughter and hearty applause as well as constant ad-
monitions from the sentry outside to quiet down or the whole
place would be shot up. The show went on for hours, as his small
audience rotated until the whole company had had the opportunity of enjoying the act.

The Baron's trip back was equally as harassing, but it had been
a rewarding evening both for the troops and for the soldier-
entertainer who thrived on performing before an audience, no
matter how small.

With the troops left mostly to themselves to while away their
spare time, the VIth Corps set up a training program to occupy
their regular hours. From the moment the Corps went on the defensive, Truscott had been busy with plans for ending the stale-

mate and breaking out of the confinement. So, too, was the German Fourteenth Army. The more severely drubbed German divisions were removed from the line, their defense perimeter adjusted, and the number of troops defending the beachhead front reduced. The Hermann Göring Panzer Division and the 114th Light Division both were transferred from the Anzio sector,[4] and the two most powerful German divisions—the 26th Panzer and the 29th Panzer Grenadier—were placed in army reserve and moved north to the Tiber. Kesselring was still fearful of an Allied amphibious operation around Civitavecchia.[5]

At the same time, the Germans were receiving replacements to beef up their battered battalions to the point where the Fourteenth Army was larger in numbers than it had been during the big February drives.[6] The replacements, however, included several Italian Army units, and the Germans had become so wary of their Axis partners by this time that these units were broken up and platooned in among regular *Wehrmacht* formations, assigned only to easily defensible positions and only during daylight hours.

The VIth Corps, too, was withdrawing, replacing, and regrouping its forces at Anzio. The weary and severely depleted British 56th Division was withdrawn from the beachhead, replaced by the British 5th Division. And, long overdue to rejoin its parent unit undergoing training in northern Ireland for the forthcoming Normandy invasion, Colonel Ruben Tucker's 504th Parachute Infantry Regiment sailed for Naples and ultimately the United Kingdom. Lieutenant Colonel William P. Yarborough's 509th Parachute Infantry Battalion also departed, as well as what remained of the original Ranger force. The British Commando units also left. But the VIth Corps was not stripping itself. Offsetting these withdrawals was a tremendous influx of replacements to rebuild those units that remained at Anzio, and, beginning in

---

[4] Truscott, *op. cit.*, 364.   [5] Bowditch, *op. cit.*, 105.

[6] On March 14, 1944, the German Fourteenth Army listed a strength of 135,698, of which 65,800 were combat troops. A month later, it listed its combat strength at 70,400.

mid-March, the veteran and respected 34th Infantry Division came up to the beachhead from the southern front. The Fifth Army also contemplated sending still another American division to Anzio, the 85th Infantry.[7] This unit had only recently arrived from the United States but had shown merit in its initial engagements.[8] It would arrive at Anzio, but months later, and only after fighting its way overland.

While the beachhead front remained static during March, the planners on both sides were hard at work. It is known that in the middle of the month, Kesselring gave orders for still another offensive to be launched down either the Albano road or from Cisterna sometime toward the end of the month.[9] Later, Kesselring postponed the attack, then abandoned the plan altogether when it was pointed out that an attack of such proportions would commit all his reserves. So the Germans continued to contain the Allied beachhead with little more than five divisions on the line.

The VIth Corps, meanwhile, was in the throes of breakout plans. The 3rd and 1st Armored divisions were removed from the line and underwent intensive training in the area of "the Pines," where such activity could be undertaken without fear of enemy observation. In this dune country some three miles east of Nettuno, the regiments could take advantage of a respite from the line to undergo the rudiments of basic training all over again. Some units were taken into the blasted towns of Anzio and Nettuno to train in house-to-house and street fighting in preparation for an attack against Cisterna.[10]

At this point in mid-March, 1944, serious consideration was given to an Allied assault aimed at reducing the German salient south of the Factory. The British 1st and 5th divisions were to

[7] Truscott, *op. cit.*, 370. [8] Clark, *op. cit.*, 339.
[9] Bowditch, *op. cit.*, 105.

[10] It must be stated that Mark Clark, who visited the beachhead on the average of once every ten days, each time would arrive with a different set of ideas for an attack, and would set the planning staffs into a whir of activity. Also, the Army Group commander—General Alexander—would almost immediately countermand his Army commander with plans of his own.

drive up the Albano road while the 45th Division was to strike from the southeast; the tanks of the 1st Armored Division were to push through the British 1st Division and exploit the advance. But after all the plans had been drawn up, the operation was called off. It soon became apparent that future operations at Anzio were dependent upon what progress was made along the main southern front, especially at Cassino.[11]

There, despite still another saturation bombing of the town and the hilltop monastery on March 15, the Germans clung to their positions. Just as the Americans and New Zealanders had tried, so too did the Gurkas and Sikhs of the Indian divisions in great efforts to dislodge the enemy from their bastion at Cassino. But to no avail. Each new attack would dent the defenses, but could not overcome the combination of men, mountains, and winter weather. And so the battle dragged on.

Finally, it was admitted by Alexander that no new attempt to crack the Gustav Line would be made at least until May 1. This new delay caused increased consternation at 10 Downing Street, but the impatient Prime Minister treated his Army Group commander much more tenderly than he did Lucas. He pleaded for an explanation but threatened no recriminations.[12] As an old Sandhurst man himself, he was more than willing to listen to Alexander's military critique of why all that time and effort must be expended at only one point in what seemed in London to be only a tenuous defense line across the Italian peninsula. He was almost apologetic in seeking an explanation from Alexander, and when he got it, the subject was dropped.

At Anzio, however, the thought of still another month of stalemate was dismal indeed. To keep the beachhead troops on their mettle and to maintain their offensive spirit, Truscott called for a series of local attacks in strength. These would improve VIth Corps positions as well as feel out the German defenses. In the British sector, two successful limited attacks carried the newly arrived 5th Division to the banks of the Moletta River and the 1st

[11] Truscott, *op. cit.*, 365.   [12] Churchill, *op. cit.*, 506, 508–509.

Division closer to Buonriposo Ridge west of the Albano road.[13] Along the easternmost sector, the 1st Special Service Force was constantly lashing out beyond the Mussolini Canal in a succession of lightning raids against German strongpoints. Only in the center of the beachhead did the front remain static, but even here there were nightly patrols to test the enemy's strength and pick up prisoners for interrogation.

It may be surprising to some, as it certainly was annoying to the German High Command, that captured German soldiers were as talkative as they were. They all but volunteered information of military value to their captors. It would appear that one reason for this was the iron discipline instilled in each member of the *Wehrmacht* carried over even after his capture. He seemed still to be looking for leadership, waiting anxiously to be told what to do. As result, most captured Germans could be pressed into service as litter bearers and ammunition carriers, at times only moments after their surrender.

Along the central sector, the static front, both sides were well entrenched, and little fighting of consequence took place during this enforced lull. Companies were rotated from front-line to reserve positions, and whole divisions relieved one another at various intervals. The biggest problem facing the front-line troops was the snipers. Pfc. Jackson Wisecarver, a machine gunner, was confronted with the knowledge that a sniper was only one hundred yards away when he took over the gun pit of another gunner. For several days Wisecarver tried every trick imaginable to get the German to expose himself, but none worked until the thirteenth day. Wisecarver had started each preceeding day with a burst of gunfire in the general direction of the sniper and throughout each day there would be an exchange of fire without results. On the last day that Wisecarver would be occupying the position, he refrained from his usual morning exchange. The sniper, suspicious at first, finally concluded that he had eliminated the American machine gunner during the night, and after a great

13 Linklater, *op. cit.*, 209.

length of time he emerged from his protective niche. It was only a short burst, but it enabled Wisecarver to turn over the gun pit to his relief without having to warn the new gunner of a sniper out front.

Our side, too, was doing its share of sniping. And one day at Anzio a Regular Army colonel showed up with what he claimed to be new sniping equipment.[14] The 3rd Division had set up a firing range in the Pines area, and the colonel headed straight for the range to test out his allegedly new equipment. He managed to miss the target completely at three hundred yards and finally gave up. But before heading back to the Palermo Base Section in Sicily, to which he was assigned, he stopped off to visit an old Army friend—General Eagles. There, at 45th Division headquarters, he confessed all.

Colonel Robert Sears was an ordnance officer, outstanding athlete, and one-time international rifle champion at the Camp Perry shoot. He had been in the Army for thirty-nine years and was about to be reassigned for retirement. He had been in two world wars, but in both behind a rear echelon desk. Now he had a son, an Air Corps pilot in the Pacific who was gloating over his combat successes, and the old man wanted at least one shot at the enemy before he was forced out of uniform. He confided to his friend that actually he was AWOL from his post at Palermo, and he pleaded for the opportunity to do the one thing he could do best—fire a rifle. All he asked was one shot against the Germans, then he could hold his own with his son in the postwar years.

Eagles put through a phone call to Colonel John Church, commander of the 157th Infantry, explained the situation, and sent the aging ordnanceman down to the regimental command post. That night, in a pouring rain, he was escorted to the front and slithered into a foxhole next to S/Sgt. Primintio Vialpando. In the darkness and the rain, the Sergeant and the Colonel got to know one an-

---

[14] There was really nothing new about the colonel's sniping equipment. Actually, it was a .22 riflescope mounted on an '03 rifle, and it was not very effective. The scope fell off after each shot.

other. Yes, there was a German sniper out front; he'd been there for days, and the Colonel was welcome to him if he could get at him.

As dawn broke, the rain let up and the sun came up over the Lepini Mountains and warmed the old Colonel's bones. He cleared his glasses and peered out front, and for an instant the sun glistened on something metallic. The Colonel had spotted his German.

He settled down to waiting. Throughout the day the enemy sniper would stick his head up a few inches, then jerk it down again. But the Colonel was patient; he had waited thirty-nine years for this. Then his chance came. The German had become careless, exposing more and more of himself in an effort to stretch his cramped body. The Colonel nuzzled his cheek against the stock of his '03, squinted down the sights at the gray-green tunic, and gently squeezed the trigger.

Now he was ready for retirement. The old Colonel had killed his German.

That night Colonel Sears thanked Sergeant Vialpando and crawled out of the foxhole toward the rear. In the morning he was off for his desk at Palermo and possibly the next boat home to be farmed out as an old soldier. But there is more to the story of Colonel Sears. Months later while he was en route home, he stopped off at a base in England and became ensnared in the transportation chaos of the early days of the Normandy invasion. Everything was going to France; the Army had no time now to bother with an old soldier heading home for retirement. In England, Colonel Sears ran into another old Army friend. He was about to take his Third Army across the Channel and force a breakthrough in Normandy. George Patton asked his friend if he would like to go along for the excitement. He would and did, and in the process another sniping stint was set up for him in Normandy. The international rifle champion now could match stories with his pilot son.

The preparations for the Normandy invasion already were causing a transportation pinch at Anzio. As early as mid-February, increasing numbers of LST's and other craft were departing the Mediterranean for ports in the United Kingdom, and by late March the Fifth Army began rationing artillery shells in an effort to build up supplies at Anzio.[15] The VIth Corps' guns were allotted only one-quarter of the shells they had been expending daily. Army G–4 explained the order by stating that the daily tonnage landed at Anzio was barely enough to maintain the forces there, and that simple arithmetic spelled out the necessity of conserving supplies to effect a build-up. British artillery ammunition supplies were further cut because of losses of ammunition ships in convoy in the Mediterranean, and the lack of artillery support for the two British divisions created increasing alarm among their commanders. Their fears were assuaged by the assignment of two American artillery battalions to support the British infantry.

The rollback in firepower came at a time when the Germans actually were increasing the volume of their artillery fire, this primarily on account of the concentration of our air effort in the Cassino sector, which made the German gunners at Anzio bolder.

British General Penney was the man who came up with a workable solution for making the most of the reduced ammunition allotments. In seeking additional support for his own 1st Division, he proposed that every gun within range on the beachhead be trained on the most threatening target before his division each day and that each gun fire two or three rounds on that target. Penney's plan was extended to every division on the line, and at various times throughout the succeeding days, hundreds of Allied artillery pieces would open up on specific targets. It was a heartening sight to the infantrymen and further indicated to the enemy the enormity of firepower lined up against them. The Penney plan was further refined to bring the guns to bear in time on target against the more likely enemy installations.[16]

15 Truscott, *op. cit.*, 359.

16 "Time on Target" (T.O.T.), firings in which the distance and trajectory of each shell are so calculated that all will land and explode on the same target at the same instant—a tremendous holocaust with a sheet of flame and splintering steel completely obliterating the offending site.

The German gunners were quick to notice the slackening in the over-all Allied artillery fire and began to counterbattery our own guns with a feeling of impunity. They also paid more attention to any changes in the topography of the beachhead, and considerable changes were being made as the VIth Corps dug in. Up until this time, only the front itself and the waterfront detachments were going underground. The middle areas—battalion, regimental, and division headquarters, ordnance, signal, and quartermaster outfits—for the most part remained above ground, well camouflaged and in some areas sandbagged in. While the Germans undoubtedly were aware of these installations, they were only rarely subjected to continuous artillery fire, and this at night from the enemy tanks and mobile guns. But when the 3rd Division, which had been undergoing training in house-to-house fighting, finally relieved the 45th Division in the line to give the latter unit some rest, its division commander wanted to bring in bulldozers to dig in division headquarters. Army regulations, however, cover every possible contingency, and in this case, General Eagles, as the senior officer of the unit in the line at the time the relief was underway, issued a flat "no." The army regulations held forth, and General O'Daniel was compelled to wait until the relief of the 45th was complete before digging in his new division headquarters. He had disregarded Eagles' warning that the activity of the bulldozers would attract enemy shellfire. The Germans did shell the area, and 3rd Division headquarters suffered some unnecessary casualties, but some two weeks later when the 45th returned to its old positions, the division headquarters personnel gladly took over the new dugouts without fear that the German gunners would pay any further attention to them.

While the 45th's three infantry regiments were relieved for the two-week rest period in the Pines, the 45th's artillery remained in their pits, and the 3rd Division's guns moved in around them. This gave the 3rd double its normal artillery support and enabled it to stage a successful limited-objective attack to better its positions. It also proved to the infantrymen of the 3rd Division that they could depend upon the artillery of other units as well as their own.

The Pines was the only area in Anzio where troops could be congregated in some safety and afforded time off the line for rest and training. The undulating wooded dunes provided a measure of protection from the enemy guns still within easy reach of the area. Yet some unit commanders attempted to reinstitute a semblance of garrison life among their troops, calling for the standing of reveille and retreat formations. Enemy guns did break up these formations, and the practice was discontinued.

The lull at Anzio turned the beachhead into a veritable magnet for gadabouts. Now that the Germans no longer threatened to push everyone back into the sea, the opportunity arose for the self-styled important persons to arrive in droves on a rubbernecking picnic. Congressmen came on so-called inspection tours, high-ranking officers from the Pentagon popped up for consultations, and the big by-line journalists who had been analyzing the war in the Mediterranean from the serene confines of Algiers began to inundate the tiny press camp at Anzio, all of them under the mistaken impression that the beachhead was safe. More than one of these persons who had no earthly reason for being at Anzio lies buried today on the hill behind Nettuno. One particularly tragic death was that of soldier-artist Sergeant Gregor Duncan, whose fine pen-and-ink drawings were a feature of the Mediterranean *Stars and Stripes* and, before the war, of the *San Francisco Chronicle*. He left behind a wife who, in order to be with him, had joined the Red Cross and was stationed, as he was, in Naples.

The beachhead was never safe as long as it remained a beachhead.

The British had a much more descriptive term for the unwelcome visits by unnecessary individuals. They referred to it as "swanning." The term is derived from that graceful bird's habit of taking short flights that create appreciable commotion but have no serious purpose. The British were as beset by the practice as were the Americans.

It was usually with great fanfare and name-dropping that the swanners would arrive at Anzio, and some of the more venture-some would work up enough curiosity and bravado to get rela-tively close to the front. One of these was a motion-picture cameraman in the employ of a weekly news magazine which was then producing film documentaries depicting the world in its eternal push onward. He and his equipment got as far as a shell hole several hundred yards behind the firing line. Here he was pinned down by enemy mortar fire and was almost stepped on by a GI checking a break in a telephone line. Corporal Thomas Bona of Wilkes-Barre, Pennsylvania, a member of a forward observa-tion party of the 160th Field Artillery Battalion, did not know whether to salute him or capture him because of his outlandish uniform. But while he repaired the break in the line, Bona an-swered the cameraman's many questions. Yes, the Germans were shooting at them. Yes, they were still well behind the front. What was he doing? He and several others were directing artillery fire against enemy installations just beyond that rise. Their battery was pouring out 105-mm. high explosive and white phosphorous shells; they were observing and correcting the fire. Of course, they had an excellent view.

At this point, the conversation took on a new perspective. Would it be possible, if the film historian set the camera and ex-plained its operation, for the forward observer to take pictures of just what was going on? This could be of vital interest to the people of the United States. He set the lens, wound the spring, and the Corporal was off to record history in its timeless flight.

A short while later, Bona returned to the shell hole, handed back the camera, and bade the man in the outlandish uniform Godspeed on his trip back to Naples. The cameraman had been to Anzio and had the pictures to prove it.

Several weeks later the Corporal and his fellow forward ob-servers—First Lieutenant Dewey Bryan of Minneapolis and Pri-vate Zenus Martindale of McAlester, Oklahoma—received V-mail letters which told of their appearance in the newsreels. All three had starred in the feature film. They had taken turns photographing one another while the cameraman had remained behind in his shell hole.

Forward observers, after all, are self-made men.

CHAPTER TEN

Breakout

BY the end of March, the regrouping of the VIth Corps was complete. A total of 14,000 replacements had been brought up to the beachhead during that month to bring the fighting divisions up to strength, and a training program had been instituted virtually before the enemy's eyes to absorb these replacements as quickly as possible as well as to work off the debilitating effects that static warfare was bound to have on the older hands of the divisions. By the end of March, the VIth Corps was ready to break out of its confinement.

Improving weather and a moderate number of unloading craft, especially the busy little LCT's which the Navy was using as lighters, were beginning to solve the VI Corps' supply problems. Too, there was the employment of gangs of civilian stevedores hired in Naples to go with the cargo aboard the Liberty ships and unload it at Anzio. Their proximity to the front as well as the knowledge that they would return to Naples with the empty ships aided in speeding up the unloading operations. Five and six Liberties were being unloaded simultaneously.

Still, Alexander was not ready to give the signal to move. He already had vetoed Truscott's plans to drive up the Albano road to retake the high ground around Carroceto and the Factory. Truscott, however, set to work on other plans and on a much larger scale.

Operation Buffalo—a plan to punch through Cisterna, move on up the Lepini Mountains into Cori, and to cut Highway 6 at Valmontone.

Operation Turtle—to push up the Albano road, take Campoleone, and threaten the approaches to Rome.

Operation Crawdad—to cross the Moletta River, take Ardea, and continue along the *Via Laurentina* in the direction of Rome.

Operation Grasshopper—to storm southeastward through Littoria, across the Pontine Marshes to Sezze, and link up with the forces moving up from the main front.[1]

A tremendous amount of time and energy went into the preparations of all four plans. Gun emplacements were dug, thousands of rounds of artillery ammunition moved up and concealed around these gun pits, miles of communication wires strung, assembly areas selected, routes of march plotted, and traffic patterns worked out for each of the four plans. It was decided that because of the comparative weakness of the two British divisions, American units would spearhead any breakout.[2] But all plans lay dormant while they waited for the troops in the south.

March moved into April. The VIth Corps stood 90,000 strong,

---

[1] Truscott, *op. cit.*, 366.

[2] Because of the critical lack of available replacements, the British divisions at Anzio were averaging barely six hundred men per battalion as compared with almost one thousand in an American infantry battalion. The long years the British had been fighting had severely sapped their manpower reserve, to such an extent, indeed, that they were breaking up regular Army divisions in an effort to get replacements for those divisions in the line.

the German 14th Army 140,000; but included in these figures were the two divisions in reserve at the Tiber on guard against that threatened amphibious assault at Civitavecchia.[3] In effect, the two armies were evenly matched in manpower.

In mid-April something new arrived at Anzio—240-mm. howitzers, and with these it was now possible for us to reach out and pulverize enemy positions well to the rear of the front line. Cisterna was a favorite target of these heavy howitzers, and with them we finally eliminated the water tower in Littoria that had been such an excellent observation point for the enemy while it remained out of reach of our artillery.

Still the stalemate continued, the ground war limited to constant patrol action. Neither side was making a move. Allied daily casualties averaged 107.5 killed, wounded, and missing for the month of April and considerably fewer than 10 per cent of this average were in killed.[4] The doldrums went on while we waited for word from the south; and no word came.

What started back in January as the primary move in the headlong dash for Rome now, in April, was purely of secondary importance. Everything now depended on the forces in the south penetrating the Gustav Line, and there, too, it was stalemate.

During April, neither Clark nor Alexander visited the beachhead.[5] In desperation, Truscott went to Caserta, where he received Fifth Army approval of his breakout plans. The date and selection of one of the four plans would be determined later. Truscott went back to his beachhead.

The month of May began in unspectacular fashion. Only patrol action and artillery duels marked the sameness. But in the south on the morning of May 1, some eight generals and two hundred officers and enlisted men surrounded Mark Clark's billet sometime after dawn. Their voices joined with the band as it played "Happy Birthday," and a sleepy-eyed but smiling three-

[3] Kesselring, *op. cit.*, 240. [4] Bowditch, *op. cit.*, 107.
[5] Truscott, *op. cit.*, 368.

star general, in his pajamas and trench coat, came out to acknowledge the salute. Mark Clark had turned forty-eight years of age.

On May 3, the Germans finally flooded the Pontine Marshes. They dynamited the dams and pumping stations, and the low-lying ground from Littoria to Sezze to Terracina—a thirty-one-mile stretch varying in width from one to five miles—soon was inundated. The farm families there were forced to move into the upper floors of their *podere*, their only means of transportation rowboats.

Alexander showed up at Anzio on May 5, was apprised of Truscott's four breakout plans, and in his gentlemanly though autocratic manner threw out all but one of them. There was only one direction the VIth Corps would be ordered to move. The only plan would be Operation Buffalo—though Cisterna, Cori, and on to Valmontone.[6]

Clark learned of this the following day and was openly annoyed at what he considered Alexander's interference with his chain of command.[7] Further, he noted that an attack toward Valmontone, while it would be of military importance, was moving the Americans in a direction away from Rome. This gave added impetus to his suspicions that the British were determined to be first to enter the Italian capital.

However, Clark on the surface acceded to the demands of his superior, but his lingering doubts about the capture of Rome led him to warn Truscott not to overlook the possibility that Operation Turtle might be put into effect at the last minute and that VIth Corps might push straight on to Rome rather than punch through the mountains to seize the Valmontone Gap to cut off the German Tenth Army retreating from the south.[8]

In any event, the date for the start of the big offensive in the south was set for May 11. A date for breaking out of Anzio must still be determined and would depend on the success and speed of the southern offensive.

[6] *Ibid.*   [7] Clark, *op. cit.,* 342.   [8] Truscott, *op. cit.,* 369.

The VIth Corps made the most of this enforced period of inactivity to get ready for the ultimate signal to go. Truscott's artillerymen worked out an intricate set of fire patterns to deceive the
enemy regarding the actual H hour for the breakout. The attack
would be preceded by the usual rolling barrage, but each morning
during the waiting period the Corps' guns would open up with a
brief but intense artillery sweep of the German defenses. The
enemy at first reacted with large-scale defensive fires, but then
finally lulled themselves into the complacent belief that these barrages were nothing more than the wasteful methods of the American military. Our morning fire missions continued but were paid
little heed by the enemy.

An hour before midnight on May 11, the two Allied armies
along the southern front opened their attack. An exceptionally
elaborate subterfuge had been going on for more than a month
while both the Fifth and Eighth armies maneuvered their assault
divisions into the line and moved up their big supporting guns.[9]
The plan called for deliberately misguiding the enemy into the
belief that we were accepting the impregnability of the Gustav
Line and would by-pass Cassino with a new landing near
Civitavecchia on May 15 by three divisions which, in concert
with the forces at Anzio, would drive on Rome. A purely ficti-
tious Canadian Corps was undergoing amphibious training along
with the U.S. 36th Division along the beaches south of Salerno.
In reality, the 36th Division was in the area, once again reorganizing for possible commitment along the southern front or shipment
to Anzio. There truly was a group of Canadian signalmen assigned
to the area, who were filling the airlanes with spurious radio messages designed to give the listening enemy the impression of great
activity where there was none. Naples was alive with dockside
activity and Allied naval craft busy skittering about the harbor
in purposeless motion.

In the meantime, more than sixteen hundred artillery pieces
were set up in the Cassino sector alone, apparently undetected by

[9] Linklater, *op. cit.,* 215–16.

the enemy in the hills above, for relatively few shells fell into the new but purposefully quiet gun positions.

For their part, the Germans—after successfully beating off three massive attacks against their bastion at Cassino—had become convinced themselves of the invincibility of their Gustav Line. They were so satisfied with their seemingly invulnerable position that the corps commander in the Cassino sector, General Frydd von Senger und Etterlin, actually was on leave in Germany listening to Hitler express his satisfaction as well as his fascination over the Cassino redoubt.[10] The Tenth Army commander, General Heinrich von Vietinghoff, was slated to start his leave on May 12, not realizing the entirely different complexion the Allied armies facing him had achieved.

The U.S. 85th and 88th divisions of the IInd Corps were deployed along the westernmost sector from the Tyrrhenian inland. They were to attack northward along the *Via Appia*. To their right, the famed colonial mountain fighters of the French Expeditionary Corps were to force their way into the Aurunci Mountains. Farther inland, the British XIIIth Corps of three infantry divisions on the line and the Italian Motorized Brigade were to push into the Liri Valley and open the way for the tanks of the Canadian and South African armored divisions. To their right, the fanatical Poles of the 3rd Carpathian and 5th Kresowa divisions were to take their turn at storming the battlements of Monte Cassino. And once again the success of the entire attack would hinge on the fall of Cassino and the hilltop monastery. This time, though, the battle for the seemingly unconquerable German stronghold would be pushed by men burning with hatred, men who had seen their homeland overrun and destroyed, men who had endured the greatest of hardships merely to get where they were. Most of them had nothing to look forward to except revenge. Their country had been ravaged, their families murdered, and each had undergone privations, fears, humiliations, and, finally, escape from prisoner-of-war camps, only to make the

[10] Majdalany, *op. cit.*, 204.

superhuman effort simply to reach the Polish Corps of General Wladyslaw Anders. They had literally volunteered for the most hazardous assignment in Italy, an assignment that had stopped the soldiers of many other nations. But the Poles were determined not to be stopped.

H hour. An hour before midnight, May 11. A half-hour before the moon came up. In total darkness the infantry and mobile guns had moved into position and waited for that darkness to erupt into a violent series of blinding flashes and horrendous explosions that would signal the start. In the fire direction control centers over a twenty-mile front, men stood at telephones, their eyes glued on chronometers, all of them waiting for the exact moment to unleash a cataclysm along the western slopes of the Appenines.

"Fire!"

And sixteen hundred guns began a symphony of horror as they tore into the darkened skies with their messages of Armageddon. The great final battle of Cassino was underway.

These sixteen hundred guns would continue lighting up the countryside for forty-five minutes, all of them preregistered on every known enemy target. Nothing would be overlooked in the deluge of splintering steel as it scanned the landscape of Italy from Cassino to the sea.

When the artillery let up, the infantry moved out.

The yearling troops of the American 85th and 88th divisions pushed out against unnamed ridges along the Tyrrhenian coast. The Algerians and Moroccans, from their bridgehead across the Garigliano, drove into the foothills of the Aurunci and beyond. The British and Indians struggled across the Rapido almost oblivious to the rain of enemy machine-gun fire that was thinning their ranks. And the Poles moved out in waves across the mountain ridges on a mission of revenge to storm the defenses of Monte Cassino.

The Allied armies in the south, after a frustration that had been welling up all winter, finally were on the move.

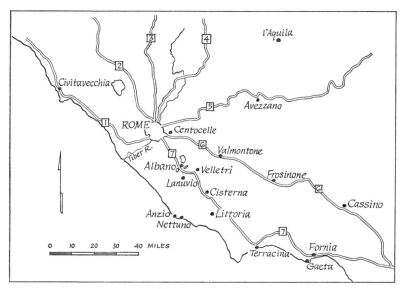

The Roads to Rome

They moved slowly at first, fought furiously for every inch of ground. Night became day and then night again, but still the battle continued. More and more divisions were thrown into the surging mass of manpower pounding against the determined German defenders and seemingly getting nowhere.

It would be dishonest to deny that the Fifth and Eighth armies faced the most formidable of foes, dishonest in that the German Army in the field was a brilliant instrument of war in the hands of skilled generals and resolutely determined field officers and noncoms whose military aptitude was of the highest degree. Dishonest, too, to deny the courage and ability of the private soldier whose steady endurance demanded the respect of the soldiers facing him. Dishonest in that it would deny the rightful recognition due the Allied soldier for defeating him. And the enemy's tenacity and determination was nowhere more ably demonstrated than in the mountains of southern Italy.

The final battle of Cassino raged for days in a momentous struggle. But on the left, the stealthy Moroccans were accom-

193

plishing a military miracle. Twelve thousand of these burnoosed Arabs, operating in independent units,[11] moved out into the night in the vanguard of the French attack into the razorback mass of the Aurunci Mountains, these rocky hills and trackless mountain wastes considered so impassable that the Germans wasted virtually no defenses among them. The natural terrain would be its own best defense. But the Goumiers, these natives of the North African Atlas Mountains, were perfectly at home in the Aurunci of Italy. They swarmed over the mountain mass obliterating what opposition they found with their knives rather than their rifles, and the orthodox French military formations raced on behind them to outflank the German defenders at the mouth of the Liri Valley.

By May 15, the Eighth Army troops struggling to keep their foothold across the Rapido suddenly felt the enemy give way. The British 78th Division came out of reserve, streamed across the river through the positions of the original attacking divisions and spilled out onto the *Via Casilina*. They were followed by the First Canadians, then the South African 6th Armored. All wheeled to attack Cassino from the northwest.

On the right, the Poles continued their hand-to-hand battle across the mountaintops, and in the early morning hours of May 18, they made contact with a patrol from the 78th Division behind Cassino. Later in the day, a detachment of Poles formally entered the ruined abbey of Monte Cassino, from which the last German defender had escaped during the night.[12] Only the dead and seriously wounded remained.

Cassino had finally fallen.

Rather than marking the end of a battle, however, it trumpeted the start of another. In the endless chain of events that constituted the campaign in Italy, the battle of Cassino can be singled out only

---

[11] A French African colonial division's basic unit was a group of seventy natives, with Frenchmen as officers. These units were called Goums, hence the term "Goumier" for a member of one of these units.

[12] Majdalany, *op. cit.*, 225.

because it took the Allied armies some five months to pass through the enemy defenses set up in the mountains to guard, not Cassino, but Rome. It was Rome that the Germans were defending; therefore Rome was the ultimate objective of the battle. Cassino, once taken, could be forgotten or remain only an interesting way station along the road to Rome.

Beyond Cassino, the battle for Rome went on.

The Fifth and Eighth armies drove on through the Gustav Line toward still another defense line the Germans had been constructing some six miles to the rear of the Gustav.[13] This one, which they originally called the Adolf Hitler Line, was intended to be as formidable a barrier as the Gustav Line. Actually, the construction of the Hitler Line was still incomplete when Von Vietinghoff's army retired to its defenses. It was apparent that the Allied advance would only be slowed, not stopped, at these secondary positions, so, in childish innocence, the name of the line was hastily changed to the "Dora Line" in an obvious effort not to besmudge the name of the Führer.

The Canadians were first to breach the new German defense line, followed by the Poles. And the Allied advance again picked up momentum.

The attack against the Dora Line opened at dawn May 23.

In the hours before dawn that same morning, the Allied guns at Anzio had carried out another of their deceptive fire missions, again without causing any noticeable enemy reaction. And then the guns fell silent and darkness engulfed the Anzio beachhead. There was nothing to indicate to the Germans that this would not be just another in the endless procession of days they were to man the defense perimeter around the Allied beachhead. A light rain had fallen during the night, but then the stars came out, and in the darkened flatness out in front of them there was no sign that the VIth Corps was getting into position to start Operation Buffalo.

The word had finally come from Alexander. The beachhead troops were to break out of their confinement. Alexander at first

[13] Clark, *op. cit.,* 349.

wanted the attack to get underway on the morning of May 21; then he postponed it twenty-four hours. Finally he set H hour at six-thirty on the morning of May 23.[14] By that time, the remainder of the 1st Armored Division and the entire 36th Infantry Division would have been moved up to Anzio to add to the Corps' strength.

An indication of Clark's determination that only Americans would be in on the capture of Rome came on the night before the breakout. He made the VIth Corps all-American. The British 1st and 5th divisions were detached from the VIth Corps and placed under the direct command of the Fifth Army.[15] And in the cellars beneath the Villa Borghese at Anzio, Clark briefed the array of war correspondents gathered before him.

"We're going to take Rome."

He went on with sweeping gestures in front of the war map explaining the movements in the south and the movements at Anzio, but his underlying theme was the capture of Rome. All-important Rome. The correspondents had been briefed better than they realized.

At a quarter to six on the morning of May 23, the Allied guns at Anzio opened up again, this time in earnest: the eight-inch howitzers, the 155's and the 105's, the Long Toms, the tanks and tank-destroyers, the mobile guns of the cannon companies, and the heavy mortars. The sandy soil at Anzio trembled beneath the reverberations of the tremendous Allied barrage as thousands upon thousands of rounds slithered through the darkened skies in the direction of the enemy, whistling as they carried their loads of destruction down upon unsuspecting heads. The series lasted for forty-five minutes, each gun firing as fast as it could be operated.

The sun was peeking over the ridge of the Lepini Mountains, but the Anzio beachhead was ringed in a pall of dust and smoke. Then, appearing first as silvery specks in the southern sky, three waves of fighters and fighter-bombers streaked in over the beachhead and headed for their immediate target—Cisterna. The town and the enemy positions around it again erupted in a violent

[14] Truscott, *op. cit.*, 371.   [15] Bowditch, *op. cit.*, 117.

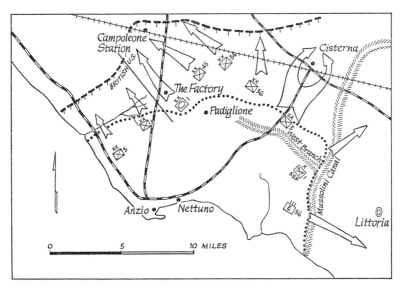

Anzio Breakout, May 23–30, 1944

shower of dust and rubble and splintered steel. The planes were gone in a matter of minutes, and the artillery took over again. The battle was underway.

The riflemen of the 3rd Division and 1st Special Service Force climbed slowly out of their holes, crept forward, then began a crouching run as their heavy machine guns spat out a covering fire. The German reaction was immediate, and the fighting was intense.

Backed by tanks and tank-destroyers, the 3rd Division opened a two-pronged assault against Cisterna to encircle the town, then reduce it. To its right, the 1st Special Service Force would attack along the banks of the Mussolini Canal and cut Highway 7 from the south. The 1st Armored Division, with a regiment of the 34th Infantry Division attached, would strike out to the left of the 3rd to cut the German defenses along the Cisterna-Campoleone rail-road line and push north to cut Highway 7 between Cisterna and Velletri. Farther to the left, the 45th Division was assigned the limited objective of bringing pressure to bear against the better

197

German divisions in the center of the beachhead line and posing the threat of a breakthrough in the direction of Campoleone. The units covering both flanks of the beachhead perimeter were to step up their patrol activity to occupy the attention of the enemy units opposing them.

The extensive mine fields, sown during the months of relative inactivity, combined with stiff enemy resistance slowed down the American attack and took a heavy toll of vehicles. But by mid-morning Frederick's Special Service Force, in their baggy para-trooper pants, were racing through the high grass heading for the far side of the Appian Way. They reached the highway shortly before noon, but in a heavy afternoon counterattack the enemy pushed them back about half a mile south of the highway. The 3rd Division's twin assault ran into heavy opposition from the outset and suffered many casualties, but by nightfall they were firmly established on their initial objectives and counting almost one thousand enemy prisoners. The 1st Armored's attack had pierced the Germans' main defense line along the railroad bed late in the afternoon and continued its drive beyond.

The 45th Division, covering the left flank of the attack, ran into extremely heavy opposition and made little headway in ground gained. But it accomplished its mission—to keep occupied the two strongest enemy divisions in the beachhead sector, the 3rd Panzer Grenadier and the 65th Infantry. Von Mackensen, believing that any Allied attempt to break out of the beachhead would come from this direction, had assigned his best divisions to cover the Albano road so that, when the breakout finally did come, these two divisions were fully engaged in a purely supple-mental battle and his weaker divisions were left to stave off the main attack, launched from an entirely different direction.

Kesselring, meanwhile, had commandeered the Fourteenth Army's two reserve divisions—the 26th Panzer and 29th Panzer Grenadier divisions, which had been in the area south of Rome—to dispatch them to Von Vietinghoff's aid in stemming the Allies' main advance in the south.[16] But the order moving these two divisions into battle was bitterly debated by Von Mackensen, which resulted in a delay in their movement; when they finally got moving, they arrived piecemeal in the south and were effectively chewed up in the Allied assault. The only reserve left for Von Mackensen was the Hermann Göring Panzer Division, which was far to the north in the area around Leghorn recuperating from its earlier battles at Anzio and actually scheduled to entrain for an assignment in southern France.[17] Instead, it was rushed southward to be pitted against its old enemies at Anzio.

The opening day of the VIth Corps' breakout battle was rewarding but costly. Combat casualties were running higher than expected, and the loss of materiel was excessive. The 3rd Division listed more than eight hundred men dead, wounded, or missing. At least eighty-six tanks and tank-destroyers had been knocked out of action. But German losses were far heavier.

The attack resumed the following morning, with the 1st Armored Division punching its way across Highway 7 and the 3rd Division closing its pincers around Cisterna. The 45th Division beat off a series of strong German counterattacks throughout the day. By nightfall, Harmon's tanks were pushing on toward Velletri.

At dinnertime that evening, General Clark was waiting at VIth Corps forward command post at Conca when Truscott returned from the front.[18] The two men went over the progress of the battle so far and studied the possibilities open to the enemy for stopping the VIth Corps drive to cut off the retreating German Tenth Army. Truscott believed that Von Mackensen would move his 3rd Panzer Grenadier Division from the center of the beachhead front as well as the 4th Parachute Division from the western end of the beachhead in an effort to guard the Valmontone Gap; also that the Hermann Göring Panzer Division would be thrown in to defend that sector. But Truscott also believed that

---

[16] Kesselring, *op. cit.*, 241–42.   [17] Linklater, *op. cit.*, 260, 277.
[18] Truscott, *op. cit.*, 374.

a strong VIth Corps effort could force its way through the gap and cut Highway 6 behind the retreating German Tenth Army, thereby sealing its escape route from the south. Clark apparently was entertaining other ideas. He questioned Truscott about the possibility of changing the direction of the VIth Corps attack to the northwest.[19] This, too, could be accomplished, he was assured. Truscott was thinking of swinging behind the *Colli Laziali* to cut off the retreating Germans farther north than Valmontone. But Clark was thinking of Rome.

Early on May 25, the 7th Infantry stormed Cisterna, and the town fell. The 1st Special Service Force pushed across Highway 7 and was at the base of the Lepini Mountains moving up on the town of Cori. The 1st Armored Division had entered the valley between the *Colli Laziali* and the Lepini Mountains, and an armored task force under Colonel Hamilton Howze cut the road leading from Cori to Artena. Task Force Brett, probing its way south through the flooded Pontine Marshes, ran into patrols from the U.S. IInd Corps coming up along the coast road from the south. The marshes had been flooded, but the water had not covered the roads. At seven-thirty on the morning of May 25 on the road southeast of Borgo Grappa, First Lieutenant Francis X. Buckley of the IInd Corps' 48th Engineer Combat Battalion extended his hand to his fellow engineers of the 36th Combat Regiment, from which Task Force Brett was formed, and Anzio ceased to be a beachhead.

Thus ended four months and three days of isolation.

Three hours later, the meeting was re-staged for the benefit of reporters and photographers, this time with General Clark in the picture. There were handshakes all around, and it became official. The Fifth Army was reunited.

This might be the end of the story of Anzio, but battles are not terminated with a handshake by members of the same army, but rather by decisive action and final victory in the field. That was still to come.

[19] Clark, *op. cit.*, 356.

Following the linkup ceremony, Clark was off to the south to revise completely the great battle still going on. Major General Willis Crittenberger's IVth Corps was to take command of the IInd Corps sector, while Keyes's IInd Corps headquarters was to move overland without delay to Anzio. Juin's French Corps would relieve the 85th and 88th divisions so that they, too, could be moved to Anzio. Juin then would continue to drive on Valmontone from the south.

As for the VIth Corps, Fifth Army G–3, Brigadier General Don Brann, was waiting at Truscott's forward command post when the Corps commander returned from the front late in the afternoon of May 25.[20] Brann was there to relay personally Clark's orders that the VIth Corps change the direction of its attack to skirt the *Colli Laziali* to the west and push straight for Rome.

Truscott registered complete astonishment. As he reported it:

> This was no time to drive to the northwest where the enemy was still strong; we should pour our maximum power into the Valmontone Gap to insure the destruction of the retreating German army. I would not comply with the order without first talking to Clark in person. Brann informed me that he was not on the beachhead and could not be reached even by radio, and that General Clark ordered the attack to the norhwest. There was nothing to do except to begin preparations.

Truscott was further astonished by Clark's apparent unfamiliarity with the existing situation at Anzio. The change of direction in the middle of a successful drive would require the most extensive and complicated shifts in troop dispositions in a congested area over a restricted road network. Clark's plan called for the 3rd Division and Special Service Force to continue driving northeast on Valmontone; the 36th Division would relieve the 1st Armored in the Velletri sector, while that division would move all its armor and vehicles across the rear of the fighting divisions to join the 45th Division in an attack through Campoleone toward Albano. The scattered elements of the 34th Division were to be

[20] Truscott, *op. cit.*, 375.

reassembled and put into the line between the 45th and 36th divisions. The plan called for the replacement of all Corps and division artillery positions, the installation of new command posts, and an entirely new communications network, all of which had to be accomplished overnight.

As Truscott put it, "A more complicated plan would be difficult to conceive."[21]

Further, Von Mackensen still had not moved his best divisions to counter the threat against Valmontone. They remained immediately in the path of the new drive to the northwest. The man who was to spearhead the new attack, General Eagles, complained that the attack would get underway at least forty-eight hours too soon, and that the divisions participating in it would suffer heavily and needlessly.[22]

Nevertheless, the drive got underway on the afternoon of May 26. The 3rd Panzer Grenadier, the 65th Infantry, and elements of the 4th Parachute divisions fought stubbornly for the next two days inflicting especially heavy casualties against the 45th Division, which was carrying the point of the attack.

Pushing through the strong German defenses in the center of the beachhead line called for monstrous efforts, especially by the combat engineers. Bangalore torpedoes had to be hauled to the front, slid through barbed-wire entanglements, and detonated to blast a path through the wire. Tanks mounting bulldozer blades were nosed through these gaps to dig lanes through mine fields imbedded with the vicious Shu mines, and fields of fire had to be cut in front of machine-gun pits. All these were the jobs of the engineers before the infantry moved out, and all of them performed under tremendous enemy fire.

First Lieutenant Richard Montgomery Strong had been an engineer and had demonstrated his ability as an intrepid fighter as well. Eventually, he had been transferred from the 120th Engineers to the 179th Infantry and had moved up the chain of com-

21 *Ibid.*, 375–76.
22 From a personal interview with General Eagles.

mand until he was given his own battalion.[23] The military career of Richard Montgomery Strong would come to an end during this breakout at Anzio. Leading his battalion forward, Strong clambered aboard a tank, firing his rifle and waving his men on behind him. He was killed aboard that tank.

The 34th and 45th divisions attacked astride the railroad line leading northwest toward Campoleone. The 45th's objective was the Campoleone station; the 34th's the town of Lanuvio far to the right. On the morning of May 27, the 1st Armored Division, which had been attacking Velletri, was relieved by the 36th Division and was moved to the left of the 45th to join in the effort to break through the German defenses before Campoleone. The attack got off to a good start. Staff Sergeant Seymour Peters led his squad against a well-defended knoll, was temporarily pinned down, then instructed his men to fix bayonets. At a signal, each man fired two clips from his rifle as fast as he could squeeze them off, then raced up the knoll to catch the enemy still crouched in their holes. The sight of twelve shining bayonets at so close a range was enough to end the German resistance.

"Kamerad!" And the knoll was taken.

But the attack slowed down and was stopped by the German commander's ability to weld together strong defending forces out of relatively small groups of stragglers and survivors of other units that had been all but wiped out. The enemy was succeeding in halting the Allied attack all along the beachhead front. At Corioli, the 2nd Battalion, 179th, suffered heavily as it drove its attack over great stretches of open terrain with no cover or concealment against enemy mortar, machine-gun, and artillery fire. Riding tanks through mine fields, the battalion pushed the enemy beyond

[23] Lieutenant Strong was one of the officers transferred from his regular unit to reconstitute the seriously depleted 179th Infantry Regiment following the big battle in mid-February, despite his rank. The paperwork was underway to promote him to a higher rank more commensurate with the command of a battalion. At Anzio, because of casualties in the front-line units, it was not uncommon for lesser grade officers and even noncoms to be placed in command of units beyond those which their rank called for.

the town, taking three hundred prisoners and accounting for an equal number of enemy dead and wounded. But there it bogged down.

The following day, May 29, enemy rear guard units were driven out of their positions at Campoleone station before noon, and two combat commands of the 1st Armored Division were moving north along the road leading to the town of Campoleone. But German strongholds that had been by-passed by the tanks were holding up the infantry units which followed. The 1st Armored's tanks now were coming under fire from both front and rear, heavy artillery fire, fire from self-propelled guns, from rival tanks, and even from the well-entrenched enemy infantry. By day's end, the 1st Armored had lost thirty-seven tanks and had retired behind the 45th Division's front line a mile north of Campoleone station.

To the right, the 34th Division was still denied Lanuvio by heavy enemy resistance, but the crux of the new VIth Corps attack on Rome was still dependent upon the speed of the 45th Division supported by the tanks of the 1st Armored. Corps chief of staff, Brigadier General Don E. Carlton, was on the phone to Eagles demanding to know what was holding up the 45th's attack and accusing the division of not being able to keep pace with the units of the 34th to its right. He chose a particularly bad time to make that accusation, since Eagles had just returned from that very sector and had observed that the 34th's famed 100th Infantry Battalion, composed of Japanese-Americans from Hawaii, immediately adjacent to the 45th was as much pinned down as were his own men. Eagles' conversation with Carlton was decidedly heated; nevertheless, Carlton was passing on Truscott's orders to press the attack.

On May 30, while Mark Clark officiated at Memorial Day services at the cemetery on the hill behind Nettuno, the 3rd Division and Special Service Force were taken from Truscott.[24] They were placed under the command of the IInd Corps, and, with the

24 Bowditch, op. cit., 121.

85th and 88th divisions, would continue the attack to seal the Valmontone Gap and sever Highway 6. The VIth Corps, reduced now to only four divisions, was to push on toward Rome. However, the Germans, too, were reorganizing, and in the giant reshuffling, Von Mackensen left a gap between his 1st Parachute Corps and the 76th Panzer Corps. The strategic Monte Artemisio, in the center of the southern defenses of the *Colli Laziali*, was left guarded by a lone artillery observer. This was Little Round Top all over again.[25]

Our generals may not have been familiar with the traditional natural defensive attributes of Cassino, but they were all too well acquainted with the tactics of the Battle of Gettysburg and the strategically important role the possession of Little Round Top played in winning that battle.

Patrols from the 36th Division reported that Monte Artemisio appeared to be undefended. General Walker conferred with Truscott and was instructed to send an entire regiment to seize the crest of the mountain. On the night of May 30, the 142nd Infantry began its climb up through the terraced vineyards and pine trees that studded the slopes, and by the following morning was in possession of Monte Artemisio. The lone German artillery observer was rudely surprised in the midst of his morning bath and captured.[26]

The 143rd Infantry followed its sister regiment to the top of the mountain, and together they beat off a series of strong enemy counterattacks launched as soon as the Germans discovered the serious penetration of their defense line. By now it was too late.

[25] On July 2, 1863, the second day of the Battle of Gettysburg, the chief of the Engineer Corps of the Federal Army, Brigadier General G. K. Warren, rode along the Emmetsburg road to find that the commanding hill looking down the entire Federal line was unmanned. Realizing the importance of the position, he sent immediately for reinforcements and placed several regiments on the hill in time to beat off a strong Confederate attack by Major General John B. Hood's division of Longstreet's Corps. The Union troops retained possession of the strategic hill, without which they would have been driven from the field and the Battle of Gettysburg could have ended in a Confederate victory.

[26] Linklater, *op. cit.*, 280.

The 36th Division had outflanked them without even firing a shot and stood on the mountaintop overlooking their defenses in the Alban Hills, defenses which they had hoped to turn into still another impregnable line to deny the Allies access to Rome. They already had begun to call these series of defenses the Caesar Line. Now they had to be given up.

A new operation instruction was issued by the Fifth Army on May 31.[27] It detailed the VIth Corps to continue its flanking movement west of the *Colli Laziali* and push on to Rome. The two British divisions along the coast would move northward to the Tiber, crushing whatever enemy resistance they met along the way. Inland, the IInd Corps was to secure the heights above Valmontone, swing to the right of the *Colli Laziali,* and continue on to Rome along the *Via Casilina.* The Special Service Force and the French Corps would remain behind to mop up whatever enemy troops had been by-passed in the dash to Rome.

But the Germans were not giving up that easily. Nowhere was their ability for reconstituting, from broken battalions and other shattered elements, rear guard units of unimpeachable fortitude more dramatically demonstrated than during these last days before Rome. Of the 377 prisoners taken at Velletri, there were representatives of fifty different companies from a variety of battalions and regiments and divisions. Yet they fought on as a cohesive unit until overwhelmed.

The Hermann Göring Panzer Division, which should have been in France by now, was still in possession of the Valmontone Gap and putting up a determined stand against the attacking IInd Corps. The 3rd Division finally reached Highway 6 by nightfall of June 1 and stormed the town of Valmontone the following day. The 85th and 88th divisions were meeting equally fierce resistance in their attempts to seize Monte Ceraso on the eastern slopes of the *Colli Laziali.*

By June 3, the IInd Corps had pushed along the *Via Casilina*
[27] *Ibid.*

through San Cesareo to Osteria Finocchio, only ten miles from Rome.

The VIth Corps, meantime, was still opposed by the larger part of the German Fourteenth Army staging its slow retreat northwestward along the Appian Way, and had to fight bloodily for every yard of ground. They passed slowly by the shores of Lake Nemi, the mythical sacred garden of Diana, goddess of feminine fertility, and they saw the smoke still rising from the Germans' wanton destruction of the galleys of Emperor Tiberius that had been salvaged from the lake bottom only a few years before and were to be preserved as a historical landmark by the Italian government.

On the afternoon of June 3, the VIth Corps took prisoner 135 Germans who had mutinied, shot two of their officers, and surrendered to the Americans. They explained that they had been provoked into the mutiny when their officers shot two soldiers attempting to withdraw from untenable positions.

By the evening of June 3, the infantry of the 34th and 45th divisions had lost contact with the enemy beyond the town of Albano, and the tanks of the 1st Armored Division rumbled along the *Via Appia* through the columns of marching infantry and headed closer to Rome.

It was apparent now that the enemy's defenses south of the Italian capital had collapsed, but there was serious doubt concerning the condition of the bridges over the Tiber. Each division driving on Rome was instructed to dispatch strong armored patrols ahead into the city to secure the bridges.[28] It was still not known whether the enemy would attempt to defend the Eternal City itself.

Kesselring, however, was more than content to extricate the remnants of his two armies from what had appeared to be a giant pincers movement that should have trapped and annihilated both armies. He was still stunned by the seeming miracle that permitted him to withdraw as much of his two battered armies as he did,

[28] *Ibid.*, 283.

more concerned now with the speedy evacuation to a new and more easily defensible line than the Tiber. He had no intention of stopping his headlong retreat before reaching the mountains far to the north of Rome.[29] Only small mobile units and self-propelled guns would be left as a rear guard, and these would be instructed to follow rapidly over the Tiber and continue to the north.

In Rome itself, tension rose as the retreating German armored units raced through the city, crossed the Tiber, and sped up the highways leading north. Here and there throughout the city bands of partisans, armed and wearing light-blue denim uniforms, staged marches and quasi-military demonstrations, only to be shot at by the retreating Germans. They would meet the same fate when the Americans arrived, for no one had been told of their existence.

[29] Kesselring, *op. cit.*, 249.

CHAPTER ELEVEN

Rome

AT four o'clock in the morning of June 4, as the American columns moved on Rome along the *Via Appia*, the *Via Casilina*, and the *Via Prenestina*, intense fighting flared up in the southern suburbs of the city. Snipers appeared to be firing from every window and from behind every clump of bushes, and the *flakwagens* of *Luftwaffe* General Ritter von Pohl's anti-aircraft brigade set up strong points on the outskirts of the city to cover the massive retreat of the German Tenth and Fourteenth armies. The advancing Americans were effectively pinned down within sight of the city limits, and beyond the ancient walls pillars of smoke were rising, indicating either demolitions or the deliberate destruction of stockpiles of supplies by the withdrawing enemy.

There had been reports that the Germans desired to make

Rome an open city. Both the Berlin Radio and the B.B.C. were broadcasting these reports, and newspapers around the world circulated stories of German envoys making arrangements through the Vatican to spare the Italian capital. Although he was determined to keep the fighting out of Rome, Kesselring was forced to make a determined stand south of the city to permit the withdrawal of his retreating armies over the flatlands north and west of the city.[1] To give up the city too soon would have caught the Tenth and Fourteenth armies well up the Apennines, where a wholesale withdrawal would be seriously impeded by the mountainous terrain.

By four o'clock in the afternoon of June 4, the American advance on Rome was still stalled outside the city. At the little airport town of Centocelle, five miles southeast of Rome, an impatient Mark Clark was demanding to know what was holding back the 1st Special Service Force.

General Frederick explained, "I'm holding off the artillery because of the civilians."

This hardly placated the Army commander, who replied, "I wouldn't hesitate to use it if you need it. We can't be held up here too long."

Clark's ever present photographers suggested he move up to the crest of the hill where the road sign "Roma" clearly indicated the proximity of the Eternal City.[2] An obedient Clark prevailed upon Frederick and General Keyes to accompany him and pose before the sign for the photographers. All those stars and flashbulbs were too great an incentive for at least one enemy rifleman, who cut loose with his Schmeisser. He punctured both the sign and the generals' aplomb as they dived into a nearby ditch and crawled back down the hill to relative safety. It gave Frederick the perfect opportunity to say, "That's what's holding up the 1st Special Service Force."

But the photographers got their picture, and eventually Clark got the bullet-riddled sign as a souvenir. At the moment, however,

[1] Kesselring, *op. cit.*, 246.   [2] Clark, *op. cit.*, 364.

he was more interested in getting into his Piper Cub and flying off to his headquarters back at Anzio. He was convinced he would not enter Rome on June 4.

But Clark's soldiers did enter Rome on June 4. The tanks of the 1st Armored Division clanked along the ceremonial *Via Appia* accompanied by a regiment of the 85th Division. They swept past the ancient ruins of the Roman aqueduct and the flat-topped pine trees, smashing through the German rear guards. The infantry-men of the 36th Division scrambled down the northern slopes of the *Colli Laziali* and fought their way up the *Via Tuscolana*. And along the traditional military route—the *Via Casilina*—two bat-talions of the 1st Special Service Force and two battalions of the 88th Division battled their way through the German defenses to enter Rome through the *Porta Maggiore*.[3]

For the second time in history, Rome had been taken from the south.[4]

Now there was an endless procession of olive-drab uniforms moving slowly down the hill alongside the Colosseum, past the Forum, and out into the expansive *Piazza Venezia*. To their left, if anyone looked up, there was the palace with its infamous bal-cony now forlorn, the balcony empty but still draped with the Italian flag. And in the darkness, as the American infantrymen shuffled by, the great square was almost silent. No welling cheers of *"Duce, Duce, Duce"* echoing off the façades of the surround-ing buildings, only the almost noiseless scuffing of thousands of rubber-soled combat boots along the pavement, the creak of a leather rifle sling as the weapon was swung from one aching shoulder to another, the clank of a canteen cap against the alumi-num container as a thirsty soldier raised the flask to his dry, dusty lips. The Americans were hushed as they walked along the same

---

[3] Linklater, *op. cit.*, 283.

[4] In A.D. 536, the Byzantine general Belisarius was commanded by Justinian I to recover Italy from the Ostrogoths. His army marched north from Reggio Calabria, fought briefly to capture Naples, then continued on up the *Via Casilina* to enter Rome without a fight.

avenues that once were trod by the sandals of the great men of antiquity, almost awe-inspired.

The onerous silence occasionally was broken by the whir of a jeep as it sped through the ranks. There was still a job to be done.

At nine-fifteen that night, there was a sharp fire fight along the *Corso* in front of the Bank of Italy across from Trajan's Column, as a German scout car was spotted and knocked out. The Americans spread out across the darkened city running into tiny bands of the enemy who had become lost or had been left behind by their retreating armies. Sometime before midnight, a group of GI's in baggy pants raced across one of the many bridges over the Tiber, firing as they ran. They routed the enemy on the other side, then fought off a stiff counterattack. And General Frederick would add another cluster to his Purple Heart; he was wounded in that brief encounter—not a bad wound, but it made his seventh.

In the early morning hours, eleven of the fourteen bridges in Rome over the Tiber were taken intact, although several had been prepared for demolition by the retreating Germans. The 1st Special Service Force had secured seven; a battalion of the 85th Division had seized the Cavour Bridge; mobile units of the 1st Armored Division were in possession of the Sant' Angelo and Umberto bridges.

Rome had changed hands.

Farther down the Tiber, the Germans had had time to destroy the bridges, and the engineers of the 34th and 45th divisions were hard at work patching them up to make them usable again. Rome was taken, but the pursuit of the enemy, now in full flight, was on. Breaking out of Anzio and capturing Rome did not end the war.

British troops at the mouth of the Tiber rounded up some two thousand Germans left stranded by their retreating companies.

The sun came up over Rome on June 5, and the city was almost deserted except for the columns of troops still coming in from the south and moving ever northward in search of new battles. The populace—swollen by the great influx of refugees to more than two and one-half million—sullen and wary at first, began to appear in the streets. The oppressively cosmopolitan Romans, so cynical, so world-weary, so unlike their demonstrative countrymen in Naples, were aloof and reserved in their welcome. It was many hours before they dropped their imperious veil of indifference and turned June 5 into a truly Roman holiday.

The change in attitude hit the populace almost as a tidal wave. After so long a wait, the realization was slow to come that their city was finally liberated. Possibly the first indication was a sign nailed up on the main doorway leading into the *Palazzo Venezia*, the doorway that had been set aside for the strutting Mussolini and his pompous underlings. Translated, the sign read, "Death to Traitors."

Little knots of the more curious gathered in the main square to be joined by others and still others, and finally great throngs of people lined the routes of march, smiling, waving, cheering, blocking traffic, offering wine and bread and flowers to the liberators. The Germans had, after all, left a trail of palpable hate behind them.

And there were girls. They helped slow down the advance.

Stripped of their cosmopolitan veneer, the Romans were as demonstrative as the Neapolitans on whom they looked down for that very reason. The mobs stormed the Regina Coeli jail and the guards were with them, throwing open the gates of the cells holding political prisoners and opening the two wings in which Italian Jews had been imprisoned by the SS. And they ransacked the yellow stucco house at 145 *Via Tasso* that had been the headquarters of the Gestapo.

In the *Piazza di Spagna* with the sun blindingly reflecting off the white Spanish Steps leading up to the Trinitá dei Monti church, the crowds milled about the ornate fountain of the sunken boat and all but wrecked the flower stalls at the base of the steps in their efforts to reap garlands for the victors. Hysteria was taking over Rome.

At the *Campidoglio* on Capitoline Hill, Clark called a meeting of his corps commanders.[5] There could be no more appropriate place than the *Campidoglio*, site of the old Roman Senate, where all laws were made. Ever since the days before the Caesars, Rome stood as a symbol of authority. Rome was the Republic, the Empire. Up the block-long incline flanked by the caged live eagle and live wolf and topped by the equestrian statue of Marcus Aurelius, Clark and his chief of staff, Gruenther, and Truscott, Keyes, Crittenberger, and Juin would receive the official welcome of a grateful city. Standing on the balcony overlooking a virtually deserted square, the tall and lean American General addressed the small number of Romans gathered there, those people so long accustomed to listening to the squat and pudgy Italian dictator. The contrast was further accentuated when the victorious commander limited himself to just one sentence: "This is a great day for the Fifth Army and for the French, British, and American troops of the Fifth who have made this victory possible."

At ten-seventeen on the morning of June 5, the Stars and Stripes and Union Jack were unfurled on either side of the Italian flag over Capitoline Hill. Then the French tricolor went up. Now it was official.

The 3rd Division, the 1st Battalion of the Duke of Wellington's Regiment, and a composite battalion of the French Expeditionary Corps were selected to garrison the newly fallen city. And the celebrating went on.

From out of hiding came the anti-Fascist Italian General Roberto Bencivenga to install himself as civil and military commissioner of Rome to collaborate with the Allies,[6] and he immediately dispatched a message to Marshal Badoglio, who had been named by the king the previous summer to head the Italian government after the downfall of Mussolini. Badoglio, in Naples, approved Bencivenga's self-appointment.

In Ravello, the little King Victor Emmanuel III was keeping his promise. Retaining the throne for himself, he turned over the

5 Truscott, *op. cit.*, 379.   6 Clark, *op. cit.*, 367.

rule of Italy to his son, Umberto. And far to the north, Benito Mussolini from his "Italian Socialist Republic" described the loss of Rome as painful.

At noon, June 5, the San Carolo restaurant was open for business as usual. The diners would be wearing different uniforms, but their appetites would be as ravenous. The proprietor, Umberto Storci, could assure the Americans of the very finest cuts of horse meat and the best of wines. His prices were startling. The Romans had yet to learn of the deliberate devaluation of the lira and of the inflationary effects of an army supplied with printing press currency. In the next few days, though, they would learn that their lira would be worth less than one-tenth of what had been its prevailing purchasing value, and the Allied soldier would take advantage of the situation while it lasted, knowing full well that prices would soar just as they had in every other city and town he had been in. Everything would go up in price almost overnight. He could reflect upon his first days in Sicily when a bottle of wine could be had for a nickel and the town prostitute for twelve cents. Over the months, he had watched and listened as the wine went up to a dollar and the trollop to ten dollars and more *"per tutta la notte."* He knew the same would happen in Rome, and that eventually the Romans would get around to the all too familiar chant he had been listening to since first setting foot on Italian soil. *"i tedeschi rubbavano tutti é poi scapati."*

It was remarkable how much the Germans could steal before they escaped. And one day, too, he knew they would probably be saying the same thing about the *"Americani."*

Still, the Romans were better off than their compatriots to the south. The food situation was bad, but not too much so. Water, gas, and electricity were functioning. Outside of a few wrecked German vehicles and damage done by our bombers around the railroad marshaling yards, Rome had come off unscathed. The Germans had not planted time bombs in public buildings and hotels and utility plants as they had done in Naples. In fact, the Germans were making quite a point of this. In the official war communiqué issued on the morning of June 5, the Propaganda Ministry in Berlin stated:

> Despite the offer of the German Command not to involve the city of Rome in hostilities in order to maintain its cultural values, United States armored formations thrust into the inner part of the city at noon on June 4 in order to take possession of the Tiber bridges. Bitter fighting ensued which was still continuing in the evening.
>
> On account of this attitude on the enemy's part, it was unavoidable that Rome should become a battlefield despite the clearly announced German intentions. The German High Command will, however, even now endeavor to limit the fighting in and around Rome to limits made absolutely necessary by hostilities.[7]

There was a modicum of truth in the propaganda communiqué.

Throughout the day, June 5, Pope Pius XII appeared at times at the window of his Vatican office and blessed the crowds in St. Peter's Square. The world had changed for Rome, but the Vatican went on as imperturbably as it had through so many other conquests in centuries gone by. The Vatican was neutral in fact as well as in spirit.

At six in the evening, the Pontiff stepped out on the balcony over the main entrance to the basilica to give public thanks to God that Rome had been spared. He thanked both the Germans and the Allies for leaving the city intact.

Throughout the day, masses of uniformed Allied soldiers found their way along the *Via della Conciliazione*, that broad new avenue lined with modern, gaudy apartment houses of cheap construction leading into the colonnaded *Piazza San Pietro*. From there, the interminable walk across the cobbled square and up the steps into the cathedral itself. But that was as far as they could go. The Swiss Guards respectfully but firmly barred anyone in uniform from the Vatican offices and apartments and even the Sistine Chapel. It was said that even if Mark Clark wished to visit the Pope in his apartments, he would have to don civilian clothes.

[7] *The New York Times*, June 6, 1944.

Within the boundaries of Vatican City the diplomatic representatives of the warring nations were changing places. The United States chargé d'affaires, Harold H. Tittman, Jr., and Britain's Francis d'Arcy Osborne were now free to leave the confines of the Vatican. The German ambassador, Baron von Weizaecker, and Japan's representative to the Holy See, Ken Harada, would take their turn in confinement.

That evening in Washington, in one of his radio fireside chats, President Roosevelt discussed the fall of Rome. It was, he said, "one up and two to go." He pointed to the steady retreat of the enemy for more than a year but warned that the Germans had not yet been driven to surrender.

For one full day, world attention was centered on the capture of Rome.

But on June 6, 1944, a different Allied army landed at Normandy, and the war in Italy was relegated to history and the innermost pages of newspapers throughout the world.

Kesselring's flight to the north, the huge movements of men and materiel up the spiny peninsula in the Mediterranean somehow did not seem to matter any more. A new and larger battlefield was opening, the long-awaited direct assault against Hitler's *Festung Europa* was now an actuality. No longer would the world overly concern itself with peripheral battles of secondary importance. The die had been cast in Normandy, and all efforts would be bent in that direction.

The long ordeal that had begun on the morning of July 10, 1943, when the British and Americans first stormed ashore in Sicily, and again in September when the Eighth Army crossed the Straits of Messina and the Fifth Army invaded Salerno with full intentions of marching straight to Rome, was over. First it was to be Rome by Christmas, then by Easter. Actually, it was Rome on a hot day in June, long after Christmas and Easter had passed and been forgotten. The terrible trials at Cassino and Anzio had built up to this, the capture of Rome. But the war would go on regardless of who possessed Rome. The Allied soldier had little to look forward to other than the continuation of what he had known for many many months: another river to cross, another mountain to scale.

On the morning of June 6, 1944, the House of Commons convened in London anxiously awaiting official word from the Prime Minister about the new cross-Channel operation, and the members fidgeted for nearly twenty minutes while Churchill took formal notice of the liberation of Rome, calling it memorable and glorious and extolling the commanders in the field in Italy. Finally he got around to what the anxious members wanted to hear: "I have also to announce to the House that during the night and early hours of this morning the first of a series of landings in force upon the European Continent has taken place . . . ."

With that, the door was closed so far as the campaign in Italy was concerned. Now everything would be centered on the operation in northern France. And with it went Churchill's remaining hopes for striking at the soft underbelly of central Europe.

The American soldiers first learned of their future role not from their commanders, but from the Italians in the streets of Rome. The Romans would recognize the divisional shoulder patch of an individual soldier, tell him of the months of anxiety while they waited for deliverance when the Allies were stalled only a short distance away at Anzio, tell him how on still nights they would lie awake and listen to the cannonading, and they would create the impression that it was somehow reproachful that we should have remained at Anzio as long as we did. Injected into the conversation would be the offhand remark, "Now, of course, you're going to France." Hearing this repeatedly, the soldier became curious.

The people of Rome knew all about it. The 3rd, 36th, and 45th divisions were going to France.

The men of the 3rd Division were the first to learn. Garrisoning the city, patrolling the streets, guarding the important buildings, and maintaining order, the 3rd Division soldiers came in contact with the Roman populace. Then the 36th and 45th were relieved on the fighting line, and the division commanders overrode the sight-seeing ban imposed by the chief of Military Government—Brigadier General Edgar E. Hume—and these men got to Rome. There, they listened to the civilians and could see officers wearing Seventh Army shoulder patches circulating about the city, each of them looking serious and important. Then came the orders to move.

First the 45th, then the 36th, was packed aboard trucks and shuttled down to the amphibious training beaches south of Salerno. The 3rd Division would give up its lush assignment and move to its special training area near Pozzuoli, the same base it had used in getting ready for the Anzio assault. In Naples, there were more and more men wearing the step-ladder shoulder insignia of the Seventh Army.

For months, General Alexander Patch had been busy in Sicily with his new command—the U.S. Seventh Army. General de Lattre du Tassigny was in Africa with the planning for his French Armée B. Their assignments—the invasion and conquest of southern France.

The troops to make up these armies would come for the most part from the Fifth Army in Italy. It had all been determined the previous December at the big power conference at Teheran. A strong Allied force was to invade France from the south in conjunction with the Normandy invasion, and it would move northward quickly to link up with the armies pushing across France from the English Channel. The winter-long stalemate in Italy coupled with the restrictive limitations on shipping had forced a change in the timetable but not in the plan. No amount of argument could sway the American and, incidentally, the Russian determination that the south of France must be invaded.

Churchill contended that the situation had changed in the Italian theater since those meetings in December, that two German armies were in headlong retreat, and that the annihilation of these armies and a push into the Balkans could be of inestimable importance to the entire war effort.[8] But Eisenhower needed the support from the south; he needed the big port of Marseilles for funneling supplies and new divisions from the States, and Marshall wanted the all-out effort to crush the German armies to be made over the broad, flat expanses of France where the mobility of the American Army could be put to its greatest use.

Churchill continued to deluge President Roosevelt, Harry Hopkins, and General Marshall with letters and cablegrams urging them to abandon the operation in southern France, and, ignoring his own intelligence agency's estimate of the enemy's strength, he painted a vivid and dramatic word picture of the debacle that was certain to follow. The beaches, he said, would be strewn with the bodies of American Doughboys and British Tommies.[9]

Oddly, there was a unanimity among the Allied high command in Italy at the time protesting what they believed would be the complete denial of total victory in Italy.[10] The Allies now had twenty-eight divisions engaged in the relentless pursuit of the two broken enemy armies. On paper, Kesselring's forces amounted to twenty-one divisions, but more than one-third of these had been reduced to virtual impotence. In fact, the German Fourteenth Army could muster only two effective divisions.[11] There was truly a golden opportunity to pound these enemy forces until they were smashed against the mountainous slopes of the Alps. But this was not to be. A change of plans at this time, regardless of where the protests originated, would not be countenanced. France would be invaded from the south, and the troops to do it must come from Italy.

---

[8] Eisenhower, *op. cit.,* 317–20.   [9] Wedemeyer, *op. cit.,* 231–32.

[10] General Alexander sent this message to London at the time: "I cannot over-emphasize my conviction that if my tried and experienced commanders and troops are taken away for operations elsewhere we shall certainly miss a golden opportunity of scoring a really decisive victory and we shall never be able to reap the full benefits of the efforts and gains we have made during the past few weeks." See also Clark, *op. cit.,* 368–69.

[11] Kesselring, *op. cit.,* 248.

Truscott's VIth Corps was selected to spearhead the new assault. And the three American amphibious divisions—the 3rd, 36th, and 45th, just as the Romans had said—would make up the sea-borne force. Yet another force was in the making. Frederick, who had been promoted to major general, was relieved of command of his 1st Special Service Force and was to form a provisional airborne division out of the conglomerate regiments of paratroopers, glider forces, and other airborne units scattered about the Allied armies in Italy.[12]

With the VIth Corps striking from the sea and Frederick's paratroopers from the skies, southern France would be invaded. Juin's French Expeditionary Corps would follow on their heels to seize the port of Marseilles. The U.S. Seventh Army and French Armée B would establish their beachhead and drive up the Rhone River Valley to link up with Eisenhower's forces within a month.

The Allied soldier went to southern France much as he went anywhere else. He went because he was told to go.

This, then, was the end of the Battle of Anzio—when, on August 12, the men who had fought there once again were aboard boats heading for still another beachhead. They left behind them thousands of white markers on the hill back of Nettuno as grim evidence of the merciless horrors of warfare as well as the nobility of the human spirit and the heights to which it can rise.

"Such is the story of the struggle of Anzio; a story of high opportunity and shattered hopes, of skillful inception on our part and swift recovery by the enemy, of valour shared by both. We now know that early in January, the German high command had intended to transfer five of his best divisions from Italy to Northwest Europe. Kesselring protested that in such an event he could no longer carry out his orders to fight south of Rome and he would have to withdraw. Just as the argument was at its height the Anzio landing took place. The High Command dropped the idea, and instead of the Italian Front contributing forces to Northwest Europe the reverse took place. Hitler was enraged at the

[12] Truscott, *op. cit.*, 399.

failure of his Fourteenth Army to drive the Allies into the sea. After their offensive of February 16, he ordered a selected group of twenty officers of all arms and ranks fighting in Italy to report to him personally about conditions at the front. This was the first and only time that this happened during the war. 'He would have done much better,' comments General Westphal, 'to visit the front himself and been convinced of Allied superiority in planes and guns.'

"We knew nothing of these changes of plan at the time, but it proves that the aggressive action of our armies in Italy, and especially the Anzio stroke, made its full contribution towards the success of 'Overlord.' "—Winston Churchill[13]

[13] Churchill, *op. cit.*, 494.

Who Was Who At Anzio

ALEXANDER, Harold R. L. G., Field Marshal General, command-
ing Fifteenth Army Group. Born December 10, 1891, County
Tyrone, Northern Ireland. Graduated Royal Military College,
Sandhurst, 1911. Served in France in World War I with Irish
Guards Regiment becoming battalion commander. Commanded
Baltic Landwehr in 1919–20 in liberation of Baltic states.

   In World War II, as a major general, he went to France with the
British Expeditionary Force in the fall of 1939 and reportedly was
the last man to leave Dunkirk in the evacuation of the beaches. In
1942 was assigned briefly to Burma Theater, then became commander in chief of the British Army in Egypt when Rommel's
Africa Korps was threatening Cairo and the Suez. Deputy commander in chief under General Eisenhower of Allied forces in
North Africa, he was named Army Group commander in the
Tunisian campaign. Led the combined armies into Sicily and later,

Italy. After the war, he served six years as governor-general of Canada and in 1952 succeeded Sir Winston Churchill as Minister of Defence. Named Earl Alexander of Tunis following his governorship of Canada.

CLARK, Mark W., Lieutenant General, commanding Fifth Army. Born May 1, 1896, Madison Barracks, New York. Graduated U.S. Military Academy, West Point, 1917. Served in France in World War I, briefly as company commander in 11th Infantry, 5th Division, in the Vosges Mountains. Wounded, he was assigned to general staff headquarters, First Army. Remained on after the war with the Army of Occupation.

In World War II, after a stint as chief of staff of the Army Ground Forces, was named commanding general of the IInd Corps in England, later deputy commander in chief of Allied forces in North Africa and participated in secret rendezvous with French leaders before the actual invasion. In January, 1943, he was designated commanding general of the Fifth Army and prepared for the amphibious assault at Salerno. In December, 1944, he replaced Alexander as commander of the Fifteenth Army Group. After the war, he headed the U.S. occupation forces in Austria and was U.S. high commissioner to Austria. In 1952, he served as commander in chief of the U.S. and United Nations forces in Korea and signed the Korean armistice in July 1953. In retirement, General Clark is president of The Citadel military college at Charleston, South Carolina.

LUCAS, JOHN P., Major General, commanding U.S. VIth Corps. Born January 14, 1890, Kearneysville, West Virginia. Graduated West Point, 1911. After Mexican Expedition, served in France as battalion commander in 33rd Division, was wounded and returned to the U.S. to finish out World War I in the Army War College.

In World War II, he was General Eisenhower's personal deputy in North Africa and Sicily, served briefly as commander of the IInd Corps in Sicily, then was given command of the VIth Corps during the battle of Salerno, replacing Major General Ernest J. Dawley. Returned to the U.S. in March, 1944, to serve as commander of the Fourth Army. In 1946 went to Nanking, China, as chief of the Army advisory group to Generalissimo Chiang Kai-shek. In 1948 he became deputy commander of the Fifth Army, Chicago.

TRUSCOTT, Lucian K., Jr., Major General, commanding U.S. 3rd Division, commander U.S. VIth Corps. Born January 9, 1895, Chatfield, Texas. Commissioned Officers Reserve Corps, 1917. In World War I served with the 17th Cavalry along Mexican border.

In World War II, he was assigned to Combined Operations headquarters in London in 1942, participated in famed Dieppe raid, organized first U.S. Ranger battalions, participated in North African campaign in the Western Task Force and as deputy chief of staff AFHQ, assumed command of the 3rd Division in March, 1943, in preparation for the invasion of Sicily. Replaced Lucas as VIth Corps commander in February, 1944. Became commanding general of the Fifth Army in December, 1944, and in October, 1945, took over command of U.S. Third Army on occupation duty. Retired in September, 1947.

EVELEIGH, Vyvyan, Major General (British), assistant to the beachhead commander. Born December 14, 1898. Commissioned Second Lieutenant, 1917. Served in World War I in France and Belgium with Duke of Cornwall Light Infantry; later, in 1919, in Russia.

In World War II, he commanded the 78th Division. After Anzio, commanded South African 6th Armored Division. Retired 1950. Died 1958.

EAGLES, William W., Major General, commander 45th Infantry Division. Born January 12, 1895, Albion, Indiana. Graduated West Point, 1917. In World War I, served in the United States at San Diego, California, Fort Sill, Oklahoma, and Camp Kearny, California.

In World War II, he was named assistant division commander of the 3rd Division in June, 1942, participating in the North African landings, the Sicilian and Italian campaigns. In November, 1943, was named commanding general of 45th Infantry Division, was seriously wounded by an exploding mine in November, 1944, during the fighting in Alsace, France, and was returned to the United States for hospitalization. Commanded Infantry Replacement Training Center, Camp Hood, Texas, starting in June, 1945. Named commanding general of 9th Infantry Division, Fort Dix,

New Jersey, in July, 1947. After service in the Pacific, he was named inspector general of the European Command in July, 1951, later director of military posts in Europe. Retired.

FREDERICK, Robert T., Brigadier General, commander 1st Special Service Force. Born March 14, 1907, San Francisco, California. Graduated West Point, 1928.

In World War II, he organized and commanded special international brigade of Canadians and Americans in June, 1942, brought the unit overseas in November, 1943, and led it in action along the main southern front in Italy until it was transferred to Anzio. Detached briefly for service with 36th Division late in June, 1944. Promoted to major general and organized and commanded 1st Airborne Task Force for invasion of southern France in August, 1944. Became commander of 45th Division in December, 1944. After a series of postwar appointments in the United States, became commanding general of headquarters command of U.S. forces in Austria in May, 1948. The following February was given command of the 4th Division at Fort Ord, California, and remained with the unit after its redesignation as the 6th Infantry (Training) Division. In May, 1951, was named chief of the joint U.S. military aid group to Greece.

GREGSON-ELLIS, Philip, Major General (British), commander 5th Division. Born August 31, 1898. Graduated Sandhurst, 1917. In World War I, served in France with Grenadier Guards.

In World War II, he served with the general headquarters of the British Expeditionary Force in intelligence, commanded the 2nd Battalion Grenadier Guards; commanded the 30th Armored Brigade and 1st Guards Brigade in 1943, assuming command of the 5th Division early in 1944. Was commandant, staff college, 1945–46; resumed command of the 5th Division until 1947, when he took over command of the 44th Division (T.A.) until his retirement in 1950. Died 1956.

HARMON, Ernest N., Major General, commander 1st Armored Division. Born February 26, 1894, Lowell, Massachusetts. Graduated West Point, 1917. In World War I, he served in France in the Baccarat sector of the Vosges Mountains, and participated in the

St. Mihiel and Meuse-Argonne offensives. Remained on after the armistice in the Army of Occupation.

In World War II, he commanded the 2nd Armored Division in the North African invasion, and was named deputy corps commander of the IInd Corps in battle of Kaserine Pass. Took over command of the 1st Armored Division during Tunisian campaign, led it in battle in Italy until July 1944. Returning to the United States, he was given command of the XXIIIrd Corps, then elected to return to Europe to command the 2nd Armored Division in Belgium, participated in the Battle of the Bulge, then in January, 1945, took over command of the XXIInd Corps. Following the collapse of Germany, he became military governor of the Rhine Province, then in June, 1945, commanded the U.S. Army of Occupation in Czechoslovakia. In January, 1946, was appointed commander of the U.S. Constabulary in Germany. He returned to the United States in April, 1947, and retired in February, 1948.

O'DANIEL, John W. "Iron Mike," Major General, commander 3rd Division. Born February 15, 1894, Newark, Delaware. Served as enlisted man in the Mexican Expedition, commissioned in infantry reserve in August, 1917, and served in France with the 11th Infantry, 5th Division, and fought in the Vosges, St. Mihiel, and Meuse-Argonne campaigns.

In World War II, he ran the amphibious training centers at Camp Edwards, Massachusetts, and in the British Isles. In September, 1942, was given command of 168th Infantry of the 34th Division and led that regiment in the North African campaign. In December, 1942, set up the Fifth Army invasion training center at Arzew, Algeria. Named deputy commander of the 3rd Division, he participated in the invasion of Sicily and later was attached to the 36th Division for the Salerno landing. In November, 1943, he replaced General Eagles as assistant division commander of the 3rd Division and assumed full command of the 3rd Division in February, 1944, at Anzio. On May 5, 1945, he received the surrender of German Field Marshal Kesselring at Saalfelden, Austria. After a stint as commandant and commanding general of the Infantry School at Fort Benning, Georgia, he was appointed military attaché in Moscow in June, 1948. In August, 1950, he returned to the United States, and the following July went to Korea to command the 1st Corps, and a year later was named commanding general of the U.S. Army Forces, Pacific. He became chief of the Military Assistance Advisory Group for Indo-China in April, 1954. Retired February, 1956.

PENNEY, William R. C., Major General (British), commander 1st Division. Born 1896. Graduated Royal Military Academy, Woolwich. Commissioned Royal Engineers, 1914. In World War I served in France and Belgium.

In World War II, he led the 1st Division in the capture of Pantelleria and other Pelagic Islands; into Italy in January, 1944, to be assigned to Anzio invasion. Retired 1949.

RYDER, Charles W., Major General, commander 34th Division. Born January 16, 1892, Topeka, Kansas. Graduated West Point, 1915. Served on border duty in Texas during the Mexican Expedition. In World War I, served in France with the 16th Infantry Regiment in the Toul, Montdidier-Noyon, Aisne-Marne, and Meuse-Argonne operations. Between wars he served as commandant of cadets at West Point.

In World War II, he was assigned as assistant division commander of the 90th Division in January, 1942, and the following May was named division commander of the 34th Division, which was then in Northern Ireland. He remained with the division through the North African and Italian campaigns until September, 1944, when he was given command of the IXth Corps, which was being activated and sent to the Pacific. On V–J Day, the IXth Corps was poised on Leyte in the Philippines ready to undertake the invasion of Japan. In September, 1945, the corps occupied the Japanese home islands.

TEMPLER, Gerald W. R., Major General (British), commander 56th Division. Born September 11, 1898, County Armagh, Northern Ireland. Graduated Sandhurst, 1917. In World War I, fought in France and Belgium with the Royal Irish Fusiliers, later served in Iraq and Palestine.

At the outbreak of World War II, he was a lieutenant colonel with the Fusiliers, served later as a staff intelligence officer at general headquarters, British Expeditionary Force, and distinguished himself in the rear guard fighting at Dunkirk. By September, 1942, he had become the youngest lieutenant general in the British Army, but voluntarily reverted to major general to lead the 1st Division in the North African fighting. He assumed command of the 56th Division after the Salerno landings until it was withdrawn from the Anzio beachhead, whereupon he took over command of the South African 6th Armored Division along the main southern front. He suffered serious spinal injuries in a mine explosion and was hospitalized in England. He had recovered sufficiently by March, 1945, to join Montgomery's twenty-first Army Group headquarters, and later became director of Civil Affairs, Military Government, in occupied Germany. After the war, he was appointed head of Military Intelligence, vice-chief of the Imperial General Staff, and high commissioner in Malaya. In September, 1955, he took over as chief of the Imperial General Staff and a year later was promoted to field marshal.

WALKER, Fred L., Major General, commander 36th Division. Born June 11, 1887, in Fairfield County, Ohio. After graduation from Ohio State College, was commissioned in the Regular Army in 1911. Served in the Mexican Expedition. In World War I, fought in France with the 30th Infantry, 3rd Division, in the Aisne-Marne, St. Mihiel, and Meuse-Argonne operations.

In World War II, he was named assistant division commander of the 2nd Division in April, 1941, later named commander of the 36th Division and brought that unit overseas and into combat. Following Anzio, he was assigned to Fort Benning to command the Infantry School. Retired April, 1946.

Those were the commanding officers, but these are the men who served above and beyond the call of duty. Each was awarded the Medal of Honor for valorous action at Anzio:

Sergeant Sylvester Antolak—3rd Division
Technical Sergeant Van T. Barfoot—45th Division
Private Herbert F. Christian—3rd Division
Technical Sergeant Ernest H. Dervishian—34th Division
Private First Class John W. Dutko—3rd Division

Second Lieutenant Thomas W. Fowler—1st Armored Division
Captain William W. Galt—34th Division
Technician Fifth Grade Eric Gibson—3rd Division
Staff Sergeant George J. Hall—34th Division
Corporal Paul B. Huff—509th Parachute Infantry Battalion
Private Elden H. Johnson—3rd Division
Private First Class William J. Johnston—45th Division
Private First Class Patrick L. Kessler—3rd Division
Private First Class Alton W. Knappenberger—3rd Division
Private James H. Mills—3rd Division
First Lieutenant Jack C. Montgomery—45th Division
First Lieutenant Beryl R. Newman—34th Division
Sergeant Truman O. Olson—3rd Division
Private First Class Henry Schauer—3rd Division
Private Furman L. Smith—34th Division
Private First Class John C. Squires—3rd Division

Bibliography

IN addition to many personal, regimental, and divisional records, official and unofficial, including the complete file of the 45th Division *News*, vols. IV and V, printed overseas during World War II, the following files, pamphlets, and publications have been referred to in the compilation of this story of the Battle of Anzio.

Historical Record, VI Corps, 1944.
G–2 Reports, 45th Infantry Division, 1944.
Altieri, James. *The Spearheaders*. Indianapolis, Bobbs-Merrill, 1960.
Bowditch, John, III, ed. *The Anzio Beachhead*. Vol. XIV in American Forces in Action Series. Washington, Government Printing Office, 1947.
Cate, J. L., and W. F. Craven, eds. *The Army Air Forces in World*

War II. Vols. II and III. Chicago, University of Chicago Press, 1949, 1951.

Churchill, Winston S. *Closing The Ring.* Vol. V of The Second World War. Boston, Houghton Mifflin, 1951.

Clark, Mark W. *Calculated Risk.* New York, Harper, 1951.

Colvin, Ian. *Master Spy.* New York, McGraw-Hill, 1951.

Eisenhower, Dwight D. *Crusade in Europe.* New York, Doubleday, 1948.

Greenfield, Kent Roberts, ed. *Command Decisions.* New York, Harcourt, Brace and Company, 1959.

Harr, Bill. *Combat Boots.* New York, Exposition Press, 1952.

Kesselring, Albert. *A Soldier's Record.* New York, Morrow, 1954.

Linklater, Eric. *The Campaign in Italy.* London, H. M. Stationery Office, 1951.

Majdalany, Fred. *The Battle of Cassino.* Boston, Houghton Mifflin, 1957.

Mauldin, Bill, *Up Front.* New York, Holt, 1945.

Montgomery, Sir Bernard L. *The Memoirs of Field Marshal Montgomery.* Cleveland, World, 1958.

Truscott, Lucian K., Jr. *Command Missions*, a Personal Story. New York, Dutton, 1954.

Wedemeyer, Albert C. *Wedemeyer Reports.* New York, Holt, 1958.

Westphal, Siegfried. *The German Army in The West.* London, Cassell, 1951.

Index

233

Anzio has been printed on paper expected to last not less than three hundred years, bearing the watermark of the University of Oklahoma Press. The type chosen for the text is Janson, a seventeenth-century Dutch design which possesses the character and strength admired by today's reader.

UNIVERSITY OF OKLAHOMA PRESS

Norman